When Gallantry Was Commonplace

American University Studies

Series IX
History

Vol. 90

PETER LANG
New York · San Francisco · Bern
Frankfurt am Main · Paris · London

Leland W. Thornton

When Gallantry Was Commonplace

The History of the
Michigan Eleventh Volunteer Infantry,
1861-1864

PETER LANG
New York · San Francisco · Bern
Frankfurt am Main · Paris · London

Library of Congress Cataloging-in-Publication Data

Thornton, Leland W.
When gallantry was commonplace : the history of
the Michigan Eleventh Volunteer Infantry, 1861-1864 /
Leland W. Thornton.
p. cm. — (American university studies. Series IX,
History ; vol. 90)
Includes bibliographical references.
1. United States. Army. Michigan Infantry Regiment,
11th (1861-1864)   2. Michigan — History — Civil War,
1861-1865 — Regimental histories.   3. United States —
History — Civil War, 1861-1865 — Regimental histories.
I. Title.   II. Series.
E514.5 11th .T47   1991   973.7'474 — dc20   91-3693
ISBN 0-8204-1259-7   CIP
ISSN 0740-0462

CIP-Titelaufnahme der Deutschen Bibliothek

Thornton, Leland W.:
When gallantry was commonplace : the history of the
Michigan Eleventh Volunteer Infantry, 1861-1864 /
Leland W. Thornton. — New York; Berlin; Bern;
Frankfurt/M.; Paris; Wien: Lang, 1991
(American university studies : Ser. 9, History ; Vol. 90)
ISBN 0-8204-1259-7
NE: American university studies / 09

The paper in this book meets the guidelines for permanence and durability
of the Committee on Production Guidelines for Book Longevity of the
Council on Library Resources.

© Peter Lang Publishing, Inc., New York 1991

Printed in the United States of America.

Melvin Joshua Lyon of Leonidas Township, St. Joseph County,
Michigan, enlisted when he was seventeen as a member of
Company D, Eleventh Michigan Volunteer Infantry. (Picture
courtesy of Wayne Mann.)

TO

Meagan L. Thornton
Jamie E. Thornton
Nathaniel L. Thornton
Nicholas R. Thornton
Rebecca J. DeGraw
Sarah Kathleen DeGraw
Andrew J. DeGraw
Benjamin J. DeGraw

Several people deserve special thanks for their generous help in tracking down information for this book: Lois G. Hendrickson, University of Minnesota Archives; L. G. Meldrum, Indiana Commission on Public Records; Terry Harmon, Kansas State Historical Society; James H. Hutson, Library of Congress; Steven Eric Nielson, Minnesota Historical Society; Sharon A. Balius, Engineering Libraries, University of Michigan; Cynthia J. Beeman, Texas State Archives; Lynn Smith Houghton, Kalamazoo Public Museum; Kathryn Kistler, White Pigeon Library and my sister-in-law Catherine Eubanks who researched the Library of Congress for me while she was working in Washington, D.C. John E. Dudd of Smyrna, Georgia; Howard W. Bordner of Washington, D.C. and Larry Franks of Sturgis, Michigan, have all shared information with me and have encouraged my work.

Dr. David Gosling and Richard Cripe of Glen Oaks Community College, Mrs. Mary L. McGue of Sturgis and my sons, Matthew and Paul, have read parts of the manuscript and made helpful and timely suggestions. My son-in-law, David J. DeGraw of Marshall, Michigan, has guided me with legal advise for which I am very grateful. Lee Barnett, State of Michigan Archives, and my former student, A. J. Hartman read the entire manuscript and saved me from numerous errors.

The book has profited by my friendship with Wayne Mann of the Western Michigan University Archives who shared his knowledge of the Eleventh Michigan with me and encouraged the writing of this book. Marelee Hawver prepared the manuscript for the printer. She has smiled through all of the changes.

My wife, Ellen, has sacrificed seven years of vacations and travel for walking over battlefields and sitting in archives. The book would not have been possible without her help and encouragement.

Table of Contents

Table of Contents

Introduction

After four months of continuous organizational activity in the summer and fall of 1861, the Eleventh Michigan Infantry was considered ready for service. On Tuesday November 26, 1861 a large crowd of civilians witnessed the assembly of the regiment in front of the station house at White Pigeon. The occasion was the formal presentation of the United States flag donated by the Ladies of St. Joseph County. As the flag was presented to Colonel William J. May, Mrs. John F. Frey speaking for the local citizens charged the Regiment to protect the flag. She placed the banner in their sacred care and said that when they returned ". . . though its brightness may be dimmed from the smoke of battle and its graceful folds pierced by bullets, we will welcome you, and it, with pride and joy, and lift our hearts in thankfulness to God for His preservation of our common country and its noble defenders."

In accepting the banner for the Regiment, Lieutenant Colonel William L. Stoughton said that even though this flag might be exposed to the battles storm ". . . those who bear it hence will never return with it dishonored. Henceforth we shall cherish it as our own, and as we defend it and the sacred cause it represents, so may our memory live in the hearts of our countrymen."

For nearly three years the Eleventh Michigan carried that banner throughout its marches in Kentucky, Tennessee, Georgia, and briefly in Alabama. When the Regiment was mustered out in Sturgis, Michigan, September 30, 1864 the flag was left in the care of its beloved Colonel William L. Stoughton. Even though the banner was faded and torn by shot and shell, those who survived to witness that day could say for as long as they lived that their Regiment never dishonored the State or the Nation. They had done their duty.

Introduction

History has not labeled this Regiment as a famous unit of the Great Conflict, however one wonders if those units which achieved fame may have had better press coverage, more eloquent survivors to write their battle reports, or unit histories published and available. No contemporary ever wrote the history of the Eleventh. Had he survived to retirement, there is little doubt that Sergeant James W. King would have undertaken the task. Until the diary of Private Ira Gillespie surfaced in print in 1965, no personal account of this nature either in letters, diaries, or memoirs had received wide circulation. No officer papers have even yet surfaced, and only those of a few of the enlisted men. So after the survivors died, there was little left to remind us of their lives.

Seventy-seven years after that flag presentation, on October 1st, 1938, Nancy Lyon, in her 90th year and surviving into her 40th year as the widow of Private Melvin J. Lyon, visited a nephew living in Jackson, Michigan. When asked what she would like to do, Nancy said that just once more, she would like to see her husband's regimental flag. Together they drove to Lansing and climbed the many steps leading to the State Capitol Rotunda where for years Michigan's Regimental Battle Flags have been on display. An attendant walking through the rotunda noticed the tall white-haired lady peering intently into the display case, and when he learned of her interest in that particular flag, of the Eleventh Michigan, he secured the key. Opening the case attracted a small crowd. The attendant explained that he wanted this lady to get a better look at her husband's flag. As the faded and damaged banner was pulled from the case, and gently unfurled, Nancy paused for a moment, then reached out with her frail hand and softly touched the cloth. Twelve years later when the nephew related to me the events of that afternoon he said there was scarcely a dry eye in the crowd.

Late next spring Nancy died, the last of her generation in our family. I was just short of seven years at the time, but living a block from her home, several vivid memories of this great grandmother have remained. The family papers were lost after her death and even though by the age of eleven I exhibited great interest in grandfather's military history, so little was remembered. Thus

Introduction

began a life long quest for the history of grandfather's regiment. Twenty-five years ago I met Leland Thornton, and with his own interest in St. Joseph County history he urged me to write the Eleventh's story. This was not to be. I am grateful to Lee for writing that which I could not.

Early in December 1861, the Eleventh Michigan - 1,000 strong - left White Pigeon for the front line in northern Kentucky. Just 340 returned to be mustered out at the expiration of their enlistment. What follows is their story.

Wayne C. Mann
Regional History Collections
Western Michigan University
June 12, 1990

Chapter One

"The most important election ever held!"

Michigan became a state just twenty-four years before the American Civil War. The first great rush of settlers in the 1830's claimed the prairie lands and oak openings of the southern counties. The frontier moved north through the heavy mixed forests in the middle of the state by 1850. The white pine forests and the lighter soils of the northern areas were not settled until after the Civil War.

St. Joseph County in the southernmost part of the state was organized in 1829. To meet the needs of the settlers with "St. Joe fever", the federal land office moved from Monroe to White Pigeon in 1831. By 1840 the population was just over 6,000, and it doubled by 1850 and nearly doubled again by 1860 when the census counted 21,000 people. It would be a hundred years before the population doubled again. In 1840 the government moved the Indians west from the reservation that had closed Mendon Township and one-half of Park and Leonidas Townships to settlement. By 1860 St. Joseph County was a proud, bustling community of farms and small villages.

The greatest economic boon to the county was the completion in 1851 of the Michigan Southern Railroad from Detroit and Monroe to White Pigeon. Burr Oak, Sturgis, and White Pigeon were on the main line with the latter village being its western terminus with car repair facilities, a turntable, and a large hotel and dining establishment. A spur track connected Constantine, two miles north of White Pigeon, with the mainline. This was built to satisfy the legislative charter requirement that the road reach the St. Joseph River on the west. Most of the local citizens believed that it was built solely to satisfy Governor John Barry who was a resident of Constantine. Three Rivers, still farther north, was linked to Constantine by a strap line. The rails were made of wood with iron straps nailed on top.

The consolidation of the Michigan Southern and the Northern Indiana railroads put St. Joseph County on the mainline of the major Detroit and Chicago railroad. By 1860 the railroad and its telegraph line brought the county into the main stream of American events. News of these events was spread throughout the area by two weekly newspapers. Although there had been numerous attempts to start more newspapers in the boom times of the frontier, they failed or moved with the pioneers. They were rather like banks in that regard.

Throughout the election year of 1860 the newspapers in St. Joseph County carried on a name-calling political debate. According to the Democratic-oriented Three Rivers *Western Chronicle*, the "black Republicans" were attempting to "make the people believe the negro question is the only issue before the people."[1] The Republican-oriented *Weekly Mercury and St. Joseph County Advertiser* of Constantine referred to the Democrats as Locofocos, Border Ruffians, and the representatives of hopelessness.[2] When the Republicians majority on the County Board of Supervisors was reduced from four to two in the local elections in the spring of 1860, the newspaper rivalry intensified. The Democrats victories in seven of the sixteen townships not only endangered the Republician control of the county government but also threatened the *Mercury's* profitable printing contract with the county.

It was the Presidential election which absorbed the local editors' attention. Even the state election which pitted Constantine's Democratic ex-governor John Barry against Republican Austin Blair of Jackson did not attract much coverage. As early as May the *Western Chronicle* referred to the Presidential Election as a crisis and predicted that it would determine whether the United States would survive as "one nation or as many small republics as chance may determine."[3] The *Western Chronicle* saw this crisis as the fault of the Republicans, especially the ex-Whig Republicans.

The *Mercury* echoed the same concern by printing Judge Salathiel C. Coffinberry's Fourth of July oration. The judge, an early settler and a much respected lawyer, asked, "Fellow Citizens, is our Union worth preserving?" He answered the question for the vast majority of the people in St. Joseph County when he said "Yes, it is! It is the offspring of the wisdom and experience of the greatest sages and statesmen, and the purest patriots that ever lived."[4]

In spite of this concern over the seriousness of the election for the future of the nation, the two newspapers were so partisan that there was no attempt to look at the issues. The *Western Chronicle* reported with relish a story about New York delegates to the Republican National Convention in Chicago who stopped in White Pigeon on their return trip home. The Michigan Southern and Northern Indiana Railroad regularly made White Pigeon a stopover to allow passengers to eat at the Railway Eating House, and this time a group of local Republicans had gathered there to receive word on the nomination. When they were told that Abraham Lincoln of Illinois was the Presidential candidate, there was widespread grumbling. When a member of the New York delegation called for three cheers for Lincoln, he got silence from the crowd. Finally someone called for three cheers for Steward and got a good response from the locals and many of the New York people as well.[5] The Democratic newspaper attempted to label Lincoln an abolitionist, connecting him with "Steward, Chase, Giddings and other abolitionists."[6] The defection of a single Flowerfield Township Republican was hailed as a sign of the future by the *Western Chronicle's* editor, Newland C. Bouton. He described Flowerfield as the county's leading abolitionist township, "the Oberlin of this county."[7]

The Republican newspaper of St. Joseph County during the 1860 election campaign was the Constantine *Mercury* edited by Levi T. Hull. Much of the news space in the *Mercury* was used to defend the spending and taxing policies of the state Republican administration. Hull devoted most of the remaining columns in attacking Stephen Douglas and John Barry, and comparatively little attention was spent on supporting either Lincoln or Austin Blair.

There were also notices of planned party activities and mention of events that had been held in the county. Typical of these events was a Lincoln pole raising in Flowerfield Township. The *Mercury* reported that a large crowd were "thrilled" by the "youthful drummer lads" in uniforms led by Abishai Hoisington of Fabius Township. The Three Rivers Wide Awakes were also there.[8] This was an organization of Republicans that specialized in torch light parades, wearing a glazed cap and cape to protect themselves from the spilled oil of the torches.

On the eve of the election the *Western Chronicle* stated in an editorial that,

> It is only four days from today, that the great battle is to be fought. The most important election ever held!
>
> It is quite apparent that a considerable portion of the masses do not believe that the country is involved in the greatest peril, at the present time, that the government has encountered since its foundation. We do fully believe it, and candidly state it.
>
> Passion and sectional hatreds have been so fearfully stimulated by demagogues and unscrupulous presses that the lovers of this Union indeed do tremble for the consequences which the coming election may precipitate upon us. There is no use in attempting to disguise the fact that in the tabooed Southern section of this Union, a settled and fixed purpose is entertained, to overthrow the government in case the sectional party succeeds in the election.
>
> The South is seemingly determined not to be *awed* or *browbeaten* into a submission to a government in which they have no voice. It is the fault of meddlesome and incendiary Northern fanatics, that such a state of things exists....[9]

In response the Constantine *Mercury* on November 1, 1860 ran a story about the whipping of a negro slave girl its front page and also articles on the dishonesty of "Honest John S. Barry." The paper's editorial was an exhortation to the Republican voters to do their duty on the whole ticket and not to trade votes.

> Let every Republican earnestly and actively discharge his whole duty, and St. Joseph County will roll up such a majority on the side of Freedom as will make the minions of Slavery - the idolaters of the little Giant - pray for the rocks and the mountains to fall down on them.[10]

Following the election the editor of the *Western Chronicle* seemingly forgot his concerns about the future. "For some time past, the columns of our paper have been almost exclusively occupied with matters of a political nature....But the election being over, we will discard politics..."[11] However, events were to bring politics back to the *Western Chronicle*. Bouton examined the causes of the sectional crisis and found that it was the fault of the abolitionist Republicans such as Steward and the division of the Democratic Party caused by President Buchanan's actions. He concluded that, although the Douglas Democrats lost the election, "their principles will prevail or the Union will be destroyed."[12] Later he cautioned patience. "Before there can be quiet in the South, there must be moderation in the North."[13]

From the election until the firing on Fort Sumter both newspapers treated secession as something of a joke and a bargaining threat. As late as the March 4 inauguration of Lincoln, the *Western Chronicle* was poking fun at the local Republicans. It reported on March 11 that "S. [Samuel] Chadwick, Esq., of this village formerly GCTRWA (Grand Commander of the Three Rivers Wide Awakes) has gone down to Washington to see 'Old Abe' inaugurated."[14]

The sectional crisis did produce two new Republican papers. The *Three Rivers Reporter* began publication on February 21, 1861, and the *Sturgis Journal* began on July 4, 1861. Wilber H. Clute edited the *Reporter*, and John G. Wait the *Journal*. The *Reporter* evidenced a new resolve. In the initial issue the editor wrote a long review of the history of sectional compromise and then asked:

This time, then we must not only Compromise with, and concede to slavery, but to rebellion and treason, also! Are we prepared to do this? Can we do this without dishonor to ourselves and incalculable danger to our country? Again we say never! No more Compromise with slavery; no more concessions to wrong or injustice extended from us through fear and cowardice; no countenance to rebellion; no parleying with traitors! We occupy impregnable ground; we have done no wrong and purpose to do none, and we may as well meet the question now as ever. If we stand firm, we shall at least preserve freedom from entire overthrow and save the Union. [15]

Notes

1. *Western Chronicle*, (Three Rivers, Michigan), 3 March 1860.

2. *The Weekly Mercury and St. Joseph County Advertiser*, (Constantine, Michigan), 13 September, 1860. Hereafter cited as Mercury.

3. *Western Chronicle*, 17 May 1860.

4. *Mercury*, 19 July 1860.

5. *Western Chronicle*, 24 May 1860.

6. Ibid, 31 May 1860

7. Ibid, 6 September 1860. Oberlin, Ohio, was one of the centers of abolitionist agitation.

8. *Mercury*, 11 October 1860. Hoisington entered the Eleventh Michigan Infantry as the Drum Major.

9. *Western Chronicle*, 1 November 1860. Underlining is Bouton's.

10. *Mercury*, 1 November 1860.

11. *Western Chronicle*, 18 November 1860.

12. Ibid, 22 November 1861

13. Ibid, 29 November 1861.

14. Ibid, 7 March 1861

15. *Reporter* (Three Rivers, Michigan), 21 February 1861. Hereafter cited as Reporter.

Chapter Two

"...true men must now stand by the country..."

The Confederate attack on Fort Sumter united the vast majority of people in St. Joseph County with the Republican administration to prevent the division of the nation. The Constantine *Mercury* anticipated events better than any other local papers. On April 11, 1861, the editor felt that both sides were preparing to fight but that both were unwilling to fire the first shot. He wrote, "Things begin to look as though they would culminate in something shortly."[1]

On that same day, the Confederate government began the siege of Fort Sumter, and on April 13, 1861, Major Robert Anderson surrendered to General Pierre G. T. Beauregard. President Lincoln on April 15 issued a proclamation recognizing the existence of "combinations too powerful to be suppressed" by the ordinary means of government and called for the states to send 75,000 militia to serve for three months to suppress the insurrection.[2]

When the telegraph relayed the President's call, Samuel Chadwick immediately hung out a U.S. flag and began recruiting a company for the army. All of the county newspapers ran the notice of Chadwick's efforts to enlist volunteers to answer the President's call. Chadwick, a Three Rivers lawyer, had served eight months as a First Lieutenant in Company E of the 1st Michigan Volunteer Infantry during the Mexican War. As he wrote Adjutant General John Robertson, "my Mexican War feeling is up...."[3] The Three Rivers *Reporter* noted on April 18 that,

"There have been printed at the Reporter office a package of handbills headed 'War! War!' for Capt. S. Chadwick, who served in Mexico."

> The President of the United States having called on the State of Michigan for
> one regiment of Volunteers and desirous that St. Joseph County shall not be
> behind her sister counties in patriotism and devoted to our common country;
> all those persons who are willing to enroll themselves for service, are re-
> quested to report their names to me immediately. Having marched against
> the enemy in Mexico, I am now ready to face traitors and rebels on our own
> soil.[4]

The *Reporter* also noted in the same issue that a Union meeting
had been held on April 17 and addressed by Rev. Dr. Bement, the
Three Rivers Presbyterian minister. It was the first of many such
meetings, designed to gain recruits for the various military units
being raised in the county. The general opinion in St. Joseph
County for Republicans and Democrats was summarized by the
Western Chronicle on April 18.

> The crisis has come, and true men must now stand by the country .... the
> rebellion has taken formidable shape, and war is inaugurated, we stand for
> the glorious old flag of our country, against all assailants, either at home or
> abroad. It is now no time to discuss measures of past policy - no time to write
> about what might have been done - the trying of measures to satisfy and ap-
> pease madmen, are over.
> The preservation of the nation is now the first thing.[5]

In the first six months after the firing on Fort Sumter, Northern
enthusiasm for the war was high. Neither the United States government nor the State of Michigan was prepared for the overwhelming response to the President's summons. Michigan's allot-
ment under the President's April 15 call for troops was one regiment. Militia regiments were to have ten companies, consisting of
one captain, one first lieutenant, one second lieutenant, four
sergeants, four corporals, one drummer, one fifer, and 64 privates.
Each regiment was to have a staff of one colonel, one lieutenant-
colonel, one major, one adjutant, one regimental quartermaster,
one surgeon, one assistant surgeon, one drum major and one fife
major.[6] Michigan's quota was easily filled by already existing uniformed militia companies. Indeed, it was primarily a question of
which companies to honor. The Adjutant General's office and the
Governor were deluged with offers of existing and new companies.

Chadwick's effort in Three Rivers was just one of many throughout the state.

Whether Governor Blair was better at judging the nature of the coming struggle or just hesitant to offend so many people by refusing their services, he did call the Second Michigan Volunteer Infantry into camp. John Robertson, Adjutant General of the State of Michigan, issued the following general order to clarify the situation.

As there appears to be much excitement abroad in relation to the organization of Military Companies, this order is published for information:

1st. That the first two regiments of Michigan Infantry will be taken from the present volunteer uniform Companies, according to the Act to provide a Military force, approved March 16, 1861. Failing to get a sufficient number from that organization, then volunteers will be received from the enrolled militia to make up the deficiency. Each regiment will consist of ten Companies.

2d. Companies forming outside the present volunteer uniformed force will keep up their organization without expense to the State, at the same time acquiring as much of the "Hardee" drill as possible, holding themselves in readiness for any call that may be made on them. Companies so organizing can be furnished with the necessary blanks for enrollment by applying at this office.

3d. The two Regiments now raising will be furnished with uniforms on arrival at their rendezvous at Detroit.

4th. Companies will not move from their present localities until ordered.[7]

This was disappointing news for the newly forming militia units of St. Joseph County and for those men who were enrolling companies. Samuel Chadwick had been working to raise a company since the first day. On Monday, April 22, he wrote Robertson that he had written the Governor on April 18 to ask what to do with his company. "I hear he [the Governor] is away from home which accounts for no answer.... I hope my company will be accepted. Will you please advise me what to do? My men are anxious."[8] The following day Chadwick wrote again.

> Last night Capt. [Isaac C.] Bassett received the blank [rolls] forwarded by you. No com. [commission] has ever been issued to him. The Co. [company] was never enrolled and no list of names exists. He is on my roll for a new company. We have today sixty names on the new roll ready for arms and uniforms. We elect officers tomorrow and will send you the roll. Bassett accepts Lieut. in the Co. I shall be in Detroit Thursday myself.[9]

However, not all St. Joseph County militia units were disappointed. The Burr Oak Guard, commanded by Captain Ira C. Abbott, was mustered with the First Michigan Infantry. Abbott was ultimately the Colonel of the Reorganized First and commanded the regiment at Gettysburg.[10] The Constantine Union Guard, commanded by John A. Lawson, became Company G of the Second Michigan. General Order No. 6, announcing the organization of the Second, was sent by Robertson on April 25, and all ten companies were in Detroit by April 27.[11]

For the other companies, the opportunity to serve looked bleak. Chadwick released his men to fill the ranks of the Constantine company and wrote to Secretary of War Simon Cameron about this time "that he was anxious to serve the country in some capacity."[12] Chadwick received an appointment as a clerk in the War Department and left Three Rivers on May 18 for Washington.

Captain William L. Stoughton, commander of the Peninsular Guard in Sturgis, received an order from the Michigan Quartermaster General on April 25 to return the "cavalry sabres, shortswords, and belts for the same."[13] Stoughton was a leader in the St. Joseph County Republican Party and the County Prosecuting Attorney. The order to return the equipment must have raised grave doubts about his abilities. On April 27, Henry McAfee, a Sturgis businessman with two sons in the Peninsular Guard, wrote to Robertson about raising

> "a picked Volunteer corps to fight in defense of my country and the Flag of my adoption and would such a company be accepted by you and the Governor. As the company here called the 'Peninsular Guard' were not accepted the Citizens here are very indignant thereat. Some blame the Captain of the company and others blame you and the Governor for their non acceptance. Curses loud and deep are uttered as our people think that of all Southern Michigan, Sturgis alone has been slighted."[14]

Possibly the citizens of Sturgis suspected that Stoughton, who had been appointed United States District Attorney for western Michigan by the Lincoln administration, was no longer enthusiastic about a military career.[15]

By the time the Second Michigan could organize, the President called for the states to furnish an additional forty-two thousand men to serve for three years. Michigan's quota under this May 3, 1861 call was for three more regiments. This requirement was met by mustering the Second Michigan as a three year regiment and by raising the Third and Fourth Michigan regiments. The Sturgis Peninsular Guard was mustered as Company C of the Fourth Michigan. Captain Stoughton decided to remain in Michigan as the District Attorney, and the Company was commanded by Captain Abram R. Wood of Sturgis. Wood was killed on picket duty at Yorktown, Virginia, April 18, 1862.[16]

The delays and false starts in organizing Civil War regiments often led to frustrations and bitter feelings. In the case of the Fourth Michigan, as early as May 8 the *Western Chronicle* reported that the Peninsular Guard would head the list of chosen companies.[17] Adjutant General Robertson did not appoint the staff officers and designate Adrian as the training site until May 16, and he did not officially name the companies until May 20.[18] The Sturgis people must have known at an earlier date that they would be part of the Fourth. They brought in their recruits from the outlying villages prematurely and then had to send them home when no orders were received to report to Adrian. The reaction of at least one enlisted man can be seen in a letter written by Eli L. Starr of Centreville.

> With feelings of most unmitigated and unqualified disgust I take my pen in hand to inform you that I have sold out my military outfit and retired to the shades of private life. The day you left a messenger from the Peninsulars came over with orders for all members of the Company at Centreville to be in Sturgis on Wednesday. You know that I gave up my proposed expedition to Detroit only on the promise of Father and Mother that I might move in the first Company that left from this County. Well, here was a chance. We were told that the Co. had rec'd orders to march into Camp at Adrian on Friday & we must be there at Sturgis on Wednesday to entrain. I told them I didn't want to go on Wednesday for I had an engagement that night but would be there on Thursday morning which as I had my outfit would be

ample time but he was anxious for me to come Wednesday. So over we Centreville boys went - got over there & found that they had received no orders to move & didn't [know] when they would but had sent out for us on the *supposition* that they were. Well, of course, they didn't want us as expected and, after very generously permitting us to *pay our own bills*, informed us that they could give no definite information as to when they would want us. We in return informed them that it would be entirely unnecessary for them to send for us on any future occasion. And after offering my military cap to them for half price, the red, white and blue neck tie thrown in, we shook the dust of Sturgis from our sandals and wended our way homeward. Thus endeth the first chapter. I had bought a big blue blanket of Jonathan for $6.00 which I shall return to him. Also a new carpet sack of Jno. Talbot (as you had mine) but this I am afraid I cannot return owing to the fact that I procured the services of R. J. Eaton, Esq. to embellish on the side of it with.

Eli L. Starr
Company A 4th Regiment[19]

Starr did finally enter the service with the Fourth Michigan as a sergeant. Most of the "Centreville boys" did not.

Secretary of War Simon Cameron was anxious that Governor Blair not over-extend his quotas. Cameron wired Blair on May 11, 1861:

Three regiments are assigned to our State, making in addition to the one regiment of three months' militia already called for, four regiments. It is important to reduce rather than enlarge this number, and in no event to exceed it. Let me earnestly recommend to you, therefore, to call for no more than four regiments...if more are already called for, to reduce the number by discharge."[20]

Blair disagreed with the War Department about the needs of the nation but was not in a position to disobey such a direct order. Therefore he appointed officers of the Fifth, Sixth and Seventh Michigan Regiments and ordered them to Fort Wayne in Detroit for a camp of instruction. In addition the non-commissioned officers of the selected companies were to attend the camp. This also had the effect of informing all companies which ones would be called if the next three regiments were needed. The camp of instruction began June 10, 1861, and broke up about August 1. In St. Joseph County another company from Burr Oak was chosen for the Seventh Michigan.[21]

However, it would be a mistake to think that everyone in St. Joseph County supported the war or thought of nothing but the rebellion. Isaac F. Ulrich, an early settler in Park Township, was a life-long Democrat and a man who was interested in politics. He served the township in various positions, most notably as Justice of the Peace. During 1861 he kept a daily journal in which he noted only four items that were related to the Civil War. On Sunday, May 5, 1861, he wrote "Cold and unpleasant. To meeting. [He had been a Methodist since 1838.] Burns preached on the subject of the present condition of the country. His opinion is to coherse the south by force of Army, good for a preacher of the *Cross*." On Saturday, August 17, he went to "Brady expecting to here [sic] address from Dr. Pratt on reestablishing peace in the Union. Republicans would not let him speak." He noted on Monday, August 19, "Military meeting at Parkville in evening." This was a meeting held by David Oakes, County Treasurer and Captain of the St. Joseph County Home Guard which was soon to be Company A of May's Independent Regiment. On Sunday, September 1, Ulrich made his final comment of the year on the war. He went to the Sunday meeting and Reverend Burns asked "who would have believed one year ago that we would have the war we now have. I did if Lincoln was elected."[22]

Notes

1. Mercury, 11 April 1861.

2. Richardson, James D, ed., *Compilation of the Messages and Papers of the Presidents*: 1789-1897 (10 vols. New York, Johnson Reprint Corp., 1969) 7:3214

3. Samuel Chadwick to John Robertson, 22 April 1861, Regimental Service Records of the Eleventh Michigan Volunteer Infantry, Records of the Michigan Military Establishment, State Archives of Michigan, Lansing, Michigan. (Hereafter cited as Regimental Service Records.)

4. *Reporter*, 18 April 1861.

5. *Western Chronicle*, 18 April 1861.

6. Shannon, Fred Albert, *The Organization and Administration of the Union Army, 1861-1865* (2 vols. Arthur H. Clark Company, 1928; reprint ed., Gloucester, Mass.: Peter Smith, 1965) 2:269.

7. Robertson, John, *General Order No. 2*, General and Special Orders, 1861-1866, Adjutant General Office, Records of Michigan Military Establishment, State Archives of Michigan, Lansing, Michigan.

8. Samuel Chadwick to John Robertson, 22 April 1861, Regimental Service Records.

9. Ibid, 23 April 1861, Regimental Service Records.

10. Robertson, John, ed., *Michigan in the War* (Lansing: W.S. George & Co., 1882) p. 167,174,758. Abbott was breveted Brigadier General of U.S. Volunteers on 13 March 1865 but not confirmed. (Hereafter cited as *Michigan in the War*.)

11. Ibid., pp. 187-188. Captain Lawson was cashiered in the fall of 1861.

12. *Reporter*, 21 August 1869. This was a history of the Eleventh Michigan Volunteer Infantry that was probably written by Samuel Chadwick.

13. J. H. Fountain to William L. Stoughton, 25 April 1861, Regimental Service Records.

14. Henry McAfee to John Robertson, 27 April 1861. Letters Relating to Raising of Companies, 1861-1878. Records of Michigan Military Establishment, State Archives of Michigan, Lansing, Michigan

15. Lanman, Charles, *Red Book of Michigan* (Detroit, E. B. Smith & Co., 1871) p. 487. See also Constantine *Mercury*, 14 March 1861, for the announcement of Stoughton's appointment.

16. *Michigan in the War*, pp. 23, 222-223, 970.

17. *Western Chronicle*, 8 May 1861.

18. *Michigan in the War*, pp. 220,222.

19. Eli Lake Starr to Brother Hank, 16 May 1861, Ness Collection, folders 64,65,66, Michigan Historical Collections, Bentley Historical Library, University of Michigan, Ann Arbor, Michigan.

20. *Michigan in the War*, p. 220.

21. Ibid., pp. 221-222, 270.

22. Diary of Isaac F. Ulrich, 1861, im passim. The originals of the diaries of Isaac F. Ulrich are in the possession of Mrs. O.E. Ulrich of Three Rivers, Michigan

Chapter Three

"Let us in if there is a possible chance."

While Austin Blair was attempting to find a way around the limitations imposed by the Secretary of War, President Lincoln was preparing to ask a Special Session of Congress for the authority to recruit an additional 400,000 three-year volunteers. The Congress received the request on July 4, increased it to 500,000 men, and passed the bill on July 22, the day after the Union defeat at the Battle of Bull Run. Finally, the Governors would have the authority to accept all of the companies that were being raised. The problem now was in the ability of the states to raise and forward the troops fast enough to satisfy Secretary Cameron.[1]

The rout of the Union Army at the Battle of Bull Run on July 21 caused the War Department to urge the governors to greater speed in forwarding regiments, equipped or unequipped, full or not. Michigan, with three regiments half-organized and their officers in the instruction camp, was in no position to act with the dispatch that Washington was demanding. The recruiting enthusiasm which had faded in June and early July was electrified by the news of the Union defeat. Once again the harassed Michigan Military Department was overwhelmed with offers and demands. Melvin Mudge of Quincy in Branch County was typical. He had organized a company in July and tried to have it accepted for service. Bull Run gave him new zeal. On July 23 he wrote: "Some of our brothers and neighbors of this place were in the late battle and we must avenge their deaths. Let us in if there is a possible chance."[2] So while public opinion in Michigan was rising to the new demands of the war, and the national administration was frantically calling for troops to be forwarded as fast as possible, Michigan was unprepared.

The telegrams between the War Department and the governors after the defeat at Bull Run reveal the panic that had seized Washington. It was his sense of danger and the desire to replace the three month regiments in the defense of the Capitol that led Cameron to greatly extend the use of independent commissions or acceptances. This device was first used in Delaware when state authorities failed to provide their quota of troops.[3] It was later used to raise specialty units, i.e. Hiram Berdan's Sharpshooters[4] and Carl Schurz's veteran cavalry.[5] The act of Congress that created the volunteer army also "provided that the President could commission individuals to raise independent commands in those states where the governors failed to perform recruiting duty."[6] However, the War Department in late July and early August issued these commissions without restraint even in states that had met every call and had offered more.

William J. May of White Pigeon received an authorization in early August to raise the regiment of infantry that ultimately became the Eleventh Michigan Volunteer Infantry. The key man in the origin of May's Independent Regiment was Samuel Chadwick of Three Rivers. Chadwick, who attempted to raise a company early in the war, later received an appointment as a clerk in the War Department. He wrote a series of letters to the Three Rivers *Reporter* from Washington in which he reported on his own activities and on the affairs of Michigan regiments with local companies. Chadwick described his position as a "good one and I am rather pleased with my success thus far."[7] On August 2 Chadwick was nominated for Assistant Quartermaster with the rank of Captain. He was at this time in charge of accepting the offers of service from independent regiments. It was also about this time that he secured an appointment as a Brigade Surgeon with the rank of Major for Dr. Samuel L. Herrick of Three Rivers.[8]

When Dr. Herrick arrived in Washington on August 4, he informed Chadwick that William May wanted to raise a regiment. While he was in White Pigeon waiting for the train, Herrick had spoken with May, who was the proprietor of the Railroad Dining House. May was a popular and well liked man. He was the colonel of two White Pigeon militia companies, the Rangers and the Invincibles. He did not seem to be interested in a military career as he never offered his two companies to the state during the early months of the war.[9] He had, however, received a major financial blow in mid-July when the Michigan Southern and Northern Indiana Railroad announced that trains would not stop in White Pigeon to allow passengers to eat.[10] This had undoubtedly led him to reconsider the possibilities of the military, especially at the rank of colonel. Chadwick "believing him [May] at the time to be a good man for the position went directly and had his name enrolled, with instructions to raise a regiment from St. Joseph County, and telegraphed the action to Col. May by order of Secretary Stanton [sic]".[11]

There can be little doubt that Chadwick in his brief moment of power in Washington arranged William J. May's commission to raise a regiment independent of state authorities.[12] Chadwick then had some difficulties which soon brought him back to Michigan to help recruit and later to serve as the Adjutant for that same regiment. He failed to receive Senate confirmation of his nomination.[13] The Three Rivers *Reporter* noted on August 17 that Chadwick was home recruiting for May's Independent Regiment. He was mentioned at that time as the prospective Lieutenant Colonel of the regiment.[14]

There were three other independent regiments commissioned in Michigan. Colonel Thomas B. W. Stockton of Flint, a West Point graduate (Class of 1823) and the Colonel of the First Michigan Volunteers in the Mexican War, had approached President Lincoln in June about the possibility of raising a regiment. Lincoln wrote to Cameron,

> I think it is entirely safe to accept a fifth regiment from Michigan, and with your approbation I should say a regiment presented by Col. T. B. W. Stockton, ready for service within two weeks from now, will be received. Look at Colonel Stockton's testimonials.[15]

Cameron immediately wired Blair that the President was willing to accept another Michigan regiment if it was led by Stockton and was ready in two weeks.[16] Blair's answer can not be found, but the regiment must not have been raised because Stockton was recruiting in early August with an independent commission from Cameron.[17]

Thornton F. Brodhead of Grosse Isle was authorized to enlist an independent regiment of cavalry. He had been the First Lieutenant and later Captain of Company A of the Fifteenth United States Infantry in the Mexican War.[18] The Detroit *Daily Advertiser* noted on August 6 that Brodhead "received a dispatch from Washington yesterday to raise a regiment of Cavalry."[19]

When the Special Session of Congress ended on August 6, Congressman Francis W. Kellogg of Grand Rapids secured a commission to enlist a regiment of cavalry. The Detroit *Daily Tribune* ran its first announcement of Kellogg's efforts to recruit his regiment on August 23.[20] Kellogg was unusually successful as the regiment was fully organized on October 2 but did not leave its rendezvous until November 14. Kellogg never took the field with his regiment. The unit became the Second Michigan Cavalry and was commanded at various times by a number of distinguished officers, including Gordon Granger and Philip Sheridan.[21]

In addition to the four independent regiments authorized to be raised in Michigan, Hiram Berdan, who was commissioned to raise a regiment of sharpshooters for the United States Army, was to raise one company from Michigan. Ultimately, he enlisted three companies from the state. The regular army was also recruiting in the state.[22] Captain Harvey Tilden of the Fifteenth U.S. Infantry opened a recruiting office in Detroit as early as July 11.[23]

The Sturgis Journal noted in September that Captain William W. Andrew of LaPorte, Indiana, with an independent commission from Kansas was recruiting a battery of Flying Artillery. It was later to be attached to May's Independent Regiment and ultimately became Battery D, First Michigan Light Artillery.[24] Another independent unit that was associated with May's Independent Regiment in White Pigeon was the Chandler Horse Guards. The Detroit *Daily Tribune* noted that "Capt. W. C. Hughes of Dayton, Berrien County, writes us from Pittsburg on the 15 inst. that the Secretary of War has authorized him to organize one squadron of two companies of cavalry 'The Chandler Horse Guards'."[25] Hughes raised four companies of cavalry in southern Michigan and was closely associated with May in White Pigeon. However, the unit was disbanded in November "on account of some irregularities in its organization."[26]

While all of these units were being recruited and organized, the Governor and the Military Department of Michigan were trying to fill the regiments designated for the state by the volunteer army authorization. Blair had to reorganize the First Regiment as a three year unit and had to fill the Fifth, Sixth and Seventh whose officers finished their training at the end of July. In addition, he soon received permission to raise the Eighth Regiment. The Governor, who in June was attempting to satisfy all who wanted to enlist, found himself in August in a desperate competition for volunteers.

This was not a problem that Blair faced alone. All of the war governors were having the same problems in the two months after the Battle of Bull Run. In most states it was much worse than in Michigan. Governor Andrew G. Curtin of Pennsylvania complained to Lincoln that his state was expected to send ten more regiments and that fifty-eight independent commissions had been granted to individuals in Pennsylvania. This had resulted in "much embarrassment, delay, and confusion" in supplying any regiments.[27] The scope of the problem for the governors can be seen in the words of James Lesley Jr., Chief Clerk of the War Department, who said, "We have accepted twice as many [regiments] from individual colonels as from State Executives."[28] Austin Blair wrote Cameron to,

> make an earnest appeal to you to recognize no more independent regiments in this state. They are introducing confusion and discord into all our affairs. Companies are divided and officers in unseemly quarrels. I will furnish all the troops you call for much sooner and in better order than these independent regiments can do and thus avert a great amount of local ill feeling.[29]

The competition between recruiters in Michigan never reached the depths that it did in some states. "Disgraceful rivalries arose which 'led would-be colonels to bribe subordinate officers to transfer themselves with their men from one regiment to another.' On one occasion, at least, a shooting affray grew out of such practices and two men were killed and several wounded."[30] However, it was bad enough for Blair.

On September 7 Cameron asked the governors how many regiments were "ready for marching orders on a few hours notice."[31] Blair replied that the Sixth and Seventh Regiments had left for Washington and that the Fifth was fully enrolled, uniformed, and ready to leave. The First, Eighth and Stockton each had about 700 men.[32] About this time the editor of the *Western Chronicle* visited May's White Pigeon camp and found seven companies with about 700 men. Captain Harvey Tilden, the United States mustering officer, had arrived in camp on September 7.[33] Apparently, Blair did not know how large May's regiment was, or he refused to recognize its existence.

By early September Cameron began to turn the independent regiments over to the state governors. On September 5, the New York and Massachusetts governors were given authority to reorganize independent regiments in their states. Curtin received control over them in Pennsylvania two days later.[34] When William P. Innes of Grand Rapids sought a commission from the War Department in September to raise a regiment of mechanics and engineers, Cameron turned the request over to Blair for acceptance.[35] This was the way he had treated Stockton's request in June. Finally, on September 16, the governors received complete control over all independent units. "These troops will be organized, or reorganized, and prepared for service by the Governors of their respective States in the manner they may judge most advantageous for the interest of the General Government."[36] The officers were to receive their commissions from the Governors. In this way Stockton's Independent Regiment became the Sixteenth Michigan, and May's became the Eleventh Michigan.

There may have been some attempt to gain control of or break up May's emerging organization in August or early September. The only documentation that supports this is a letter from Samuel Chadwick written from White Pigeon. Chadwick, writing to an unnamed correspondent who was probably Adjutant General Robertson, said "A letter was sent [by] me from this place yesterday to Detroit intended for Gov. Blair. Please call at the P.O. and take it out & present to the Gov." A postscript that must contain the main points of the letter to the Governor was added at the bottom.

> Let me suggest that these companies that are raised for May's Reg't be attached to the other Regiments raised. The Dept. will allow the Gov. to add from two to five co's. Then he can raise the 10th Reg't out of the surplus. There are *three full* co's. and large skeletons for the rest.[37]

On September 11 the Democratic party newspaper, the *Western Chronicle*, charged that Governor Blair "had done everything possible to crush the regiment [May's]."[38]

Sometime before Secretary of War Cameron's September 16 order to officers holding independent commissions to report to the Governor of their state, a move was made to secure three hundred men from May for Colonel Stockton's regiment. May went to Detroit to fight the order that would have destroyed the regiment. He was in Detroit on September 16 because on that date Captain David Oakes of Company A telegraphed May and Governor Blair that "Capt. Tilden has sent a dispatch to the War Dept. for marching orders for your regiment representing that it has the minimum number of men present."[39]

While Captain Tilden was trying to keep the Governor from breaking the regiment by putting it under War Department orders, Colonel May was attempting to strengthen his political base in Michigan. The Detroit newspapers were reporting that William L. Stoughton of Sturgis was to be the Lieutenant Colonel. Stoughton had been the Captain of the Peninsular Guard which was serving with the Fourth Michigan. He was serving presently as the U.S. District Attorney for Western Michigan; in other words he was a power in both the State and National Republican Party.[40]   May must have been partly successful because the number of men that he was ordered to send Stockton was reduced to eighty-three, the minimum for one company.

On September 17, May was back in White Pigeon to explain the situation to the regiment. Whatever the Colonel said, it was understood that if eighty-three men did not volunteer to leave the regiment and join Stockton, then the entire regiment would have to go.[41] The Colonel also tried to entice non-members of the regiment to join Stockton thereby reducing the number that would go from the regiment. He offered ten dollars to any man outside of the regiment who would volunteer.[42] By 11:30 a.m. the eighty-three volunteers boarded the train to the cheers and goodbyes of their former comrades.

May wasted no time in consolidating his new arrangement with Governor Blair. In the afternoon after sending the volunteers to Stockton, the regiment elected their officers. This formality was usually a foregone conclusion. The man who organized the regiment became the colonel, and his nominations for the other staff officers were duly elected. However, the situation was not normal for May's Independent Regiment. From the beginning Colonel May had introduced Samuel Chadwick throughout the recruiting area as the future Lieutenant Colonel. On his return from Detroit May proposed William Stoughton for the position as the Detroit newspapers had reported he would. Stoughton was easily elected. He was well known and highly respected. Benjamin Doughty of Sturgis was elected major, and Germain Mason of Constantine was chosen Adjutant. May confirmed his appointment of Addison Drake as Quartermaster, William N. Elliott as Surgeon and Holmes Pattison as Chaplain.

The Three Rivers *Reporter* was quick to protest this slight to Chadwick. Reporting the election on September 21, the *Reporter* said,

> Mr. S. Chadwick did not, as was anticipated by nearly all the citizens in this part of the state, and most of the soldiers in the Independent Regiment, receive the appointment of Lieut. Colonel. That measure was either right or shamefully wrong.[43]

The *Reporter* went on to suggest some cheating. The Adrian *Daily Expositor* put it more succinctly with "S. Chadwick of Three Rivers has been diddled out of the Lieutenant Colonel of Col. May's Regiment after it was once assigned to him."[44] Strangely, none of the men of the regiment mentioned the election in their letters written shortly after the event. It appears that the enlisted men were not particularly upset by the election results. The final act in the officers election story came with the Governor's inspection on October 8. Germain Mason was somehow induced to step down as Adjutant, and Chadwick accepted the position.

For Holmes Pattison of Colon the appointment as Chaplin presented some real problems. His rank in the ministry of the Methodist Episcopal Church was not high enough to allow him to serve Communion. He wrote to his Bishop, Matthew Simpson, asking to be ordained as an Elder. Chaplin Pattison showed an important aspect of the regiment and its Colonel when he wrote:

> [The men] seem quite anxious to commemorate the broken body and shed blood of our blessed Redeemer in camp once in three months according to the custom of our church. Again our Col. in conversation with me yesterday on those subjects expressed a very strong desire to have all members of the Church organized and formed into Classes and Class Meetings and Prayer Meetings held regularly in camp. Unless I am ordained an Elder I shall not be able to administer the Sacrament of the Lord's Supper to the men as they now strongly desire.[45]

Captain Benjamin G. Bennet of Company D was detailed to accompany to Detroit the men tranferred to Stockton. While in Detroit he read an account of the flag presentation to Stockton's regiment before they left for Cleveland. The *Free Press* article ended with the statement that, "It is understood that at Cleveland the regiment is to be joined by a portion of Colonel May's Regiment which has been transferred to this one."[46] Bennet was quick to see a threat in the article, and the next morning's issue carried his letter to the editor of the *Free Press*.

> The paragraph in your paper of yesterday morning may work an injury to Colonel May's Regiment, although inadvertently on your part. Your article might perhaps carry the impression that Colonel May's Regiment had been

attached to Stockton's. Such is not the case. Colonel May sent one company of eighty-three men to join Stockton in Cleveland; and there are yet in camp at White Pigeon over 700 men who have been mustered into the service. All apparent variances between Governor Blair and Colonel May have been amicably arranged, and the former now wishes to see the 'St. Joe Regiment' filled up and put in the field. Recruiting is going on rapidly, & the regiment will be full by Monday next. [47]

On October 8 Governor Blair arrived in White Pigeon to assure the men of his good intention.

....the regiment was put through its drill by Lieutenant Colonel Stoughton, reviewed by Colonel May and the Governor, then formed into a hollow square to hear the Governor speak. He assured them that he had the best interests of the regiment at heart and that he was in no way unfriendly to their efforts to complete their organization. He knew the men were among the finest the State had to offer, and called upon them to do their best when they met the enemy. [48]

The threatened dissolution of May's regiment was finally ended.

Notes

1. For President Lincoln's message to Congress, see O.R., Series III, Vol. 1, pp. 311-321. The message was carried in most local newspapers.

2. Melvin Mudge to Robertson, 23 July 1861, Regimental Service Records, Letters relating to the Raising of Companies, Eleventh Michigan Infantry, Box 139. Records of the Michigan Military Establishment, State Archives of Michigan, Lansing, Michigan.

3. O.R., op. cit., p. 124.

4. Ibid., p. 270.

5. Ibid., p. 140.

6. William B. Hesseltine, *Lincoln and the War Governors* (New York: Alfred A. Knopf, 1948) p. 184.

7. Three Rivers *Reporter*, 6 June 1861.

8. Ibid, 21 August 1869. This is the same history of the Eleventh Michigan Infantry that was cited in Chapter Two. See also Applications for Brigade Surgeon, Record Group 107, Records of Office of Secretary of War, Box 118. These applications do not always have a letter of application from the individual but are more in the form of letters of nomination. Dr. Herrick wrote a personal letter of application on 10 August 1861 and had letters of recommendation from Colonel Dwight A. Woodbury of the Fourth Michigan Infantry and Senator Samuel C. Pomeroy of Kansas.

   This file also contains an application for Dr. William N. Elliott of White Pigeon with no personal letter. His application does have letters of recommendation for Colonel Woodbury and Senator Pomeroy. However, his file contains a letter of recommendation from Governor Blair. There is no evidence that Elliott, who served as the Surgeon for the Eleventh Michigan, ever sought a position as Brigade Surgeon at this time.

9. *Western Chronicle*, 17 May 1860. There is no evidence that these militia units were offered for service in the Civil War. In the early days of intense excite-

ment when most militia leaders were writing the Adjutant General to accept their companies, May did not try to have his men accepted for service or at least the letters do not exist.

10. Three Rivers *Reporter*, 11 July 1861. The company was apparently moving this operation to their newly constructed passenger house at Goshen, Indiana. *Annual Report of the President and Directors of the Southern Michigan and Northern Indiana Railroad Co., March 1, 1861* (New York: W. H. Arthur and Co., 1861). p. 31.

11. Ibid., 21 August 1869. Chadwick mistakenly referred to Secretary of War Edwin M. Stanton when he meant Simon Cameron.

12. There would appear to have been an "old boy network" of Mexican War officers operating to commission all three of Michigan's independent regiments.

13. There were in Michigan a strange series of newspaper articles that may help explain why Chadwick was not confirmed. In the August 10th (the paper was two days late) issue of the Constantine *Mercury*, the acid-tongued editor Levi Hull wrote the following article:

> We notice that Samuel Chadwick of Three Rivers had been nominated as Assistant Quartermaster. We also learn that Isaac B. Hussey, formerly of Niles, has been appointed Assistant Quartermaster. Hussey used formerly to visit this village frequently and is known to many of our citizens as a whiskey drinking bloat. His latest public transaction was as one of the officers and operators of the Boone county (Indiana) Bank swindle.

Chadwick had been recognized in the company of a poor character. This same article ran word-for-word under the heading of "Bad Appointments" in the Detroit *Daily Advertiser* two days later. On August 14 the Lansing *State Republican* ran this notice:

> Sam Chadwick. This individual, who had been nominated Assistant Quartermaster has been promptly discharged by the Secretary of War, upon representation being made by responsible parties that he in not a suitable person.

In turn, the *Mercury* ran this same notice on August 22 with the following remark: "We should really like to know the charges and specifications, and whether from some cause the Republican is not slightly malignant." Two days after the *State Republican* article the Adrian *Daily Expositor* noted that "J. J. Newell of this city has been appointed Assistant Quartermaster in the army in place of Samuel Chadwick of Three Rivers whose nomination was recently announced but not confirmed."

14. Three Rivers *Reporter*, 17 August 1861.

15. Lincoln to Cameron, 13 June 1861. O.R., Series III, Vol. 1, p. 269.

16. Cameron to Blair, 14 June 1861, Ibid., p. 271.

17. For first notice of recruiting see Detroit *Daily Advertizer*, 6 August 1861. The *Western Chronicle* ran a notice that Stockton was recruiting an independent regiment on the same day that it printed May's announcement. *Western Chronicle*, 14 August 1861. Stockton's regiment became the Sixteenth Michigan Volunteer Infantry. *Michigan in the War*, pp. 359, 783, 940-941.

18. *Michigan in the War*, p. 553, 783.

19. Detroit *Daily Advertizer*, 6 August 1861. *Michigan in the War*, p. 553 said the First Cavalry commenced recruiting on August 24, 1861 at Camp Lyon near Detroit.

20. Detroit *Daily Tribune*, 23 August 1861.

21. *Michigan in the War*, pp. 614-627. Kellogg also recruited the Michigan Sixth Cavalry on an independent commission from the War Department. Ibid., p. 569.

22. Ibid., p. 744.

23. Detroit *Daily Advertizer*, 11 July 1861.

24. Sturgis *Journal*, 12 September 1861.

25. Detroit *Daily Tribune*, 16 August 1861.

26. *Michigan in the War*, p. 744.

27. Curtin to Lincoln, 21 August 1861. O.R., Series III, p. 539-441. For more on this problem, see William B. Hesseltine, *Lincoln and the War Governors* (New York: Alfred A. Knopf, 1948), pp. 181-191.

28. Lesley to General John A. Wright, 6 August 1861, Ibid., p. 390.

29. Blair to Cameron, 19 August 1861, Ibid., p. 428.

30. Fred Albert Shannon, op. cit., p. 261. *New York Tribune*, 11 September 1861.

31. O.R., III. Vol. 1, p. 489.

32. Blair to Cameron, 7 September 1861, Ibid., p. 490.

33. *Western Chronicle*, 11 September 1861.

34. A. Howard Meneely, *The War Department, 1861: A Study in Mobilization and Administration* (New York: Privately printed, 1928). p. 210-213. This was a PhD thesis at Columbia University.

35. O.R., III, Vol. 1, p. 497.

36. General Order No. 78, Ibid., pp. 518-519.

37. Letters relating to Raising of Companies, Regimental Records. This is a extremely strange letter. Other evidence cited in Chapter Four will show that the first three recruits arrive in White Pigeon on August 20, and Company B was the only full company in camp on August 22. Companies A and C arrived on August 24. Chadwick, who had issued the commission that started the regiment and was being introduced by May as the future Lieutenant Colonel, was instructing the Governor on the means to destroy the unit.

38. *Western Chronicle*, 11 September 1861.

39. Regimental Service Records. Oakes as Captain of Company A must have been the senior officer present on September 16. The *Western Chronicle* reported that May had gone to Detroit on regimental business on September 11.

40. *Western Chronicle*, 11 September 1861. "The Free Press [Detroit] reported that Stoughton was the Lt. Colonel but no one in the regiment knew this." The *Chronicle* went on to point out that Chadwick was being introduced in St. Joseph County by May as Lieutenant Colonel.

41. James W. King to Sarah Jane Babcock, 17 September 1861. James W. King Papers, Regional History Collections, Western Michigan University, Kalamazoo, Michigan. Hereafter cited as King Papers.

    Daniel DeVine Rose to Sarah Rose, 18 September 1861, possession of Leland W. Thornton, Centreville, Michigan. Hereafter cited as Rose Papers. King was not present for May's speech, but Rose was. Rose and King were good friends as their later letters show. So probably King was only repeating what he was told by Rose

42. Rose Papers, 18 September 1861

43. *Reporter*, 21 September 1861

44. Adrian *Daily Expositor*, 24 September 1861

45. Holmes A. Pattison to Bishop Matthew Simpson, 26 August 1861, Papers of Bishop Matthew Simpson, Box 7, Library of Congress, Washington, D.C.

46. Detroit *Free Press*, 17 Septembewr 1861.

47. Ibid., 18 September 1861.

48. Wayne C. Mann, "The Road to Murfreesboro: The Eleventh Michigan Volunteer Infantry from Organization Through its First Battle" (M.A. thesis, Western Michigan University, 1963), p. 26. (Hereafter cited as Road to Murfreesboro).

Chapter Four

"I have joined Col. May's regiment."

William J. May had a few busy weeks after receiving his commission to raise a regiment. By August 14 the local newspapers announced that May had a commission. On August 17 the Adrian *Daily Expositor* not only ran the notice of the regiment but also added that Reverend Benjamin E. Doughty of the Sturgis Methodist Church was to be the Major and Addison T. Drake of Sturgis was Quartermaster. By September 11 the Lansing *Republican* ran a notice of May's Independent Regiment in White Pigeon which was to be armed with Enfield rifles and have the "finest quality uniforms."[1]

In that same week May received permission from the superintendent of the Michigan Southern Railroad to use the company's facilities at White Pigeon as a training camp. The dining house became the "victualing department" and the 640-foot-long car house was the barracks. The grounds were the drill and parade fields. Editor Bouton proclaimed it to be "by far the best and healthiest [camp] in the state."[2] The editor of the Constantine Mercury visited the camp and wrote:

> Messrs. Shurtz, Laird and Wallis have the contract for feeding and lodging the men, and from all we have seen and can learn, are giving the very best satis-faction. The tables are loaded with good, substantial, well cooked food, neatly prepared and arranged. The lodgings are in buildings temporarily fitted up for the purpose, and are comfortable. Those who lodged upon the State fair ground at Detroit last Spring, think the lodgings at White Pigeon luxurious.[3]

The White Pigeon camp was originally called Camp Goodwin but, after the arrival of Captain Harvey Tilden of the United States Army as the mustering officer, the name became Camp Tilden.[4]

The one problem that May did not have was in finding men. Across southern Michigan there were still units that had been re-cruited early in the summer and found no place in the Fifth, Sixth, and Seventh regiments. After the Battle of Bull Run, communities and individuals redoubled their efforts to enlist men to preserve the Union. The *Western Chronicle* reported that over two hundred men in the county had enlisted in the two and one half weeks since Bull Run.[5] These were the type of men who joined May's Inde-pendent Regiment.

One company that organized early and had yet to find a regiment was Melvin Mudge's from Quincy in Branch County. Mudge went to Detroit early in July and received encouragement from the Michigan Military Department to raise a company. On July 22 he wrote Adjutant General Robertson. "A better company of boys was never raised. If there is or as soon as there is a place, give it to us and oblige the Quincy Rifles."[6] After the news of Bull Run Mudge wrote, "Let us in if there is a possible chance."[7] Mudge asked about a possible assignment to the Eighth Regiment. On July 29 DeGamo Jones, Aide-de-Camp to General Robertson, wrote Mudge a curt note, "No companies have as yet been assigned to the Eighth Regiment. Should your command be designated you will be officially notified."[8] But the Quincy captain had waited long enough. He wrote Robertson on the same day asking why his company had not been assigned. Then he gave his own opinion of the reason: "We think there will not be much chance for us for the fact that we have no Ex Governor or Congressman or any other wire working politician to interceed for us. Yet we did cast our vote for Governor Blair ...."[9] For Mudge and the Quincy boys, May's commission to organize a regiment independent of state con-trol was a new opportunity. They changed their company name from the Quincy Rifles to the Quincy Wolverines and arrived in White Pigeon on August 22. They were the first full company in camp.[10]

David Oakes, former Supervisor of Sherman Township and the incumbent Republican St. Joseph County Treasurer, was one of the principal recruiters in the county. As early as April 20 Oakes wrote the Adjutant General asking how to organize a company and for a set of military books.[11] He had visited the Peninsular Guard at the Fourth Regiment's training camp in Adrian with William Stoughton, the former captain.[12] In late July he began recruiting the St. Joseph County Home Guard. Oakes was especially active in the northeastern section of the county. His company must have been of good size when he approached the State in late July for a place. However, he too was rebuffed by the Michigan Military Department. On August 3 De Gamo Jones wrote Oakes that, "There are always more companies organized than will suffice to fill the Regiment requested."[13]

Oakes tied his company to May's regiment. It was Company A although it was the second or third company to arrive at White Pigeon. His association with May's efforts can be seen in the notice of the recruiting meeting held in Park Township on August 19.

> A meeting was held at Parkville, on Monday evening, for the purpose of raising recruits for Col. May's Independent Regiment. The occasion was enlivened by the presence of Capt. Oaks [Oakes] with several members of his Company, and Martial Music. The meeting was addressed by Drs. Beck and Howard, and Messrs. Oaks, Crosette and others. Several names were added to the Muster Roll. The feeling throughout the county is decidedly in favor of having Col. May's Regiment, at the disposition of the War Department in as short a time as possible. Meetings are being held all over the county. A meeting was held in Cass County last night, which was attended by several persons from Three Rivers.[14]

The St. Joseph County Guard moved to White Pigeon on September 2 with a vast parade of people.

> Capt. David Oakes' Company, from Centreville, went into rendezvous at Camp Goodwin, White Pigeon, on Monday last, with, as we are informed, one hundred and sixteen men. On their way they paid our village [Constantine] a visit. They were in wagons, accompanied by a large number of their friends and neighbors, and with their banners and two good bands of music made a sight worth seeing. The Company is made up of the very best material - strong, robust men, used to labor - they will go into camp and be

easily transformed into the very best soldiers. The size and apparent strength of the men was the admiration of everyone. [15]

Calvin C. Hood, a Sturgis merchant, began recruiting a company for May's regiment at some date between the fifteenth and twenty-second of August. Hood's company arrived at White Pigeon about the same time as the St. Joseph County Home Guard and became Company C. Ira Gillaspie of Sturgis recorded his decision to enlist in Hood's company and how he went about doing it.

August 20, 1861 - I come to the conclusion that I would volunteer my cirveses to my country. I sot down and wrote a letter to Sam Slyter requesting him to come to Sturgis and go with me. I talked with my wife on the subject and she did not want me to enlist but she feared I would be drafted for thare was a goodeel of talk about drafting. She said I might do just as I saw fit. I explained to her the state of our country that it is in need of all true patriots to sustain her goverment but all did not convince her that I aught to enlist. I went to my employer told him my intentions. He said you are write Ira for your country needs you. Saturday evening I went out to my fathers on a viset. He lived in the town of Sherman about seven miles from Sturgis. My father and mother was very much aposed to my enlisting. They admitted that our country needed men but their plea was that thare was anuff without me but I had fully made up my mind to enlist so thare was no stoping me.

August the 22 - I come home and found out that the fier we had seen from fathers was the burning of the Railroad Block. Next day I went to work for John Collance abossing the job of clearing away the reck of the fier. My wife said all she could to me to convince me that it was not my duty to go to war. Next day when Capt. C. [Calvin] Hoods Company was marching about town in the afternoon they was colected in front of the recruiting office. I went over opened the dore went up to the desk and told Henry Plat [Platt] that I had been to see Mr. [Mathias] Falkner. He had told me the termes of enlisting as followes said he if you enlist you will draw 26 dolars every two months and you wife will draw 12 dolars every 2 months and said he at the end of the war you will be entitled to 160 acres of unocupied land and one hundred dolars. Now Henry is this fact or not. Said he it is. I told him to hand me his pen. He done so. I put my name to the muster role. I was a soldier. I then went back to my work untill the company was formed in line to be mustered into the cirveses when I went over to the offices agane and fell in and was mustered in with the rest.

When I got home I found that the news had got thare before me. My wife was acrying. I told her to console herself that the war would soon be over and our country at peace but she thought I had aught not to have enlisted. I told her that the drafted men was not used as well as volenteers and in battle they was shuved write ahead and used for brestworks for volenteers. She could not think of having me drafted. I got a leter that evening from

Sam stating that he would come out and see me anyway and maybe he would enlist and go with me. Enoch [Gillaspie] had enlisted after I did contrary to my wishes or his folkes eather. [16]

Another company that was raised in the closing weeks of August was the Bronson Guard of Bronson in Branch County. The Captain was Benjamin G. Bennet of Burr Oak. Bennet had served as the First Sergeant of Company G of the First Michigan Volunteer Infantry. He was a former editor of the *Western Chronicle* and was the ticket agent at Burr Oak for the Michigan Southern Railroad at the time of his enlistment in the First Infantry. He was not mustered out of the service until August 7. As a veteran who had been at Bull Run, Bennet was a popular speaker at recruiting meetings and was always favorably reviewed by the local newspapers. The *Mercury* reported on an August 31 meeting in Constantine at which "Grove" Bennet was the principal speaker.

> Pursuant to notice, there was a public meeting held at Case's Hall, in this village, on Saturday evening last. The meeting came together at seven o'clock and was organized by electing B. G. Bennet, chairman, and L. T. Hull, secretary. Hon. H. H. Riley addressed the meeting upon the matters now agitating the country and the duty of all loyal citizens in the present exigency. He was followed by B. G. Bennett, who gave a brief and graphic account of the battle of Bull's Run, July 28th [sic], at which he was present and an actor. His remarks were listened to with the utmost attention. At the conclusion he made a statement of the facts relative to Col. May's commission from the U. S. War Department to raise an independent regiment. That it was a reality, and could not fail of being filled up if the people acted in as good faith and as earnestly as the War Department and Col. May were acting. [17]

The first notice that Bennet was raising a company appeared in the *Western Chronicle* on August 22. When the editor of the Sturgis *Journal* visited the camp at White Pigeon on September 4, Bennett's Company D was there.

By September 11 when the editor of the *Western Chronicle* again visited Camp Tilden, there were three more companies: the Three Rivers Light Guard, the Hudson Riflemen, and the Schoolcraft Rifle Rangers. [18] The Three Rivers company was a community effort. Both Three Rivers' newspapers had reported the meetings and called for an all Three Rivers company. Many leading citizens spoke at these meetings, and some joined the company. Henry N. Spencer was the Captain. He was forty-three years old and had been a Justice of the Peace in Lockport Township (1846-1856). At the time of his enlistment he was the Sexton of Oakdale Cemetery. Spencer was also the Superintendent of the Three Rivers Presbyterian Sunday School. This church was very active in its support of the war. Eighty members or relatives of its members served in the army.[19] The *Western Chronicle* reported that the company was mustered at Three Rivers by Samuel Chadwick, who was referred to as Lieutenant Colonel.[20] To the cheers of neighbors and friends and the music of a band, the Three Rivers Light Guard left for White Pigeon to become Company E.[21]

The Hudson Riflemen had a more complex history than the previous companies. It was the amalgamation of two Lenawee County companies. Sylvester B. Smith, a Morenci bookkeeper, organized a company by early June. He carried on a long correspondence with the Adjutant General through June and July attempting to have his company accepted for service.[22] However, by September Smith's unit must have been seriously under strength, as he joined with the Hudson Rifles led by Joseph Wilson of Hudson. The two units became Company F of May's Independent Regiment. Smith served as Captain and Wilson as First Lieutenant, but the company retained the Hudson name.

It is possible that Smith's company split on the issue of joining the Independent Regiment in White Pigeon. This was the type of situation that caused Governor Blair to write Secretary of War Cameron that, "Companies are divided and officers in unseemly quarrels."[23] The Morenci company must have been close to full about this time as Smith wrote Robertson that he had a full company. Yet they had to join the Hudson unit to go with White Pigeon.[24] The combined Morenci-Hudson unit also came close to splitting on the same issue. A local hero from the Fourth Michigan who had escaped from a Richmond prisoner-of-war camp arrived home to recruit for the Fourth Michigan Infantry just as Smith and Wilson were planning to join May. An unnamed correspondent reported to the Detroit *Free Press* about a debate within Smith's company.

> An independent company has been raised here by Capt. Smith, and today after some sharp debate, the company voted, forty-four to four, to join Col. May's regiment now rendezvousing at White Pigeon rather than one of the state regiments. Eighteen members were absent when the vote was taken but will probably go with the majority.[25]

It would appear that Smith and Wilson had about seventy men. Smith's company had the latest muster date of any company, September 11. The Hudson Riflemen became Company F. Since companies were usually named for their arrival time in camp, May must have been holding the sixth position for Smith.

Company G was also a unit with a curious history. Twenty-two year old Thomas Briggs, of Schoolcraft in Kalamazoo County, recruited the Schoolcraft Rifle Rangers. The men were mostly from southern Kalamazoo and northern St. Joseph counties. Briggs recruited them to join Stockton's Independent Regiment.[26] For reasons that cannot be discovered, the company was in White Pigeon by September 11 with Briggs as Captain but with only 44 men.[27]

However, by September 24 Charles Moase was listed as the Captain and Briggs was First Lieutenant. Moase was twenty-six years old and had served as Second Lieutenant of Company G, First Michigan Infantry. He had sailed as a seaman on a whaling ship at twenty-one and became a locomotive fireman at twenty-four.[28] He was clerking in a store in Bronson when he joined the First Michigan. Moase had opened a recruiting office in the railroad depot at White Pigeon shortly after being mustered out in Detroit on August 7.[29] He was the "Acting Adjutant of the regiment" until the organization and the election of officers.[30] Apparently, when Moase failed to be elected Adjutant, Briggs was persuaded to step down for the veteran of Bull Run.[31]

John R. Hackstaff, the editor of the Coldwater *Democratic Union*, organized Company H. Hackstaff was well acquainted with St. Joseph County as he had started a number of short-lived Democratic newspapers in Sturgis and White Pigeon in the late

1840's and early 1850's.[32] In 1859 he began the *Democratic Union* which was remembered in Coldwater as "a spicy paper."[33] The Company was recruited almost exclusively in Branch County. Hackstaff was one of the first officers to resign, and he seems to have been very ill from the beginning. Moase in later years testified that Captain Hackstaff was an invalid in White Pigeon and that the entire command fell on First Lieutenant Samuel Mills.[34]

Company I was raised in the Monroe County area as the Chandler Guard by Nelson Chamberlain. Chamberlain was a veteran of the Mexican War. He wrote to Robertson on September 21 that he had enrolled a full company.[35] Ten days later he was planning to bring them to Detroit for mustering into the service. At that time he again wrote to Robertson:

> I have now enlisted 70 or 80 men which I wish to bring to Detroit to be mustered into service. We hope to complete the company this week, but if we should not succeed in this, we will bring into the service as many as we have, with the understanding that we have officers in proportion to our number of men.[36]

Chamberlain closed by asking for free railroad passes to bring the men to Detroit.

On October 4 Robertson accepted Chamberlain's company for he wrote: "By direction of the Governor you are hereby authorized to bring to Fort Wayne the seventy or eighty men you mention in accordance with the proposition contained in your letter of the 1st inst."[37] Captain Chamberlain must have had a sudden change of mind because on October 5 he wrote a terse note: "I have joined Col. May's Regiment."[38] He arrived in White Pigeon with fifty-one men and was the last company to join May.

The Adrian *Daily Expositor* announced on August 25 that "W. [William W.] Phillips of this city has obtained seventy-five recruits for Col. May's independent regiment."[39] Phillips worked western Monroe and eastern Hillsdale counties for additional men. He was in White Pigeon by September 23 with sixty-four men. This unit became Company K and was full when the regiment left for Kentucky with only a few men from St. Joseph County.

There were two other units associated with May's Independent Regiment in White Pigeon: the Chandler Horse Guard and Andrew's Flying Artillery Battery. Captain W. C. Hughes of Dayton (Berrien County) was recruiting two companies of calvary from southern Michigan. Adjutant General Robertson's history of Michigan military units has only a brief account of the Chandler Horse Guard.

> At Coldwater there was a battalion of cavalry recruited under the direction of Major Hughes, designated the 'Chandler Horse Guard.' It was mustered into the service with four companies, fully eqipped and mounted, but on account of some irregularities in its organization, was disbanded before leaving the state.[40]

However, there are only records showing the mustering out of service in Coldwater of two companies.[41] Hughes apparently left the state with the two companies that he was originally authorized to raise. He must have left the two additional companies in White Pigeon with May. May wired the War Department as early as August 17 for permission to add a squadron of cavalry and Andrew's Battery to his regiment.[42] Chief Clerk James Lesley, Jr. ordered the Colonel to "add Andrew's battery, not the cavalry."[43] Colonel May told an audience in Hudson on September 14 that his regiment would have its own artillery and cavalry.[44] May was probably just using the cavalry as a recruiting tool at this late date unless he planned to present the War Department with a fait accompli when he was ordered to the front. These were the two companies of the Chandler Horse Guard that were mustered out at Coldwater on November 22 by the Michigan Military Department for "irregularities in its organization." Most of the men listed in the mustering out list were from St. Joseph and Branch counties. At least one of the "Chandler Horse Guard" joined May's regiment after being mustered out as cavalry. Robert Thomas joined Company B on November 23.[45]

More closely associated with the regiment was the artillery battery raised by William W. Andrew, a thirty-year-old La Porte, Indiana, lawyer. This unit ultimately became Battery D of the First

Michigan Light Artillery.46   It was recruited in Branch and St. Joseph counties with nearly half of the men from Union City in Branch County.   Apparently some move was made to replace the officers while they were still in White Pigeon.   Benjamin Wells wrote to his wife about the artillery company:

> ...there is mutiny in the camp. What it will amount to, I will not venture to say at the present. There has been considerable excitement in the Artillery company for some days past. And yesterday they were to be mustered into United States service. And it appears their first Lieutenant had not been elected by the company but had been appointed by the Col. The company are all opposed to his appointment and when they were called on to muster, every man refused to take the oath and have the would-be-Lieutenant mustered as such. The company are all determined not to be mustered unless they have the choice of their own officers. This caused a great deal of excitement in camp.[47]

The battery did leave White Pigeon with the Eleventh on December 9, 1861. However, they were quickly separated from the regiment at Louisville. Captain Andrew and Second Lieutenant Alonzo S. Nichols resigned in January, 1862. Later they would organize and serve as Captain and First Lieutenant of the Twenty-first Battery of the Indiana Light Artillery.[48]

Notes

1. Lansing *Republican*, 11 September 1861.

2. *Western Chronicle*, 11 September 1861.

3. Constantine *Mercury*, 25 September 1861.

4. This is probably the same Captain Tilden who had a recruiting office for the Fifteenth United States Infantry in Detroit. There is a curious postscript to the character of Tilden which was published in the Constantine Mercury on 30 January 1862.

   "In the lengthy report of the Potter investigating committee on the disloyalty of Gov. employees, we find mention of the somewhat notorious (in this vicinity) individual whose name heads this article.

   The witness, Alfred B. Mullet, is a clerk in the Treasury Dept. and is acquainted with H. Tilden, lately appointed captain of the regular army. About the time of the attack on Ft. Sumter he told the witness that 'all the trouble was brought on the country by the Black Republicans - that the South was right, and that he hoped they would whip the Gov to hell.'

   This is the same Capt. Tilden who mustered in May's Regiment, and after whom Camp Tilden was named. He was not noted for loyal or disloyal sentiments while at White Pigeon but for drinking large quantities of whiskey & getting highly drunk as a natural consequence."

5. *Western Chronicle*, 8 August 1861.

6. Mudge to Robertson, Regiment Service Records, 22 July 1861.

7. Ibid., 23 July 1861.

8. DeGamo Jones to Melvin Mudge. Letters Out from Adjutant General's Office; Vol. 1, April 1861 - February 1863. Records of the Michigan Military Establishment, State Archives of Michigan, Lansing, Michigan, p. 254.

9. Mudge to Robertson, Regimental Service Records, 29 July 1861.

10. *History of Branch County, Michigan* (Philadelphia: Everts and Abbott, 1879), p. 66. They were not the first soldiers to arrive at White Pigeon. James Martin recalled his enlistment when he wrote his regrets for not being able to attend the 1928 Regimental Reunion. He was 86 years old.

   "I would like to meet with the old Boys once more. It was 67 years today Aug. 20 that I enrolled at Coldwater and went direct to White Pigeon that night.

   There were three of us. We stayed at the old Hotel and slept on the floor. We had our meals there for two or three days and were assigned to Co. D until our Company H was organized.

   I believe we were the first to arrive at Camp Tilden.

   Remember us to...any old comrades, not many of them will be ready for inspection in the morning."

   James Martin to James Todd, August, 1928, Regimental Reunion Records, 11th Michigan Infantry, Kalamazoo Museum, Kalamazoo, Michigan.

11. Oakes to Robertson, 20 April 1861, Regimental Service Records.

12. Three Rivers *Reporter*, 13 June 1861.

13. DeGamo Jones to David Oakes, Letters Out from Adjutant General Office, op. cit.

14. *Western Chronicle*, 21 August 1861. This is the same meeting that Isaac Ulrich noted in his diary. (see Chapter Two)

15. Constantine *Mercury*, 5 September 1861.

16. Daniel B. Weber, ed, *The Diary of Ira Gillaspie of the Eleventh Michigan Infantry*, (Mount Pleasant, Michigan: Central Michigan University Press, 1965), p. 7. Mathias Faulkner was First Lieutenant of Company C, and Henry Platt was Sergeant-Major of the Regiment. (Hereafter cited as Diary of Ira Gillaspie)

17. Constantine *Mercury*, 5 September 1861.

18. *Western Chronicle*, 11 September 1861.

19. History of St. Joseph County, Michigan (Philadelphia: L.H. Everts and Co., 1877), pp. 139, 145, 147.

20. *Western Chronicle*, 5 September 1861. The company was mustered on September 4. However, all troops in the original enlistment were dated to have mustered 24 August 1861 when the minimum number had arrived at White Pigeon except Company F which was dated 11 September 1861. See Record of Service of Michigan Volunteers in the Civil War, 1861-1865 Eleventh Infantry. (Kalamazoo, Michigan: Ihling Bros. and Everard, n.d.) passim. Hereafter cited as Michigan Volunteers, Eleventh Infantry.

21. Ibid., 11 September 1861.

22. Smith Letters, various dates, Regimental Service Records.

23. O.R., Series III, Vol. I, p. 428. See page 23 for full quote.

24. Adrian (Michigan) *Daily Expositor*, 25 August 1861, 14 September 1861.

25. Detroit *Free Press*, 13 September 1861.

26. Three Rivers *Reporter*, 1 August 1861.

27. *Western Chronicle*, 11 September 1861.

28. Records of the Department of the Interior, Pension Office, Pension File of Charles Moase, National Archives, Washington, D. C.

29. Constantine *Mercury*, 22 August 1861.

30. Records of the Department of the Interior, Pension Office, Pension File of Samuel C. Mills, National Archives, Washington, D. C.

31. Although Briggs had only forty-four men in September, I checked the original membership of Company G in *Michigan Volunteers: Eleventh Michigan Infantry*, their place of residence and enlistment date. Moase did not muster out of the First Michigan until August 7, and the first announcement of his recruiting efforts was August 22. I credited Briggs with the enlistment of 76 men and Moase with 13. Twelve men could not be clearly assigned to either recruiter by date or place of enlistment.

32. History of St. Joseph County, op. cit. p.44.

33. Coldwater (Michigan) *Republican*, 4 February 1876.

34. Records of the Department of the Interior, Pension Office, Pension File of Samuel C. Mills, National Archives, Washington, D. C.

35. Chamberlain to Robertson, Regimental Service Records, 21 September 1861.

36. Ibid., 1 October 1861.

37. Letters Out from Adjutant General, 4 October 1861.

38. Chamberlain to Robertson, Regimental Service Records, 5 October 1861.

39. Adrian *Daily Expositor*, 25 August 1861.

40. *Michigan in the War*, pp. 744-45.

41. Regimental Records, Miscellaneous Organizations, State Archives of Michigan, Lansing, Michigan.

42. Telegrams Collected by the Office of the Secretary of War, 1861-1882. Microfilm 473, Roll 97, Telegrams received by the Secretary of War, August 1 - November 14, 1861, National Archives, Washington, D.C., p. 185.

43. Telegrams Collected by the Office of the Secretary of War, 1861-1882. Microfilm 473, Roll 75, Telegrams sent by Secretary of War, July 25 - September 10, 1861. Volume 159-160, National Archives, Washington, D.C., p. 310.

44. Hudson (Michigan) *Gazette*, 14 September 1861.

45. Michigan Volunteers, Eleventh Infantry, p. 93.

46. Record of Service of Michigan Volunteers in the Civil War, 1861-1865 First Light Artillery (Kalamazoo, Michigan: Ihling Bros and Everard, n.d.), pp. 64. This record of Battery D states an absolute falsehood in the opening line in attributing the organization to Coldwater and in stating the names of the officers responsible for the organization. This fabrication began with John Robertson in *Michigan In the War*, pp. 526-527.

47. Benjamin F. Wells to Melissa H. Wells, 2 November 1861, Benjamin F.Wells Papers, Michigan History Collection, Bentley Historical Library, University of Michigan, Ann Arbor. This is a large set of letters between Benjamin and Melissa H. Wells, The sender will be identified in the text. Hereafter cited as Wells Papers.

48. *Report of the Adjutant General of the State of Indiana*, Vol. 3 (Indianapolis: Samuel H. Douglas, 1866), p. 438.

Chapter Five

"...those who bear it hence will never return with it dishonored."

Of the men who enlisted in May's Independent Regiment, Ira Gillaspie left the most complete record of his decision to join the army. He decided as early as 20 August to "voluteer my cirveses to my country."[1] Having made his own decision he wrote his best friend, Sam Slyter of Rome, Indiana, to enlist in the same company. It was only then that Gillaspie talked to his wife and parents about his decision. They were opposed to his enlistment but feared that he would be drafted if he did not volunteer. Only his employer encouraged him to join the army. When he signed up on 23 August, Gillaspie very carefully checked what he had been told about his pay by Mathias Faulkner, First Lieutenant of Calvin C. Hood's company. He was assured that he would receive thirteen dollars per month, and his wife would receive an additional six dollars from the township. On mustering out he was promised one hundred and sixty acres of land and one hundred dollars. Considering that agricultural workers were paid only fifty cents per day, this was not bad pay. Gillaspie also recruited Sam Slyter's brother-in-law, Phillip N. Rasler of La Grange County, Indiana. On the other hand he opposed the enlistment of his own brothers, Enoch and Martin, both of whom joined the Eleventh anyway.[2]

If Ira Gillaspie joined for a mixture of pay and patroitism, seventeen year old Borden M. Hicks of Three Rivers had other reasons. Years after the war, he confessed:

> I heard the shrill notes of the fife, the rattling of the snare drum, saw the boys marching up and down the street and heard the Drill Master shout in

clarion tones, "Left-Left-Left,' then, and not till then, did I realize that our
Southern Brothers were causing an unholy war. My heart was set on fire with
an intense desire and longing to serve my Country, to go down south to Dixie
land, and shoot those misguided southern 'fire-eaters' back into the Union.
Not a bit of it. Rather my heart was on fire with a desire and longing to be a
soldier. All I wanted was a chance to don a uniform, to march and fight, to
do some heroic deed and to come back home and be admired by the girls, as
a Hero.[3]

Daniel D. V. Rose, an eighteen year old Mendon farm boy,
seems to have joined to save the Union from destruction by the secessionists. On several occasions he wrote his mother expressing
this view.[4] Nineteen year old James W. King's letters have much
the same feeling, although he did once enlarge on the idea. In a
letter to his future wife, Sarah Babcock, King spoke of soldiers sac-
rificing their "life blood to sustain the rights and liberties of a free
government for them [the people back home] to enjoy in after
years."[5]

No evidence indicated that any members of the regiment were
abolitionists. The members of the Hoisington family were not
sympathetic to the abolitionist cause and were probably typical of
the feeling in the regiment. Melissa Hoisington Wells wrote her
husband, Benjamin F. Wells of Company E, that an acquaintance
of theirs had married. "She married a man by the name of Har-
wood. He is her own cousin and a widower with four children and
a black Republican in the bargain. I wonder that she would stoop
so low as to marry a black Republican...."[6] Her brother, Wallace
Hoisington, was the First Sergeant of Company E. When the
regiment reached Louisville, Kentucky, he wrote the *Western
Chronicle*:

I saw slaves yesterday, for the first time in my life; there is nothing of that
shabbiness and poverty in their appearance that sensation writers are so fond
of blowing about, on the contrary, all I saw of the colored population here,
were well dressed.[7]

In general, the members of the regiment had little interest in slavery, but they were against secession. With over a thousand men in

White Pigeon training for war, there were over a thousand reasons for being in May's Independent Regiment.

A Civil War volunteer regiment was a close knit group of relatives, friends, and neighbors commanded by officers whom they knew and respected before they joined the army. The decision to enlist was often based on this network of friends and relatives. Ira Gillespie was responsible for the recruitment of his two friends although he tried unsucessfully to prevent his brothers from enlisting. When Abisha Hoisington enlisted as the Drum Major of the Eleventh, he was followed by his son, Wallace, and his son-in-law, Benjamin F. Wells. Addison Drake, the Quartermaster, and William Elliott, the Surgeon, were brothers-in-law as were Calvin C. Hood, Captain of Company C, and Henry S. Platt, the regimental Sergeant Major. There were several sets of brothers and cousins serving in the regiment. Some of them were business partners before the war.[8]

The Eleventh Michigan was in White Pigeon for nearly four months. This was an unusually long time for a volunteer regiment to spend in its rendezvous camp. This was due in part to the opposition of Governor Blair and in part to the slowness of equipping the regiment. Normally once the minimum number of men enlisted, a mustering officer would arrive and swear the regiment into Federal service, and then they would be forwarded to the army. Early in the war Secretary Cameron directed the governors to establish camps of instruction for militia units to prepare them for federal service. Regiments were to be instructed in drill, discipline, and tactics. After the call for five hundred thousand volunteers, Cameron proposed a system of four national camps of rendezvous and instruction where Regular Army officers would train the troops. Both the Army and the governors opposed this plan. General-in-Chief Winfield Scott did not want to provide the officers, and the governors wanted to retain control for as long as possible. Scott and the governors won. "Newly formed regiments were organized, equipped, and inspected at their home station and then sent directly to the army to which they were assigned. Whatever training they received, therefore, was at the home station under the command of the regimental officers."[9]   In this regard the Eleventh was probably better off than most volunteer regiments.

Captain Harvey Tilden of the Fifteenth Infantry of the Regular Army was in White Pigeon in late August and immediately had the regiment's training under way. About September 1, Ira Gillaspie wrote "we comensed Batalion drill in large field none by the name of Swans Meddow. It lay a little east of town with the railroad passing by one side of it. Capt. Tilden of the U.S.A. drilled us."[10] The Eleventh also had eleven veterans of the First Michigan Infantry that had been at Bull Run.[11] Most of these men had been noncommissioned officers in the First but were commissioned officers in the Eleventh. They had only served three months, but they knew how to drill. Alfred Q. Brown remembered where "a three month man drilled all of the officers as we loafed on the ground."[12] Company I had the most experienced soldier in forty-five year old Robert Anderson, a twenty-one year veteran of the British Army with an additional two years in the United States Army.[13] Some of the men and officers had prewar experience with state militia units. William L. Stoughton was chief among these as he had been the Captain of the the Sturgis Penisular Guard. These militia units were primarily drill and parade units but that was exactly what the volunteer regiments were trained to do. The object of the drill was to allow officers to move their regiments quickly from column of march into line of battle. Training in the Civil War was not like the modern basic training. There were no long marches in full field packs, no firing on the rifle range, and no training in cooking or making camp. There really was no training that would help the regiment survive the next three years. In the long run disease and bad food proved more dangerous than the Confederate guns.

The type of training that would have prepared them for the rigors of their military life was impossible at White Pigeon since the regiment received absolutely no military equipment until the very end of their stay in Michigan. As an earlier historian of the Eleventh Michigan observed, "They had, indeed, almost nothing but their willingness to go to war."[14] The lack of weapons was the most serious shortage militarily, but the lack of uniforms was more important to the morale of the men. Daniel Rose wrote to his mother that he would have his "likeness taken...and sent home" when the uniforms came.[15] As early as October 2 Robertson sent May a copy of a telegram from U.S. Quartermaster General Montgomery C. Meigs ordering uniforms to be sent to the regiment[16] For the next several days expectant soldiers met every train arriving in White Pigeon in hopes of receiving their uniforms. They were disappointed daily. The uniforms were lost among the supplies piling up in Pittsburg. Finally on October 19 the uniforms arrived and the *Three Rivers Reporter* noted:

> The uniforms of the Independent Regiment have at last been dug out of the immense mountain of freight which had accumulated at Pittsburg by reason of some obstruction of the railroad. We will venture an opinion there never was a gladder set of fellows than these when the long expected and anxiously looked for cars containing the woolen freight hove in sight. [17]

When the uniforms were finally distributed, there were no trousers for the enlisted men. This caused a wag at the *Constantine Mercury* to comment that "if no trousers come, the regiment may be very respectably uniformed a la highlander."[18] There was an element of disgust in Benjamin Wells' letter to his wife on November 2: "As far as the uniforms there is not much use of saying anything about them. The non commissioned officers have part of theirs but the rest of them are not here and I do not know when they will come."[19] A week later Colonel May was asking Robertson to find out what the problem was with the equipment. The Adjutent General discovered that the government contractor in Philadelphia had failed to complete the order. The state then arranged to have Sykes and Company of Detroit complete the equipment order. By the end of November the remainder of the uniforms and most of the individual equipment such as canteens and haversacks finally arrived in White Pigeon.[20] However, Ira Gillaspie reported that they were not issued their "uniform caps" until December 2 which was a week before they left for Kentucky.[21] The uniform when complete consisted of an overcoat, a dress coat, pants, two pair of drawers, a vest, two shirts, socks, shoes, a forage cap and a tall stiff

black felt hat embellished with a plume.[22] Sergeant Borden Hicks
recalled that the dress coat had brass shoulder scales which the
men called frying pans. He also remembered:

> As no sheverons were issued to us we bought tape and put them on our-
> selves, not quite as artistic as the Government issue, but they told onlookers
> that we were officers and did not belong to the common herd. Then we
> asked for furloughs to go home, and see the girls in our new togery and,
> when we got there, we made a bee line for the photographers and did not
> rest till we had our pictures taken in all the panoply of war.[23]

The question of arms for the regiment was a more serious matter. There was a great shortage of all kinds of military equipment
at the beginning of the war, and after six months it was worse. The
United States government and the Confederate government and
all the states in and out of the Union were trying to buy weapons.
The major sources were the European nations. As a result the European governments were able to unload outdated muskets, and
American soldiers were forced to rely on them.

The Michigan Military Department made it a policy not to supply arms until a regiment was ordered forward. This policy was a
major problem in the training of volunteer regiments. On November 22 Robertson ordered the Michigan Quartermaster to forward
1,000 muskets and accessories with a "proportion to be Rifles for
the flank companies."[24] Sergeant Borden Hicks and a Branch
County history identified them as Belgian muskets.[25] However, a
photograph of Melvin J. Lyon, Company D, which was taken in the
early months of his enlistment, shows him with an Prussian
"Potsdam" musket.[26] Soon after arriving in Kentucky, Colonel
May certified that the regiment needed 40,000 Buck and Ball
cartridges and 60,000 percussion caps for Prussian muskets of 69 to
72 caliber. On January 8, 1862 May reported to General Thomas
Wood that he had sent 108 Prussian muskets to Louisville for
repair. He went on to say that:

> I could have with propriety have sent all we have as they are certainly unfit
> for any practical service and it would not be just to send a Regiment into an
> engagement with such imperfect [weapons] as at every drill more or less of

them brake... I hope if possible you will procure us some other *good* guns in place of them...[27]

There was one agreement about these muskets; they were of poor quality. Hicks stated that it was "the gun that we feared more than we did the rebels as it was sure to hit us everytime it was fired, whether the three buck shot and round ball with which it was loaded hit what we aimed at, or not."[28] However, Companies A and K were issued some other type of weapon, probably a rifled musket. Aaron B. White of Company A wrote to Dan Rose, who had been left in Michigan as a hospital attendant, "While at Louisville, our rifles were changed for such old muskets as the other companies had. You had better believe that we were all pretty mad. The darned things don't shoot worth a cent."[29] The final judgement on the Prussian muskets was written by Captain Benjamin Bennet, one of the Bull Run veterans.

> The guns with which our regiment is armed are miserable things - absolutely good for nothing. The men have no confidence in them, and if called into action would be loth to stand fire where they knew there was not an even show. For my part, I hope we shall not go into battle until we get better arms.[30]

Nevertheless, the importance of receiving the weapons for the enlisted men was reflected by Ira Gillaspie who said, "The men began to feel like real soldiers."[31]

There was just enough happening at White Pigeon to keep the vast majority of the men interested and involved. However, twenty-seven men deserted during this period, and, since only thirty-nine desertions occurred in the entire three years, the morale must have been low during the long wait. For many of those whose homes were along the railroad routes it was possible to go home every weekend or to have visitors from home. Ira Gillaspie who was from Sturgis was one such fortunate soldier. One Sunday he was doomed to disappointment however. He had received his Captain's permission to go home, but, when he was ready to leave camp, he could not find an officer to give him a pass. He stayed in White Pigeon, but the next time it happened he just left.[32] There was some feeling that things would be better if the whole operation could just be moved a few hundred miles from home.[33]

It was not all hard work and frustration. Most of the enlisted men were only eighteen or nineteen. The average age for the Eleventh was only twenty-one. So there were high-jinks and a lot of rough housing. Melvin Mudge remembered in later years that the regiment hit the hen houses and bee hives of St. Joseph County pretty hard during their White Pigeon stay. Company A stole a barrel of beer from one of the local establishments only to have it stolen in turn by Company B.[34] There was some drinking and drunkeness although the amount is difficult to gauge. James King wrote that after the regiment was paid some of the men were having "quite a spree." "There are double guards stationed all around the camp to keep the boys from running up town. But a great many get out and get intoxicated."[35] King often expressed his dislike for drinking and considered it a great weakness. However, Captain Calvin Hood opposed drinking in a more active manner. He took some men from Company C and "cleared out sevral whiskey shops" in White Pigeon.[36] As with any large group of young men there were fights and other dangerous actions that resulted in injuries. One of the artillery men smashed his foot "a fooling with the turn table on the railroad."[37] The most serious accident of the White Pigeon period occurred on December 6 when the sutler, Marshall M. Wells, shot Charles Leonard of Company C in the jaw. Leonard had purchased a pistol from Wells. As the sutler was showing Leonard how to load it, the gun accidently fired. Leonard was not seriously wounded.[38]

If some of the men were having second thoughts about being soldiers, an even greater number of parents were having them. As early as September 10, a private in Company B secured his discharge on the grounds that he was a minor. Borden Hicks' father tried to prevent his leaving Three Rivers.

> ...Now my father stepped in and said, 'I will not consent to your going.' So I arranged with the Captain to send a Corporal and Guard to my home and arrest me. Well do I remember as we marched out of the front gate, my father

saying, that by this act, I ceased to be a son of his, and, that from now on he disowned me."[39]

The process of releasing volunteers because of their age came to an end when it was tried on Captain Bennet of Company D. Nineteen year old Henry Twiford voluntarily joined Bennett's company. Soon after they arrived in White Pigeon Twiford's parents visited him. They asked Bennett to write them concerning their son as he did not know how to write. Bennett agreed to do this. Two months later they returned to White Pigeon with a writ of habeas corpus for their son's release from the army on the grounds that he was a minor. Bennet wrote to Adjutant General Robertson in Detroit relating the events and asking for instructions. Bennet pointed out the seriouness of the question in that nearly half of the regiment was under twenty-one.[40] Robertson's reply is not in the regimental records, but Henry Twiford remained in the army. Only one other man was discharged for being a minor after Bennet's letter.

On November 26, when the regiment drew their weapons, the Ladies Aid Society of Three Rivers presented the Eleventh with a national flag on behalf of the ladies of St. Joseph County. It was a very expensive, silk flag with thirty-five stars. The staff was mounted with a bronze globe on which was perched an eagle. This was a solemn ceremony. The flag was for the vast majority of people more than a symbol. It was the embodiment of all the past and future of democratic government. Men would die to protect their flag from the enemy. Lieutenant Colonel Stoughton accepted the flag for the regiment. He told the Ladies Aid Society, "those who bear it hence will never return with it dishonored."[41]

On the same day that they received their weapons and flag, General Don Carlos Buell sent an order to Adjutant General Robertson to move the Eleventh to Kentucky. Even at this late date, there was a report in the Constantine *Mercury* that the regiment was going to be disbanded.[42] The *Mercury* had never been friendly to the unit or to May. The story was probably based on the fact that the Chandler Horse Guard was mustered out of the service on November 22 at Coldwater. The two companies of calvary had been closely associated with May's Independent Regiment before the state gained control of the regiment. The Editor of the *Mercury* must have felt foolish when the paymaster arrived on December 2 and paid the regiment thirty-seven thousand dollars for two months and ten days of service. The following day Robertson ordered the Eleventh to Kentucky.

> The Eleventh Regiment Michigan Infantry now stationed at White Pigeon commanded by Colonel William J. May will proceed with as little delay as possible by Michigan Southern Railroad and thence via New Albany and Salem Railroad to Lafayette and Indianapolis and thence to Jeffersonville. Colonel May will then cross the Ohio River to Louisville, Kentucky where he will report to General D.C. Buell Commanding the Department of the Ohio. Colonel May will provide himself with the necessary provisions to subsist his Regiment on the march and for two additional day(s) after his arrival at Louisville, so that there may be no danger of his command being short of subsistance.[43]

On the evening of December 9, 1861 the Eleventh Michigan boarded thirty-one passenger coaches at White Pigeon. At 12:15 a.m. on December 10, the regiment left for Kentucky. They would not return until September 25, 1864. More than two hundred of them would never return, and none of them returned unmarked by the experience. But finally the long wait was over, they were on their way to Dixie to end the rebellion.

Notes

1. Diary of Ira Gillaspie, p. 3.

2. Ibid, p.3 Enoch Gillaspie deserted at Bardstown, Kentucky, on December 27, 1861. See Ibid p. 16.

3. Borden M. Hicks, "Personal Recollections of the War of the Rebellion", *Glimpses of the Nation's Struggle*, Sixth Series, Papers Read Before the Minnesota Commandery of the Military Order of the Loyal Legion of the United States, January 1903-1908 (Minneapolis, Minn.: Aug. Davis, 1909) p. 520. Hereafter cited as Hicks, Recollections.

4. Rose Papers, passim..

5. King Papers, 6 March 1862.

6. Wells Papers, 27 April 1862.

7. Western Cronicle, 25 December 1861.

8. St. Joseph County (Michigan) Circuit Journal, 1858-1868, Regional History Collection, Western Michigan University, Kalamazoo, Michigan, pp. 90, 95, 109. This is a record of a suit involving William J. May and William N. Elliott as business partners.

9. Armin Rappaport, "The Replacement System during the Civil War", in *Military Anaylsis of the Civil War*, ed. by Editors of Military Affairs (Millwood, N.Y.: KTO Press, 1977) p. 125.

10. Diary of Ira Gillaspie, p. 9.

11. The Veterans of the First Michigan Infantry who served with the Eleventh were:
    1. Bennet, Benjamin G. - Michigan Volunteers, Eleventh Infantry
    2. Catlin, Edward - Michigan Volunteers, Eleventh Infantry
    3. Cushman, James - Michigan Volunteers, Eleventh Infantry
    4. Flynn, Thomas - Michigan Volunteers, Eleventh Infantry

5. Gilbert, Cyrus W. - Military Service Records, National Archives
6. Heath, Lewis W. - Michigan Volunteers, Eleventh Infantry
7. Knappen, Edward S. - Michigan Volunteers, Eleventh Infantry
8. Mills, Samuel - Michigan Volunteers, Eleventh Infantry
9. Moase, Charles - Michigan Volunteers, Eleventh Infantry
10. Newberry, Charles W. - Michigan Volunteers, Eleventh Infantry
11. Plumb, Carlos - Diary of Ira Gillaspie, p. 8

12. Alfred Q. Brown to James Todd, 15 August 1930. Todd Letters, Kalamazoo Museum, Kalamazoo, Michigan.

13. Michigan Volunteers, Eleventh Infantry, p. 5.

14. Road to Murfreesboro, p. 22.

15. Rose Papers, 18 September 1861.

16. John Robertson to William J. May, 2 October 1861, Letters Out from Adjutant General's Office. op. cit.

17. Three Rivers Reporter, 26 October 1861.

18. Constantine Mercury, 24 October 1861.

19. Wells Papers, 2 November 1861.

20. Road to Murfreesboro, p. 29.

21. Diary of Ira Gillaspie, p. 11.

22. Road to Murfreesboro, p. 29.

23. Hicks, Recollections, p. 522.

24. Order No. 29., General and Special Orders, 1861-1866. Adjutant Office, Records of the Michigan Military Establishment, State Archives of Michigan, Lansing, Michigan.

25. Hicks, Recollections, p. 522; History of Branch County, op. cit., p. 66.

26. Road to Murfreesboro, p. 30.

27. Colonel William J. May to General Wood, 8 January 1862, Regimental Order Book, Regimental Records, Record Group 94, Box 1999, National Archives,

Washington, D.C. (Hereafter cited as Regimental Order Book.) The underlying of 'good' is May's.

28. Hicks, Recollections, p. 522.

29. Aaron B. White to Daniel D.V. Rose, Rose Papers, 26 December 1861.

30. Sturgis Journal, 16 January 1862.

31. Diary of Ira Gillaspie, p. 11.

32. Ibid, pp. 10-11.

33. Walter Hoisington to the Western Chronicle, 2 October 1861.

34. Reunion speech of Melvin Mudge, Coldwater (Michigan) *Republican*, 4 September 1869.

35. King Papers, 6 December 1861.

36. Diary of Gillaspie, p. 12.

37. James G. Genco, *To the Sound of Musketry and the Tap of Drum: A History of Michigan's Battery D Through the Letters of Artificier Harold J. Bartlett, 1861-1864* (Rochester, Michigan: Ray Russell Books, 1983) p. 7.

38. Diary of Ira Gillaspie, p. 12 and King Papers, 6 December 1861.

39. Hicks, Recollections, p. 521. The story had a happy ending as Hicks recalled that his father was so proud of him when he was promoted to Second Lieutenant that his father came to Murfreesboro for a visit.

40. Benjamin Bennet to John Robertson, 9 November 1861, Regimental Service Records.

41. Three Rivers *Reporter*, 30 November 1861.

42. Constantine *Mercury*, 28 November 1861.

43. General Order No. 119, General & Special Orders, op. cit.

Chapter Six

"...we did not enlist to be a government pack mule."

The Regiment reached Salem Crossing near LaPorte, Indiana, about daybreak on December 10 and changed cars to the south-bound New Albany and Salem Railroad. James King wrote that he "enjoyed the trip very much."[1] Ira Gillaspie noted that they "passed thrue Tippycanoe Laffyett and sevral other smart little places Indianapolis for one."[2] Sergeant Major Henry S. Platt was less impressed. He wrote:

> ...a more dreary looking country...one can scarely imagine. It was one continous line of water and marshes. The few towns we passed through seemed to be standing knee deep in mud and water, and the inhabitants were in perfect keeping with the town. They have one redeeming quality, however, they are all loyal and good union citizens, judging from the hearty cheers and waving of handkerchiefs with which we were greeted as we passed along.[3]

At Indianapolis the men were to receive hot coffee. Unfortunately, those who were served received only cold coffee with no sugar or milk. After eating only bread and cold meat, they were anticipating the coffee. There was grumbling, but some of the men of Company C provided that unit with an acceptable substitute. They liberated a barrel of cider while the officers were having dinner.[4]

The regiment reached Jeffersonville early Wednesday morning. They finally got their hot coffee which "reveved us very much",[5] and they heard their first front line rumor: "that Buckner was but a few miles from Louisville with a larg force of rebils."[6]

About eleven o'clock in the morning they crossed the Ohio River by ferry to Louisville. They were finally in Dixie but a friendly Dixie. As the Eleventh marched across town with the regimental band playing, they were cheered "on evry hand by little and big women and men from evry corner and from evry dore and window by our union friends."[7] King wrote that "Crowds of people thronged the streets. Ladies with their silks and satin ribons [sic] flying, men in military dress, [and] Negroes by the wholesale. I saw more colored people yesterday than I ever saw in my life and most of them slave."[8]

The march from the river to the outskirts of Louisville where the Regiment camped was a distance of six or seven miles according to Borden Hicks. It was the longest march they had made with their knapsacks, and "all they contained, besides some things strapped on the outside. They were not heavy when we started," but at the end of the march "they weighed a ton."[9]

In Louisville the regiment was issued camp equipment "which not only embraced everything known for camp life at that time, but also five Sibley tents to each company."[10] These were huge conical tents designed for twenty men. They were heavy and difficult to handle. After several mishaps the companies managed to pitch the tents in rows at least "as straight as a rail fence."[11] Hicks recalled:

> ... as we looked inside of the tents, our future homes, we wondered what we were going to sleep on, no feather beds, not even straw. Did the Government expect us to sleep on the bare ground? One old man who seen service in the Mexican War, assured us that soldiers always slept on the ground. That settled it, and we bravely though with much discomfort, carried out his assertion - our first night under canvas.[12]

Company A was more resourceful than Hicks' Company E. King wrote:

> The first charge we made after getting Secesh was on a hay stack. We needed somthing to put in our tents for bedding. The Colonel told us to take it, and, if he was a Union man, he would pay for it. If not, he would not. We enjoy ourselves better here than in Pigeon.[13]

Ira Gillaspie "askes Martin my brother what he thought of soldering now. Him and his partner J. Morehouse just shook their heads and grinned like kids."[14] As a result of sleeping on the "wet mudy groung...we caut a tremendious cold. Such coughing you never herd as was herd in our camp."[15] On December 16 the regiment had their first drill with their knapsacks on, and they "made so much nois coughing that one could not hear the comands." [16]

During the week that the Eleventh stayed in Louisville, the men had an opportunity to see a big city. Captain Bennet summed up their feeling when he wrote that "I was very happily disappointed in the City of Louisville. It is a much larger and handsomer city than I supposed; indeed, it is magnificent. Broadway is, I think, the finest street I ever saw..."[17] The men lost no time in taking in the sights and the entertainments of the city. James King described the city in great detail after spending a day walking around. He was most impressed with the post office which he called a "splendid pile."[18] John Bloom of Company E attended the theater and probably did not go by himself.[19] The theater remained a popular site. Later Dan Rose sent his brother a "picture of [John Wilkes] Booth the great tragedian in Louisville."[20] They realized here that they were just green recruits when "we was startled by a heavy fiering of musketry on south of us. It was some Regt. fiering at targots but we was just raw anuff to think everything was rebils."[21]

On December 18 the regiment moved to Bardstown, Kentucky. It was a small town on a spur of the Louisville and Nashville Railroad about forty miles southeast of Louisville. Bardstown was used as a recruit rendezous and was under the command of Brigadier General Ebenezer Dumont of Indiana. They made about ten miles the first day, and it was tough going. The road was a good macadamized one, but they had never taken a long march. Gillaspie complained that "our feet got very sore."[22] However, the weather was pleasant, the sights were interesting, and the road still had cheering people. Company E, remembering their "sore experience in carrying our knapsacks through the city of Louisville..., informed the Captain that we did not enlist to be a Government pack mule."[23] The men threatened to break their muskets and go home. "The Captain very graciously listened to our terms and hired a team."[24] On the third day the Colonel hired enough teams to carry all the packs. Nevertheless, Gillaspie wrote: "My feet were dreadfull sore and even bloody on the heels."[25]

As the regiment marched into Bardstown, they passed an Indiana regiment, camped at the fairgrounds, and the Indiana boys lined the road in ranks and gave them six cheers which they returned. They went to camp about a half mile south of town. Their first long march was over, and they had done forty miles in three days. This would not be much later, but it was quite an accomplishment at this point. Furthermore, there were seven other regiments near Bardstown, and another eight were expected at any time. They were with other soldiers. Their band joined the other regimental bands. Indeed, Colonel May gave the band two hundred and fifty dollars to buy more horns.[26] They began daily musket practice.[27] This was really soldiering.

On December 22 it rained. "It seems as though the very heavens had sprung a leak. The rain pours down in torrents and every thing is afloat"[28] This was also soldiering; to be "penned up here with 18 or 20 men in a small tent."[29] They were eating camp fare now - no more dinners at the Dining House. It was army crackers, which were known as hard tack, coffee, and bacon. Sergeant Ephraim G. Hall of Company I described the situation:

> We have arrived at a tolerable degree of perfection in Hardee's Tactics and have been until quite lately drilling on Hard Tacks. For the benefit of the unintiated I would explain that these latter are an edible compound made as supposed of a pulverized sandstone and slake[d] lime, judiciously mixed. In shape and appearance they are not unlike soda crackers sold in bakeries at the North and issued under the head of 'rations,' but are very useful for a variety of purposes. A soldier who has been fed for sufficient lenght of time upon these is supposed to be proof against a musket ball or indeed any load of shot except perhaps a rifled cannon ball. They should prove very serviceable in the event of it being necessary to erect hasty fortifications and are also very useful as targets as the balls striking against them fall flatten to the ground and are afterward gathered up. Thus preventing an unnecessary waste of lead.[30]

Some of the more enterprising companies managed to buy turkeys for their first Christmas dinner away from home, but most just had boiled beef, coffee, and hard tack. However, they were in good

spirits. If nothing else they were in a strange land with strange cus-
toms. King wrote a description of his trip to Bardstown with Orderly Sergeant Aaron B. Sturgis.

> After passing the guard we took the road that led to the village. Every few
> rods we would neet a negro. Some were riding mules. Others mounted on
> ponies. Some were on foot. All as happy as could be for this is the negroes
> holidays. They are all dressed in their best, many of them splendidly. They
> have nice shirt bosoms [and] starched collars. Their boots are blacked and a
> white handkerchief is almost sure to be seen protruding from some one of
> their pockets. They go from one plantation to another. Thus gathering and
> feasting and dancing the time away. They do no work from Christmas eve
> until the day after New Years. Every little child we met in the street would
> shout Christmas Gift. They do not wish you a merry Christmas as we at the
> North do but it is all Christmas gift. [31]

Some blacks came to the camp to entertain the men "with their fi-
dles temboreans and banjoes and they had a publick negro show.
They shure are naturalls."[32]

Their good cheer was not to last. First, it became apparent that
they would not "stay here about a week when we will be pushed on
farther down in Dixie."[33] They were in a training camp. On December 24 Brigadier General Thomas J. Wood became camp
commander. Wood was a Kentucky-born regular army officer. He
graduated from West Point in 1845 and served in the Mexican
War. Early in the war he had been employed as a mustering officer
for Indiana voluteers.[34] Wood immediately issued orders to bring
the troops around Bardstown into a state of readiness.

Headquarters U.S. Forces

Bardstown, Ky. Dec. 26, 1861

General Orders
No. 4

I. Hereafter, the troops of this command including Regimental and Company officers will turn out under arms at Reveille. The men will appear with
their cartridge boxes on. Immediately after the calling of the roll, the company commanders will cause the ranks to be opened and pass along the ranks
to see that the men conform to this order.

II. Immediately preceeding dress parade daily or in case, there should not be for any reason, a dress parade, then immediately preceeding retreat, company commanders will make a minute and careful examination of the arms and ammunition in the hands of the men. Every gun must be carefully inspected and every cartridge box opened and ammunition minutely examined.

III. Company commanders will by timely requistion keep the amounts of ammunition in the cartridge boxed up to forty rounds as also keep their men properly clothed and equipped. Regimental commanders will be held responsible that this directive is strictly carried out.[35]

Wood inspected the Eleventh on Christmas Day. One result was that the regiment was ordered to remove their shoulder scales "and that order suited us all."[36]

On December 29 the regiment moved five miles south of Bardstown to join the other regiments of Wood's command. The night before they left Samuel Hibberlee of Company C was on guard duty, and he must have been a bit jumpy. Ira Gillaspie recorded that "about 12 pm at night whang went one of the guards guns. The releaf was very quickly turned out and the whole camp wakened. Hear is the post screamed Sam Heberly [sic] for he was the one that gave the alarm. After clost examination it was discovered that Sam had shot a mule."[37]

The new camp site was named Camp Stoughton. It was bounded by a beautiful hardwood grove with pine covered hills in the background. James King said, "It was all new to me. I never saw anything like it."[38] He was impressed with the sight of the camp with five regiments. He wrote:

To the East of us is the Turnpike. Across this is a cleared field and on this is encamped four regiments of Infantry. Three of them are from Indiana and one from Ohio. I wish you could see this camp at night when their lights are all burning. It is a splendid sight . . . . We have things very comfortable here. We have stoves in our tents which makes it seem little like living.[39]

However, this enjoyment of being part of the grand design to suppress the Rebellion was not to last long, for it was in Bardstown that the smallpox finally caught up with them. Gillaspie noted on the day that they arrived at their new encampment, "Several of the boys come down with the smallpox."[40] They had been fleeing from that killer since White Pigeon.

When George F. Grather of Company A died of typhoid fever on October 19 in White Pigeon, the only response had been one of grief. This had been the first death in the regiment.[41] Every man and officer attended Private Grather's funeral and another thousand citizens from the surrounding county came. King wrote that "all seemed to feel the mournfulness of the occasion. He enlisted with us at Centreville to share in the dangers and privation of a camp life, but alas he has fallen before he met the enemies of his country."[42] This can be contrasted with the reaction to the death of Joseph Turner of Company H, who died on December 7 of smallpox. "Thare was a man died in the hospittle. Some said he had the small pox. It rased an aufull exciement amongst the boys. Some were on the point of leaving. Well it come very near causing a general mutine."[43] Indeed, as early as November 20 a rumor had spread through St. Joseph County that the regiment had smallpox. A soldier had been taken sick while visiting Mottville, and the local doctor had diagnosed the illness as the deadly disease. After a few days Regimental Surgeon William Elliott had to issue a public denial. Probably only Dr. Elliott's reputation in White Pigeon stopped the rumor. As it turned out the soldier did not have smallpox.[44]

Army regulations required vaccination of recruits against smallpox, and the rule was followed closely enough to prevent a large scale outbreak of the disease during the war. Regulations also required revaccination if it was deemed necessary. However, doctors were much less appreciative of the need for this step. "Vaccination was often neglected at the training camps maintained by the states."[45] This would seem to be true in the case of the Eleventh.

What prevented another panic by the public when Turner died of smallpox was the order to move to Louisville. Nevertheless the regiment was forced to leave a number of men in the hospital at White Pigeon. Daniel Rose of Company A was left in White Pigeon as a hospital steward. He said "about thirty that is sick and those that takes care of them" were left behind.[46] Rose may have had some difficulty in distinquishing smallpox and chickenpox. He wrote "Some of them has the chicken pox (or the smallpox). We have lost two boys with it and there is one more dangerous case but the rest of the boys are getting along finely."[47] Dr. James Mandigo of White Pigeon visited the camp on December 8 at the request of the White Pigeon Township Board of Health. He identified seventeen cases of smallpox.[48] He also placed the camp and its personnel in quarantine. Rose complained that "the citizens are so fraid that the doctor will not let us go up town."[49] The offical line of the Regimental Surgeon was that all of the cases were chickenpox.[50] Ultimately, the Regimental Letter and Order Book would list twelve men who died of smallpox between December 7, 1861 and March 12, 1862. During this same period there were twenty-nine deaths from measles, eight from typhoid fever and twenty-six from pneumonia. In all there were one hundred and sixteen deaths by disease during the first year.[51] The regiment's smallpox ratio was much higher than the army average, which was five cases per thousand.[52]

Brigadier General Wood was taking no chances with the possibility of a smallpox epidemic in his command. He told Adjutant Chadwick: "You have got the smallpox, and you must go into some by-place till you are quit of it - a mere matter of caution, mere matter of caution, Adjutant."[53] The regiment immediately moved back into the woods about a mile, but this was not enough to allay the fears of contagion.[54] On January 2, the same day that the Eleventh was moving back, Wood established a camp of instruction, called Camp Morton in honor of the Governor of Indiana. On January 5 the Eleventh was ordered to Camp Morton, two miles north of Bardstown.[55] It was during this march that disaster struck the health of the regiment. When the men stopped for a rest near one of the Indiana regiments, about fifty of the Indiana sick, mostly measles cases, passed through the ranks of the Eleventh. Shortly after this incident the first measles cases were reported.[56]

The new camp was on the property of a man who was supposedly the brother of the innkeeper in Arlington, Virginia, who had killed the "Noble Elsworth."[57] King described the farm in favorable terms:

> "When we arrived here we found everything deserted. A large plantation house stood on the premises surrounded by numerous outbuildings. There has [been] a great display of taste been laid out on this farm. A fine lawn extends in front of the house and set with a fine grove of locust trees."[58]

The regiment took steps to improve on what they had. In less than a week they built a brick oven that supplied fresh bread rather than hard tack. The men also "confiscated about 200 rods [rod = 16 feet] of fence to make walks of on account of the mud."[59] Rose and a number of the men who were left in White Pigeon arrived in Bardstown on January 25.

Many of the men became discouraged at this point. This last move was in the wrong direction. Sergeant Aaron Sturgis summed up their feelings, "...we were going away from the enemy."[60] The weather was not good. Heavy rains and snow turned the drill field into a quagmire. Duncan Stewart recorded on January 18 that they "Had dress prade at 4. The mud is knee deep."[61] They were in quarantine, and they suspected that it was the result of some interstate rivalry. Indeed, the men were most bitter about the quarantine which they felt was unfair. Benjamin F. Bordner of Company D summed up the suspicions of many of the Eleventh.

> I think we will stay here to watch and guard Bardstown. All the troops have left for Bowling Green except [the] 11 Mich. They are left behind just because General Wood wants the Indiana troops to have all the praise I will tell you how they served us when we came to Bardstown. Old Wood was very glad to see us so he ordered us to move five miles south. We moved on Sunday. We camped in a field near three Indiana regiments. In two or three days the hoosers commenced to find fault that they did not like to camp as near to the 11 Mich. because they had the small pox so we had to move back and be left behind. Now I will tell you something about them. The night before we moved the news came that there was six buried out of the hooser reg. they died with small pox so that shows that they had...the small pox before we got here.[62]

The worst of the whole affair was that they were dying and nothing seemed to help. They were helpless and left behind.

Many of the enlisted men were young farm boys or had grown up in isolated rural villages. They had never been exposed to many of the usual childhood diseases and now had to face them with their energy drained by a poor diet and primitive living conditions. Rose listed the diseases among the troops as smallpox, chickenpox, measles, and mumps.[63] Gillaspie recorded on January 31 that "We are loseing an aufull site of good men from illness. We hve in camp the small pox measles black toung newmoinia vericoloid all in our Reg. at one time."[64] Captain Bennet wrote the *Western Chronicle* to clarify the situation for the folks at home. He said the condition of the regiment was critical, but everything possible was being done for the sick.

> I do not write this for the purpose of creating a panic at home nor will I follow the example of some and charge our surgeons with inefficiency and incapacity, but I think it will be well to let the truth be known. During the last week we have lost, on the average, near three a day, and this despite the utmost exertions of the surgeons.[65]

He added that since more than half the men had colds due to the weather, it was fortunate that the mortality rate was not higher. However, he concluded with the hopeful note that since so many had had the measles the worst should be over.[66] By the time Bennet's letter was being printed, things were improving. The sick list was rapidly decreasing.

Relieving the worry of people at home was a major concern of many of the letter writers from the Eleventh. Charles Teal of Company K wrote:

> We...[were] mortified at hearing from home a report of the 11th Michigan being all taken prisoners. Such I am happy to state is not the case, nor was there any such attempt made, also that the Regiment suffered most dreadfully from small pox neither of which is true. Yet there are some cases of sickness, such as bad colds, just as you can find in any other Regiment with the same number of men.[67]

James King was typical of many of the soldiers when he wrote:

> I expect you hear strange stories about us. Captain just rceived a letter stating that he was dead and both of the Lieut's, when in fact he has not been

sick a day. Other letters state that we are dying off thirty or forty a day when in fact there had been very few deaths. I can not see where such reports originate.[68]

One of the biggest problems with information to the home folks was a lack of any centralized control. The newspapers printed letters from anyone and in no particular order. As an example, the *Western Chronicle* published a letter from Charles Rice on March 3 that had been written on January 23. Rice wrote that the Regiment was rumored to have smallpox and had been forced to move away from the other troops. This information was six weeks out of date. Indeed, when Rice's letter was printed, the Regiment was on the march to other duties.[69]

For the officers of the Eleventh there was another danger at Bardstown that proved just as fatal, at least to their military careers, as smallpox. On January 22, May, Stoughton, and Doughty were ordered to report for their officer examinations. Later, the company officers were examined. These tests were at the direction of the War Department and were designed to eliminate the most incompetent officers that the states had appointed. The tests were not severe, but they did create a fear of failure. This, along with the sickness in camp, would have been enough to generate hostility among the officers. The worst feeling seemed to be between Captain John L. Hackstaff of Company H and Captain David Oakes of Company A. Their rivalry dated back to the White Pigeon days and possibly even earlier. Oakes had been a Republican office holder, and Hackstaff had been a Democratic newspaper editor. Hackstaff especially used the St. Joseph County newspapers to attack Oakes and other officers of the regiment. As it turned out, only Captain William Phillips of Company K actually failed the examination. He resigned on February 19. Hackstaff, who had been seriously ill since White Pigeon, resigned on March 11.

By the end of January not only was the health of the regiment improving but also the general fortune of the Eleventh. Colonel William Lytle of the Tenth Ohio Infantry became the commander of the Bardstown encampment on January 20. Lytle was a Mexican War veteran, and on February 8 he appointed Chadwick his adjutant general. The Eleventh had a friend in a high place as a result of the Mexican War "old boy" network. The effect was almost immediate. Lytle ordered Companies D and E of the Eleventh into Bardstown as the Provost Guard, and the Regimental Band soon followed.[70] On February 28 a squad from Company C under Lieutenant Mathias Faulkner was assigned to guard the property of Governor Wickliff on the Springfield Turnpike, and another squad under Lieutenant Benjamin Reisdorff of Company I went to the property of a Mrs. Rowan. The Regiment had some duties besides just endless drill.

It is difficult to assess the nature of the quarantine of which the Eleventh was complaining. As early as February 5 the entire regiment marched into the main Bardstown encampment to witness the hanging of Sam Calhoun of the Second Kentucky Infantry for the murder of a local farmer. Duncan Stewart of Company E was detailed from Provost Guard duty to work in the Commissary Department, where he handled rations for all the troops in the Bardstown area.[71] It was an unusual quarantine.

On February 24 Colonel John C. Walker of the Thirty-fifth Indiana wrote to the Department of the Ohio Headquarters that:

> The Medical Director at Bardstown informed me a few days ago, that there was no small pox in the 11th Michigan Regiment, Col. May, and that it would inspirit the men and improve their health to assign them some light duty. I will therefore take the liberty of recommending that the 11th Michigan Regiment be ordered to this post [Munfordsville, Ky.] and assigned to Guard duty in this vicinity.[72]

They were not forgotten; they just had smallpox. Even before Colonel Walker asked for the Eleventh to be sent to Munfordsville, the Regiment was ordered to move closer to Bardstown. On February 25 they set up camp at the Jackson farm. "One of the most pleasant places I ever saw. A large brick house stands to the rear of our camp. In front of this house is a wide lawn covered with shade trees...On this lawn we pitched our tents."[73] There were no regrets about moving. Ira Gillaspie wrote:

I went over to the burying ground whare we had buryed some 80 of our men in one spot. Thare will be many a sad and lonly home sites in Michigan because of this field and its contents. The report is that we will move tomorrow. I hope it is so for I have a dislike to our camp since so many of our boys have died hear."[74]

On February 27 an order came for the regiment to move to Munfordsville, and Adjutant Chadwick was ordered back to Michigan for recruiting duty. Chadwick took care of the regiment's interests, but he always watched out for himself. On March 2 the order to Munfordsville was rescinded and the following day they were ordered to Belmont Furnace to relieve the Third Minnesota. The people of Bardstown had a fond memory of the Eleventh Michigan. A year later a member of the Second Michigan passed through Bardstown and wrote the *Constantine Mercury* "Bardstown must be known to you through the Mich. 11th which was encamped in close vicinity to the town for three or four months. From what I could learn, the 11th was very well liked there."[75]

Notes

1. King Papers, 11 December 1861.

2. Diary of Ira Gillaspie, p. 13.

3. *Journal*, 26 December 1861.

4. *Journal*, 26 December 1861.

5. Diary of Ira Gillaspie, p. 13.

6. Ibid.

7. Ibid.

8. King Papers, 11 December 1861.

9. Hicks, Recollections, p. 522-523.

10. Ibid.

11. Ibid.

12. Ibid.

13. King Papers 13, December 1861.

14. Diary of Ira Gillaspie, p. 13.

15. Ibid.

16. Ibid.

17. Bennet to *Western Chronicle*, 8 January 1862.

18. King Papers, op. cit.

19. Bloom Diary, 13 December.

20. Rose Papers, 3 March 1862.

21. Diary of Ira Gillaspie, p. 13.

22. Ibid.

23. Hicks, Recollection, p. 523.

24. Ibid.

25. Diary of Ira Gillaspie, op. cit.

26. *Western Chronicle*, 15 January 1862.

27. King Papers, 26 December 1861.

28. Ibid.

29. Ibid.

30. Monroe (Michigan) *Commercial*, 30 January 1862.

31. King Papers, 26 December 1861.

32. Diary of Ira Gillaspie, p. 14.

33. King Papers, 22 December 1861.

34. Ezra J. Warner, *Generals in Blue: Lives of the Union Commanders* (Baton Rouge: Louisiana State University Press, 1964) p. 569. Hereafter cited as Generals in Blue.

35. Regimental Letter and Order Book.

36. Diary of Ira Gillaspie, p. 14.

37. Ibid.

38. King papers, 29 December 1861.

39. Ibid.

40. Diary of Ira Gillaspie, p. 15.

41. Regimental Letter and Order Book.

42. King Papers, 22 October 1861.

43. Diary of Ira Gillaspie, p. 12.

44. *Western Chronicle*, 20 November 1861.

45. George Worthington Adams, *Doctors in Blue* (New York: Henry Schuman 1952) p. 219.

46. Rose Papers, 11 December 1861.

47. Ibid.

48. Misc. Papers of St. Joseph County Board of Supervisors, Regional History Collections, Western Michigan University, Kalamazoo, Michigan.

49. Rose Papers, op. cit.

50. Walter [Wallace] Hoisington, *Western Chronicle*, 4 December 1861.

51. Regimental Letter and Order Book.

52. Adams, op. cit., p. 219.

53. *Reporter*, 18 January 1862.

54. Gillaspie, p. 15 and Diary of Duncan Stewart, Company E, Eleventh Michigan Infantry, January 1, 1862 to May 31, 1862. (Diary is in private collection of Stewart Talbot, Vicksburg Michigan) Here-after cited as Stewart Diary.

55. Gillaspie, p. 15 and Regimental Letter and Order Book and Stewart Diary, January 1862.

56. Road to Murfreesboro, p. 52. - There is a problem with the outbreak of the measles as Gillaspie reported on December 30 that " sevral more of the boys was down sick with the measles."

57. King, 12 January 1862.

58. Ibid.

59. Rose, 27 January 1862.

60. Aaron B. Sturgis to *Journal*, 30 January 1862.

61. Stewart Diary, 18 January 1862.

62. Benjamin F. Bordner Letters, 5 January 1862. Ness Collection, folders 64, 65, 66, Michgian Historcial Collections, Bently Historical Library, University of Michigan, Ann Arbor, Michigan. Hereafter cited as Bordner Letters.

63. Rose Letters, 27 January 1862.

64. Gillaspie, p. 17.

65. *Western Chronicle*, 19 February 1862.

66. *Western Chronicle*, 19 February 1862.

67. Monroe *Commerical*, 16 January 1862.

68. King Papers, 17 January 1862.

69. *Western Chronicle*, 3 March 1862.

70. Regimental Letter and Order Book. The order was for Companies C and I, but Companies D and E went. There is no explanation for this change.

71. Stewart Diary, passim.

72. Office of the Adjutant General, Volunteer Organizations, Civil War, 11th Michigan Infantry, Box 1998, National Archives, Washington, D.C.

73. King Papers, 28 February 1862.

74. Gillaspie, p. 18.

75. Mercury, 30 April 1863.

Chapter Seven

"What do you think of such guns as that."

Belmont Furnace was on the Louisville and Nashville Railroad, and the job of the Eleventh was to help guard this important supply line against Confederate cavalry attacks. However, the first task was to get there. Although Belmont is only about fifteen miles west of Bardstown, it proved to be a difficult march. It rained steadily for about a week before the march began. On March 6 the regiment started at about one o'clock in the afternoon in a snow storm. They quickstepped through town on the turnpike and then turned off on a mud road. From then on it was "tuging and pulling all the rest of the day [until] 10 o'clock."[1] The men had a cold supper that night. They did about ten miles the first day, but, unfortunately on the winding trails of the Kentucky hills, they were only about four miles closer to Belmont.

The next day was worse. They crossed and recrossed streams, went down creek beds, and worked up and down ravines. "We traveled three miles to reach one."[2] They were now so far back in the Kentucky hills that the natives had not heard about the war. Some of the inhabitants asked the soldiers why they were all dressed alike. That night they camped on the banks of Wilson Creek with five miles to go. After thawing their boots and standing in the freezing mud to eat breakfast, they began the last leg. Finally, the Minnesota boys sent their wagons out to help bring them in about noon. One of the Eleventh wrote that he thought the Minnesota men were the best that he had seen yet.[3] His judgement might have been influenced by those wagons.

For Ira Gillaspie the march was a disaster. On the day before the Regiment left, he was detailed to dig two graves in the Bardstown cemetery. On the way back to camp he stopped at a grocery and had a couple of beers and a cake. That evening he was sick and believed that he had been poisoned. The next morning his brother Martin came down with smallpox. Gillaspie insisted on leaving with the regiment although Lieutenant Faulkner wanted him to go to the hospital. "So I started with the rest of the boys in the Reg. but I tell you I wished myself back a good many times before night. Lieutenant Faulkner caryed my napsack a part of the way for me. I was most aufull sick for that to happen you may depend." Gillapsie said they camped on the bank of a creek "whare the railroad crost."[4] The next day he and another sick soldier pumped a handcar back to Bardstown to the hospital. Faulkner was at this time in charge of the company as Captain Hood had been furloughed home for twenty days because of illness. This willingness of an officer to carry an enlisted man's pack said a great deal about the nature of a volunteer regiment.

The Eleventh was on guard duty in the area of Belmont Furance until April 28. These seven weeks were a pleasant interlude for the men. The Kentucky spring was beautiful, and the duty was light but important. Fortunately, they did not have to defend themselves or the railroad with the smoothbore muskets. The regiment was spread along the track at various critical points. Company E was at Sheperdsville, Company D at Nolin River bridge, Company C at Belmont Station, Company A at Elizabethtown, and two companies near the Headquarters at Belmont Furance which was off the mainline about three-quarters of a mile. The other three companies were at intermediate points. The regiment was "scattered over nearly forty miles of ground."[5]

According to Bordner he was on guard duty once every ten days with "plenty to eat and drink."[6] The camps were visited daily by throngs of farmers from the local area to sell their produce at reasonable prices. The war had cut off their usual markets, and they were eager to trade with soldiers, even Union soldiers. The result can be seen in a description that Benjamin Wells wrote to his wife:

"I am well and hearty and getting fat everyday. I weigh 145 lbs. which is more than I ever weighed before... we have been here nearly six weeks and as we have but little to do and pretty good fare for Soldiers we are fleshing up."[7] They had set up a regimental oven again to supply soft bread. Duncan Stewart who was stationed at Sheperdsville was frequently detailed to go by train to Belmont for his company.[8]

The men spent their off duty hours rambling over the surrounding countryside, writing letters, and reading. The reading material had a wide range. Charles Forbes of Company C was found "reading an interesting novel. The Lost Trappers."[9] Duncan Stewart spent an afternoon reading Shakespeare.[10] Benjamin Wells' wife sent him eight issues of his "Frank Leslies."[11] The Eleventh had rather eclectic taste. Another big attraction was the photographer. The "daguerrian car" was at Belmont Furance, and many of the men took the opportunity to have their "likeness" taken to send home.[12]

If the residents of Bardstown were mostly Unionists, the Kentuckians along the railroad were not. "We are here in one of the hotbeds of rebellion. Sometimes one of them will hurrah for Jeff Davis and then he is sure to get himself nicely whipped ..."[13] Wells bloodied the nose of one such rebel sympathizer.[14] Duncan Stewart reported "a fight between Jerome Van Nordstrom and a couple of Ky'ns. The Ky'ns drew a knife."[15] Although only two fights were reported between the men of the Eleventh and pro-Confederate Kentuckians, there were undoubtedly more. There were probably a number of fights between members of the regiment. Gillaspie reported one at the auction of the personal property of John A. Angle, Company C, who died on March 20.[16]

Company C, which was recruited largely in Sturgis, had a record of attacking whiskey shops and dumping the whiskey. Captain Calvin Hood was usually the leader of these expeditions. On the evening of April 7:

Sargt.Twitchell [Enos M. Twichell] and Paten [Henry Patten] with some 5 or 6 others went over to an oald negro den whare they kept whiskey to sell to the soldiers... They wanted to pore it out but the darkey would not tell whare it was so the boys had to pull some of them up by the neck to make them tell whare the whiskey was. When the rope began to choke them they was ready to tell all. The boys took the whiskey to shampoo the negroes with. It got into their eyes and made them scratch for certain.[17]

Two weeks later Captain Hood decided to make a clean sweep. After dress parade he picked out a squad of ten, including Sergeant Smith A. Benedict, Henry Patten, Stephen A. Caner, Peter Doyle, John L. Ryan, and Gillaspie.

...[Hood] told us he wanted us to folow him. We told him we would folow him any whare he wished to and do any thing he might ask of us. I could see he was right angry about some thing. . . Sargst. Benidick was boiling allso. We went over to the sutlers and thare halted with our arms held hy. Capt. Hood went in and comenced breaking and throwing out what whiskey he had. After we had done with him we went about 1/2 a mile to an oald Irishmans which was suspisioned. We searched his primaces but found none to speak of. He was allmost scared to death. He amused us boys a goodeel for he jumped when we waved our guns in the air. The mud is nee deep hear and we ended up neck deep in it. We went about 2 1/2 miles further whare we found all most 3 barrels of the oald stuff. We nocked in the heads and turned it out disregarding the entretyes of the women for women was all thare was thare. The men had all vamoosed. We went on about a mile and a 1/2 further whare we found a cople more barrels and some half dosen women but no men. We served it the same as the other. One woman went to snatch out a pitcher full and one the boys hit her vesel and the contents went into the ladys bosom. She screemed and yelled but the Capt. told her to be quiet and go. We went about 3 miles in another direction whare we was directed by our last victoms. We searched the house but found none. We called for some thing to eat which we got in a hurry I tell you.[18]

The only clue as to Hood's behavior on this last occasion was that Charles Graves of Company C was as drunk "as you can get and stand" at dress parade the day before the raid, and Mrs. Hood was present at the parade.[19]

When Jerome Morehouse of Company C became sick on March 22, Ira Gillaspie diagnosed it. "I saw that Jo Morehouse was worse. I went and examined him and it was plain to see that he had smallpox. He was taken to the pesthouse at once." Gillaspie had had enough. "I then went to work and vacksonated all of the boys that was not already so."[20] Morehouse was back in five days, and he did not have smallpox. This type of non-professional diagnosis was undoubtably the source of many of the rumors of smallpox in the regiment. Once the disease had occurred it was seen in every spot. Fortunately, no one became ill as a result of the "vacksonation." However, it would appear that some of the Eleventh had not been vaccinated even at this late date.

Another activity that seems to have occupied the men a great deal was to speculate on how long the war would last. After the Union victories at Forts Henry and Donelson in February and at Island No. 10 on April 8, plus the opening of the Peninsular campaign, the general opinion was that the war would not last long. Ben Wells wrote his wife that the regiment would probably not go any farther south. "We will not move many more times ere we move for home. I think the war will soon close."[21] In one squad there was a debate on this subject, and "one man said four years but we laughed him down to dirt."[22] There was an element of anxiety in the debates and speculation. They had been in the army for eight months and had not heard an enemy gun. The fear was that the war would end, and they would never be in a battle.

There were two changes in the affairs of the Eleventh in early April that gave them new hope of seeing action. One was the resignation of Colonel May. William May was well liked by the men and had passed the tests of the examining board. However, he had been sick in September of 1861 and was very sick in March of 1862. Captain Bennet wrote to the *Western Chronicle* that "Col. May's health, for months has been poor, and it is possible that he has not been as active as he otherwise would, but that he has willful neglected the regiment is utterly false."[23] This letter was a reply to the editor of the *Three Rivers Reporter* who had written a critical article about May. By the end of March there were rumors that May was about to resign. Captain Spencer, who was in Three Rivers on leave, reported this and so did Major Doughty who was in Sturgis. There was a very revealing interview between James King and Colonel May on March 12. King, who had been left behind in Bardstown as a hospital clerk, reported to May for duty at Belmont Furance.

> I went into the building occupied by the officers and found him [May] in his
> room. He wished me good morning, asked me how the sick were getting
> along up at Bardstown. I told him that four of them had died since the regi-
> ment left. My God said he how many of our boys are to die? Would to God
> I had never seen a Regiment.[24]

King was a very astute young man of unusually keen judgement.
His assessment of May was also revealing.

> A great many blame Colonel May but I believe if there ever was a kind
> hearted man and one who tries to do right, Col. May is one. I have seen bet-
> ter managers than him but he has a heart.[25]

On March 29 May wrote to Adjutant General Robertson to recommend the promotion of First Lieutenant Patrick Keegan of
Company H as the Captain in place of W. W. Philips. May added a
note: "I have been very sick or should have sent this in sooner. I
can now be up but not out of my room."[26] On April 1, 1862,
Colonel William May resigned his commission and left the army.

Lieutenant Colonel William Stoughton was appointed to replace
May. He had been extremely active as the Lieutenant Colonel as
May had relied on him a great deal. As early as March 11 the orders were sent with Stoughton's signature. Even in Michigan
Stoughton dealt with many matters, such as public relations, which
would normally be the role of the Colonel. King assessed the mer-
its of the two men in the following terms. "I think Lieut. Colonel
Stoughton a better military man than May and the Regiment will
probably do better under his management than May's."[27]

Once Stoughton's appointment as Colonel was confirmed by
Governor Austin Blair, the speculation turned to the Lieutenant
Colonel's position. Although Adjutant Samuel Chadwick had been
a frontrunner for the postion in the early days of the regiment's recruitment, he was not considered now to become the Lieutenant
Colonel. The primary reason for this was the opposition of
Stoughton. He and Chadwick did not have good relations from the
beginning. On April 10 there was a petition from all of the regimental staff officers (except Chadwick) and the Captains of Companies B, C, D, and E to Governor Blair asking that Stoughton be

appointed Colonel and Captain Nelson Chamberlain of Company I be appointed Lieutenant Colonel.[28] This was not a regiment election, but it was probably as close to one as they could have in the field. Chamberlain was a Mexican War veteran and from the eastern part of the state. However, Austin Blair had other plans for the lieutenant colonelcy. Nathaniel B. Eldridge had served previously as the Major of the Seventh Michigan Infantry. He was a former doctor and was practicing law when the war began. After the affair at Ball's Bluff, Eldridge wrote a letter which was printed in the Lapeer County newspapers blaming Brigadier General Charles P. Stone for the disaster. Stone placed Eldridge under arrest, but after six weeks of waiting for a trial, Eldridge resigned his commission and returned to Michigan. Blair immediately appointed him to the State Military Board. Eldridge apparently used this position to seek a command.[29] He wrote Adjutant General Robertson on April 17 that he would accept the Lieutenant Colonelcy of the Eleventh Michigan, but a command would have been more welcome. He wrote again on May 7 seeking confirmation of his appointment to the Eleventh.[30] He was at this time forty-eight years old. Eldridge seemed to be well received by the Eleventh. Chamberlain stayed with his company, and there were no bad feelings.

The other change that occurred at Belmont was the exchange of the Prussian smoothbore muskets for Springfields. King wrote, "One thing I must give Col. Stoughton the praise. He has exchanged our muskets for the latest style of improved Springfield rifle."[31] This was certainly an auspicious beginning for the new Colonel. The 1861 model of Springfield was a .58 caliber, muzzle-loading rifle that fired the new conical, lead bullet called mini balls. The rifle was fifty-eight inches long and with the bayonet weighed almost ten pounds. In the hands of an experienced rifleman these weapons were accurate at a distance of six hundred yards. Rollin Eaton of Company A wrote home after firing his new rifle for the first time. "I shot mine 40 rods (640 feet) yesterday and put 4 balls hand running in an 8 inch circle [with] level sights then I raised the middle sight and shot 125 rods (2000 feet) at a small tree and hit that 3 times in sucession that is the furtherest any of us has shot them yet. They are warented to be corect 1 mille. I can hit a turkey 3 times out of 4 [at] 80 rod for all day. What do you think of such guns as that."[32] These were the weapons that revolutionized battlefield tactics by the end of 1863. Duncan Stewart's company turned their old muskets in on April 11 but did not draw the new ones until April 15. After turning in his musket, Stewart "slept that night for the first time without arms."[33]

As early as April 6 the rumor was out that the regiment would be ordered to Nashville, Tennessee and brigaded.[34] On April 23, Adjutant Chadwick "told us that we had orders to move. The news was what we all wanted to hear."[35] Company E was packed and ready to go on April 25 when word came "to stay until tomorrow." On the twenty-sixth they packed the big Sibley tents and all the gear, when the order came that they would leave on April 28. They unpacked "and had a good game of ball."[36] On Monday the twenty-eighth "We was caled up very early and comenced giting ready to move. By 6 am we was on our way to the depoe whare we was soon halted. We had to sit hear and wait untill after 3 oclock in the afternoon for the train to take us to Louisville." The regiment spent all night getting there as the "engineer was drunk and then some. He would run like all possesed and then the train would barely move along."[37] The train derailed at least once. But hurry up and wait is also part of soldiering.

At seven o'clock in the morning the regiment marched through Louisville to the docks and boarded the "E.H. Fairchild." Here they waited until five o'clock in the afternoon before leaving. Captain Spencer of Company E was left behind and had to follow along the bank until New Albany where he was rowed out to the "Fairchild." At West Point, Kentucky, the regiment exchanged cheers with Battery F, First Michigan Artillery, in which Norman S. Andrews of Three Rivers was a First Lieutenant. Adjutant Chadwick wrote an account of the incident for the Three Rivers people.

> ...great anxiety prevailed among the boys to reach West Point before dark that we might look on the face of 'Norm' Andrews once more. As the papers of Louisville had advertized for proposals to move our regiment, the battery

had anticipated our approach, and as the flag bearer stood on deck and waved our flag, and whistle sounded, flash went one of 'Norm's' guns, and the roar of welcome from its mouth incited our boys to cheer after cheer as we neared the bank. Thus, although we did not see our friends and take them by the hand, we heard from them, and gave them in return music from the band and cheers without number.[38]

The Ohio River was flooded and looked "more like a vast lake than a river."[39] The Cumberland was about as large as the St. Joseph River only much deeper. The men were impressed by the cliffs that towered hundreds of feet over the river However, when the "Fairchild" started plowing upstream on the Cumberland River, the trip became a bit choppy, and many of the men reported going to bed sick. The symptoms sound a great deal like seasickness. On the second day they passed Fort Donelson. Here for the first time they saw a battlefield. King said the trees "looked as though ten thousand lightnings had played among the branches. Twas through these trees our gallant boys poured their shot and shell..."[40] They arrived in Nashville about ten o'clock and spent the night on the boat. The regiment now "was really in the southland of the rebils."[41]

Notes

1. Stewart Diary 6 March 1862.

2. Ibid.

3. *Mercury*, 3 April 1862.

4. Diary of Ira Gillaspie, p. 20.

5. King Papers, 14 March 1862.

6. Bordner Letters, 20 March 1862.

7. Wells Papers, 18 April 1862.

8. Stewart Diary, passim.

9. Diary of Ira Gillaspie, p. 22.

10. Stewart Diary, 31 March 1862.

11. Wells Papers, April 1862.

12. King Papers, 14 March 1862.

13. Wells Letters, 24 April 1862.

14. Clayton Wells, *My Father, Benjamin F. Wells* (Ann Arbor, Michigan: The Alumni Press, 1929) pp. 13-14.

15. Stewart Diary, 21 April 1862.

16. Diary of Ira Gillaspie, p. 23.

17. Ibid, p. 23.

18. Ibid, pp. 24-25.

19. Ibid, p. 24. There is also a report of the Pennisular Guard making a raid on the whiskey shops in Sturgis before they left for their rendezvous camp at Adrian for service with the Forth Michigan.

20. Ibid, p. 22.

21. Wells Papers, 18 April 1862.

22. Diary of Ira Gillaspie, p. 16.

23. *Western Chronicle*, 12 March 1862.

24. King Papers, 14 March 1862.

25. Ibid.

26. Regimental Service Records. Lewis Childs, First Lieutenant of Company I, was ultimately given the promotion as Captain of Company H. His commission dated from March 12, 1862.

27. King Papers, 6 April 1862. Oddly enough no other item of surviving correspondence mentions May's resignation or Stoughton's promotion.

28. Regimental Service Records.

29. John I Knapp and R.I. Bonner, *Illustrated History and Biographical Record of Lenawee County, Michigan*, (Adrian, Michigan: The Times Printing Co., 1903) p. 233-234.

30. Regimental Service Records.

31. King Papers, 14 April 1862.

32. Letter of Rollin Eaton, Boyer-Watkins Family Collection, A-176, Regional History Collections, Western Michigan University, Kalamazoo, MI, April 15, 1862.

33. Stewart Diary, 11 April 1862.

34. King Papers, 6 April 1862.

35. Diary of Ira Gillaspie, p. 25.

36. Stewart Diary.

37. Diary of Ira Gillaspie, p. 26.

38. *Reporter*, 24 May 1862.

39. King Papers, 3 May 1862.

40. Ibid.

41. Diary of Ira Gillaspie, p. 26.

Chapter Eight

"...the oald bandit and traitor...had plundered the town and gone."

The orders that moved the Eleventh Michigan Infantry to Nashville were just a small part of Major General Don Carlos Buell's strategy to capture Chattanooga. Soon after he became commander of the Department of the Ohio, Buell had proposed an advance down the Cumberland and Tennessee River valleys rather than through the Cumberland Gap. It was not until Grant captured Forts Henry and Donelson in February that Buell was authorized to move on Nashville as a means of attacking Chattanooga and East Tennessee. On February 14 he occupied Bowling Green and two weeks later Gallatin and Nashville. Buell was pulling troops south as he moved. Therefore, when the Eleventh went on guard at Belmont, other regiments were ordered even farther south. The Confederate army under General Albert Sidney Johnston did not stop in Tennessee but concentrated at Corinth, Mississippi. On March 11, Major General Henry W. Halleck become the commander of the newly organized Department of the Mississippi. Halleck's new command included Buell's Army of the Ohio, and he ordered Buell to join Grant at Shiloh, Tennessee. Buell's leading division met with Grant's command on April 6, the first day of the Battle of Shiloh. Following that battle Buell's Army of the Ohio became the Centre Corps of Halleck's force in the advance on Corinth.

Buell's Third Division under the command of Brigadier General Ormsby M. Mitchel had not gone to Shiloh but had been sent to Murfreesboro, Tennessee. Mitchel was to rebuild the bridge on the Nashville and Chattanooga Railroad. When the bridge was finished, Mitchell's division of 9,000 men advanced to Huntsville, Alabama, on the Memphis and Charleston Railroad. On April 11 when he captured Huntsville, Mitchel's division was farther south than any other Union troops in the Western Theater. He immediately spread his command along the railroad from Stevenson to Decatur. Confederate cavalry units unable to secure forage in northern Mississippi and Alabama began to operate behind Mitchel's isolated position. These raids and his supply problems forced Mitchell to concentrate on holding the railroads. On June 18 Buell arrived in Huntsville with four divisions. When the Eleventh Michigan unloaded from the boat in Nashville on May 3, this was the general situation in which they were to operate until July of 1862. Buell was moving his entire operation to the corridor from Nashville to Huntsville.

The Eleventh marched into the city and were welcomed by their old commander from Bardstown, Brigadier General Dumont. "We herd him really burn the tail off the rebils and he did it good."[1] From the beginning the Michigan boys did not like Nashville. King wrote on the first day that "the people here are nearly all secessionists and look upon us with coldness."[2] Three months later they still felt uneasy about Nashville. Ben Wells said upon being ordered to Bowling Green: "I am glad we are away from Nashville for I did not like the place very well."[3] Lott Woodworth of Company E had the experience of being spit on. He wrote "a woman spit in my face. Had it been a man I would have killed him."[4] On this first visit to Nashville the men would not have to endure abuse from the locals for long. On the night of May 4 they were ordered to march to the Columbia depot. The Regiment arrived at the depot at midnight, but the train did not arrive until late afternoon on May 5. They were probably getting used to hurry up and wait.

The reason for the hurried departure from Nashville was a dispatch from General James Negley at Columbia who reported the sight of a large force of Confederates. The Eleventh was ordered to Franklin but went on to Columbia.[5] When the train reached the Duck River, the railroad bridge had been burnt. The regiment crossed the river on a pontoon bridge built by the First Michigan Mechanics and Engineers.[6] This was the first pontoon bridge the men had seen. They marched the final five miles into Columbia arriving about one o'clock in the morning. After sleeping in the court house that night, the regiment made camp about two miles out of town.

The next day five companies (A, D, F, H, and I) were detailed to escort a wagon train of supplies to Huntsville. After marching twenty-five miles or so they were met by the train guards from Pulaski. Although they had sore feet, they also had "all the turkeys and geese we wanted to eat."[7] The other five companies were detailed to search a cedar swamp for rebel cavalry after they had spent the night waiting in ambush. They returned to camp without seeing any rebels except "a cople of posoms. We shot them anyway."[8] On May 12 a squad from Company B became lost while scouting beyond the picket line. They wandered into the fire zone of the picket line held by Company I, and their pickets fired into the squad from Company B. One man was wounded but not seriously. The men who had fired came back to camp to report, and "they were 2 mity shaky boys never haveing shot a body before they was really week in the nees and sick of heart."[9] Gillaspie then realized a great truth about himself and the entire regiment. "I could not help but think that I have never shot a body yet either. I supose that I will soon."[10]

One of the things that the Michigan men caught onto very soon after their arrival in the Confederacy was that any kind of northern money was good. Captain Bennet described the situation from Nashville.

> Nashville is quite a city, but has been literally ruined by secession. Trade of all kinds was a prefect stand still when our troops arived there, and I don't believe there was ten dollars of good money in the whole town. The currency was composed of Shinplasters of all kinds. The banks issued bills as low as five cents. The railroads issued checks, 'good for freight or passage,' and butchers and grocers all issued bills of all denominations - below $1.00 - while 'Confederate Scrip' made up the currency above $5.00, and anyone who refused to this trash was deemed a traitor and punished accordingly.

Under Federal rule, Nashville is fast improving; stores are opening, goods coming in, and farmers are bringing forward their cotton and tobacco, and getting good money. Merchants, Hotel Keepers, and all refuse 'Confed. Scrip' now and snap at "Uncle Sam's Green Backs' like trout at a fly ... Enclosed I send you a specimen of Southern money, which you must keep on exhibition. It was taken as change, by one of our boys, who spent a "Constantine" bill! Any kind of money - even Constantine and Tecumseh goes current here.[11]

It did not take the enlisted men long to write home for "wildcat bank" money that their fathers had been stuck with since the Panic of 1857. Dan Rose wrote, "In this state the people take any kind of northern money . . . send me just as much poor money as you can for I can get rid of it."[12]

The round of duties at Columbia included scouting and guarding wagon trains to Pulaski. One of the highlights of their stay was the arrival of Andrew Johnson, the Union Governor of Tennessee, and ex-Governor Brown for a speech. The train also brought the Sixty-ninth Ohio Infantry, and the two regiments escorted the governors to their hotel with the Eleventh's band playing. However, there were also the "sights" as General Sherman used to call them. In Columbia the local brothel was known as the White House. When Gillaspie was on guard at the railroad depot, he reported that "the inmates of the White House emograted to Nashville. Francis and Elizy hated to go and leave the boys but they were compeled to by the town marshall."[13] Soon after the girls left so did the Eleventh. However, the regiment was ordered to Murfreesboro. On the last day of May, just before the regiment left, Duncan Stewart of Company E reported to the hospital in Columbia. In his diary he noted that he had had a bad headache since May 27. He died at the Columbia Hospital on June 30, 1862.[14]

From Murfreesboro the Eleventh would begin chasing cavalry and mounted guerilla bands. They knew this was important work and something that had to be done if the Union was to be restored. Burke Foreman wrote to a friend that "they mostly think that the THING called secession is about wound up though I confess I can't see through yet. There are a good many guerilla bands roving through Kentucky and Tennessee yet. If these bands can be broken up then the war would soon be done."[15] General Dumont was organizing an expedition to do exactly that. On June 11 Dumont's column left Murfreesboro with the Sixty-ninth Ohio, Seventy-fourth Ohio, Twenty-eighth Kentucky and Eleventh Michigan infantries, ten pieces of artillery, and five hundred cavalry.[16] According to Ben Wells, the column was joined by the Eighth and Twenty-first Kentucky Infantry.[17] They went to Woodbury and then McMinnville. From there they started for Pikeville, but the cavalry discovered that the rebels had left, and Dumont decided to return to Murfreesboro. The column was on the crest of the Cumberland Mountains in a barren land about eighty miles from their base. When the troops returned through McMinnville, they were supplied with several thousand pounds of fresh bread, which Dumont ordered the people to supply, or the town would be burnt. "The bread was ready but not of the best quality but as the saying is hunger is the best of cooks."[18] There was a note of pride in Well's description of the end of the march.

> A little after dark it began to rain and rained pretty hard for several hours but we went. The boys seemed to feel first rate for they were singing and hurrahing all the time it rained. We got into camp about 1/2 past four in the morning and a more tire and worse used up set of boys I never saw. There were but a few men in the Reg. that would have gone 3 miles further. This is what in the Military is styled forced marching: but few troops in the service have made better time under similar circumstances than we made on this march.[19]

They had marched nearly two hundred miles and still had not fired a shot at the enemy. At this time the Eleventh had 501 enlisted men present for duty. The entire force, present and absent, was 866 with 189 men sick or on furlough. The regiment had lost 163 due to death, discharge, or desertion. In the six months since coming south the effective force was reduced by half, and they had not been in combat.

On June 21 the Eleventh went back to Nashville to become part of the garrison. During the next two weeks squads from various companies were detailed for short term duties. A detail of forty men under Captain Calvin Hood of Company C and Lieutenant

Ephraim G. Hall of Company F took 1400 prisoners that were captured at the Battle of Shiloh from Nashville to Cairo, Illinois, by
steamer.[20] The troops that were in camp resumed regular daily
drill. In one instance, these drills came close to costing Colonel
Stoughton his life. On June 25 he was watching the men practice
the manual of arms for firing formations when Daniel Shippy of
Company D accidently fired his rifle and killed the Colonel's
horse.[21] For most of the men the two weeks in Nashville were an
endless round of guard duty, camp duty, and drill, relieved by visiting the sick in the hospitals, blackberrying, and, as John Bloom
said, "back at my old trade - doing nothing."[22]

All that changed on July 9, 1862 when the regiment was ordered
to Kentucky to help capture Colonel John Hunt Morgan and his
Confederate cavalry. Major General Kirby Smith, the Confederate
commander at Chattanooga, had been holding eastern Tennessee
against three Federal divisions. Now that Buell was joining
Mitchel, Smith ordered two of the most dashing Confederate cavalry commanders to put pressure on Buell's supply line to
Louisville. They were very successful in this work. While Colonel
Nathan Bedford Forrest was to attack the railroad between Buell
and Nashville, Morgan was to disrupt Buell's supply line to
Louisville and those of Federal Brigadier General George W.
Morgan at the Cumberland Gap. Forrest left Chattanooga on July
6, moved through McMinnville, and captured the Ninth Michigan
and the Third Minnesota infantry regiments at Murfreesboro on
July 13. Forrest had 1200 prisoners, 50 wagons and teams, a battery of artillery, and a quarter of a million dollars worth of Buell's
supplies. Many people in St. Joseph County thought that the
Eleventh had been captured at Murfreesboro as the regiment had
been ordered there July 1 but for some reason did not go.

Morgan left Knoxville on July 4 and five days later captured the
small Federal garrison at Tomkinsville, Kentucky. For the next
three weeks he kept the commander at Louisville, Brigadier General John T. Boyle, in an absolute panic. On some days Boyle sent
cries of alarm and demands for men and weapons to Lincoln, Stanton, Halleck, Buell, and the governors of Indiana and Ohio, plus

the Mayor of Cincinnati. President Lincoln summed up the situation in telegram to Halleck on July 13: "They are having a stampede in Kentucky."[23] The Eleventh left Nashville at nine o'clock in the evening of July 9 and arrived in Bowling Green at daybreak. On the tenth Morgan hit Glasgow, and the Eleventh went to Cave City by rail. After marching all night the regiment entered Glasgow at seven in the morning of July 11, but "Morgan and his band had fled from us."[24] The men were back in Cave City again on the thirteen for breakfast and took the train for Munsfordville and the Green River bridge. Morgan was expected to try for the bridge at Munsfordville. Instead he struck Lebanon on July 11 and then went to Harrodsburg, Versailles, and Georgetown, arriving on the seventeenth at Cynthiana. On the afternoon of the July 13, the Eleventh started for Lebanon by train, but the bridge at New Haven had been burnt. They learned from Captain Greene of the Bardstown Home Guard that Morgan had left Lebanon. So it was back to the main line and to Shepardsville by July 14 and then to Louisville on the fifteenth. At this point Stoughton was ordered to send five companies back to Bowling Green, but he only sent Companies E and I, which he reinforced from the men left behind in Nashville.

In the long run the only thing that really counted for the Eleventh were the dispatches. The Assistant Adjutant General in Nashville, Oliver D. Greene, gave the Eleventh most of the credit for saving the bridges at Bowling Green and at Green River. He also took plenty of credit himself for sending the Eleventh. On July 12 Greene wired Colonel James B. Fry, Buell's Chief of Staff, that "I heard of his [Morgan] movement and his direction in time to get the Eleventh Michigan to Bowling Green and save that bridge. Foiled in that, Morgan tired to get at Green River Bridge but the Eleventh Michigan and the troops from Louisville were again on hand to save the bridge."[25] Green also warned Fry that "heavy movement is taking place up near Murfreesboro via McMinnville from Chattanooga."[26] This was Forrest's column which captured Murfreesboro two days later.

The regiment was ordered to Louisville and camped a few miles out of town on the Frankford Pike. They did not get much rest as "Thare was a aufull excitement amongst the people hear fearing and atackt from Morgan."[27] The men were pretty excited, too, and there were constant false alarms that brought out the entire regiment. On July 16 the regiment was ordered to Frankfort as part of the infantry force being organized under the command of Colonel Cicero Maxwell of the Twenty-sixth Kentucky Infantry.

Maxwell came from Louisville with the Eleventh to take command. Brigadier General Green Clay Smith, who had been in command at Frankfort, was ordered by General Boyle to take the cavalry troops and move immediately to Georgetown, seventeen miles east of Frankfort. Smith, who had previously been the Colonel of the Fourth Kentucky Cavalry, stated later that he was prepared to march on Georgetown with 1,320 infantry and cavalry before the order came giving the infantry to Maxwell. At two o'clock on the morning of the eighteenth Maxwell moved his command: consisting of the Eleventh Michigan; the Fifty-fifth Indiana; Company B, Second Battalion, Sixteenth U.S. Infantry; some cavalry; and two sections of artillery towards Georgetown. Smith left at the same time for Lexington to assume command to the troops in that area. Smith and Maxwell were then to cooperate to defeat Morgan who was in Cynthiana but was expected to come their way. The infantry column arrived in Georgetown at eleven o'clock in the morning only to find that Morgan had left during the morning of the seventeenth. When Smith reached Lexington, he heard that Morgan was in Paris. He sent an order to Maxwell to march the infantry to Paris to meet him. Smith left Lexington with a force of 595 men and overtook a regiment on the road with another 500 infantry. Maxwell left Georgetown sometime between one and three o'clock on the morning of July 19. When he was about half way to Paris, Smith informed him that Morgan was there but was expected to leave by way of the Winchester road. Smith urged Maxwell to hurry his march indicating that he would attempt to hold Morgan until the infantry column could come up.

For the first time since Morgan had crossed into Kentucky, there was a Federal force within striking distance with sufficient strength to defeat or to hold him until more troops could arrive. This depended on Smith holding Morgan and on Maxwell arriving. Neither happened. Smith could not cover both the Lexington and Winchester roads, and, when his advance met Morgan's rearguard on the Lexington road, Morgan simply left by the Winchester route. Maxwell brought his column within four miles of Paris by eight o'clock in the morning when he was informed by a civilian that Morgan was in Paris and prepared for battle. Maxwell consequently formed his troops in line of battle and stayed there for two hours. In his report he said it was here on the Georgetown road that Smith's message to cover the Lexington road reached him. Maxwell later marched his command cross country towards the fairgrounds on the Lexington road, but before reaching there he was informed by another civilian that Smith had driven Morgan from town. The infantry column then proceeded directly into Paris and arrived at 10:30 in the morning. Morgan was gone with few losses, or as Gillaspie put it: "the oald bandit and traitor ... had plundered the town and gone."[28] Smith was determined to follow Morgan even though the troops were exhausted. However, a member of the Paris Home Guard informed him that Morgan had been reinforced with another 2000 troops and was returning to attack. Smith dug in and sent out a strong scouting party which could not find the Confederate raiders.

On the morning of the nineteenth Smith left with the cavalry for Winchester and at eleven in the evening the infantry followed. Maxwell and the infantry arrived in Winchester about five o'clock in the afternoon of July 20. Maxwell had pressed all of the available wagons that he could find along the route to carry troops. Smith was still determined to follow Morgan, and he ordered Maxwell to follow with 150 selected infantry. Maxwell prevailed upon Smith to allow him to bring all of the Eleventh and the regular army company if he could secure enough wagons to haul them. Smith left for Richmond with the cavalry, and Maxwell followed with the infantry in wagons. "We moved on ratelte bang, jolteit a whang over the pike towards the city of Ritchmond."[29] The fatigue began to tell on the men, and their mood was probably not the best. At Boone's Ferry on the Kentucky River the "Reglar Capt. drew his revolver on one of the Co. F men. In an istant some half dosen of us boys was at a ready for the Capt. Had he of shot it probley would have bin his very last shot. On that you can depend. Gen. Smith huried him off fast."[30] The column reached Richmond on the afternoon of the twenty-first. It was the end of the race for the Eleventh. Smith went on with the cavalry, while Maxwell and the infantry went back to Lousiville.

The Eleventh reached Lexington on July 22; the men were still a bit testy. Gillaspie reported a confrontation with the Sergeant-Major of the Fifty-fifth Indiana Infantry who was trying to "steal some feed and horses of us."[31] Two days later they were still in Louisville and still feeling a bit aggravated. Gillaspie said, "I went to town and saw the Provo Guards take sevral off to the work house but would not trouble us Mich. 11th boys."[32] No doubt much of this newly discovered combativeness was due to frustration. After chasing Morgan for over three hundred miles, the regiment had him at Paris, but the commanding officer let him slip away.

Officially, it was Smith who was blamed for Morgan's escape at Paris. General Boyle wrote Buell on July 25 after Morgan had left Kentucky that: "Smith ought to have taken him."[33] Whether Boyle was referring to the action at Paris or the subsequent cavalry chase across Kentucky is not clear. However, he was not pleased and four days later wrote Buell again and asked "Don't you want General G. Clay Smith."[34] Exactly what happened outside of Paris, Kentucky, on the morning of July 19 and, therefore, who was at fault for the failure to bring Morgan to battle can not be clearly determined from the official sources.[35] Second Lieutenant Henry S. Platt of Company I laid the blame on Maxwell. According to Platt, Stoughton requested Maxwell to take the column into Paris rather than forming line of battle four miles south of town on the wrong road.[36] This could have possibly resulted in the capture or death of more of Morgan's raiders but probably would not have stopped

Morgan's flight. Cyrus Gilbert wrote that "we would [have] cut his retreat off at Paris if the Genrel [had] tried. I bleave that he was about half secsh and so does all the rest that was along. His name was Smith. It is said that they were both free Masons."[37] King repeated what many of the men must have said when they returned to Nashville. He wrote:

> The part of the regiment who were in pursuit of John Morgan returned without capturing the enemy. At Paris, Ky., they came up with the enemy were ordered to hold their piece [sic] and not to fire on the enemy and so allowed this black hearted traitor to escape. I never saw a more exasperated set than our men and officers. General Smith was the officer in command. A more dastardly piece of cowardice or trajtorism I do not know which to call it - has not been transacted in a long time.[38]

Ben Wells wrote his wife a similar account:

> They had a long chase through K.Y. after Morgan . . . . At Paris they might have captured his whole force of 2000 men had it not been for a cowardly Genl. who had command of our force when he got within canon shot Gen Smith drew his men up in line of battle and waited for Morgan to attack him: when he well knew that Morgan would do no such thing our Regt was in line 1/2 mile from the road where Morgan's whole force had to pass and there they stood in the rain one whole night and they were all anxious to move to the road and come in ahead of the rebels: our Col. and Gen Smith had some pretty hard words about the affair the Col. wanted to march to the road and commence the attack but the Gen would not let him say it would bring on a general engagement. The Col. told him that was what he came there for and there was no use of marching men to death to get in sight of the enemy and then fold their arms and let the traiters get away unmolested and he for one would do it no more. Our men were disappointed when they found that the rebels had escaped: If they had only shot Genl Smith they would have rid the country of as big a scoundrel and coward as Morgan himself.[39]

Well's account seemed to describe the actions of Maxwell rather than Smith, and there is nothing in Colonel Maxwell's report about any personal contact between his column and General Smith until they entered Paris. Morgan reported that "As my command was filing out of Paris on the Winchester pike I discovered a large force of Federals coming toward the town from the direction of Lexington. They immediately countermarched, supposing no doubt that my intention was to get in their rear. This enabled me to bring off my entire command without molestation, with the exception of two of my pickets, who were probably surprised...."[40] Although Smith was undoubtedly not responsible for keeping the Eleventh from striking, it does not appear that he worked very hard to give them the opportunity. Colonel Maxwell of the Seventh Kentucky must shoulder the blame for holding the infantry out of the action.

General Boyle made some attempt to keep the Eleventh under his command. He wrote Buell on July 25 that he planned to send them to Russellville "to drive rebel bands from Logan, Christian, Trigg, and Todd Counties."[41] Two days later he received a curt order from Buell: "Have the Eleventh Regiment Michigan sent to Nashville without delay."[42] The regiment arrived in Nashville on July 29. They had been soldiering now for eleven months and had yet to see combat.

Notes

1. Diary of Ira Gillaspie, p. 26.

2. King Papers, 3 May 1862.

3. Wells Papers, 22 July 1862.

4. This is a gloss written in Lott Woodworth's copy of *Michigan In The War*. It is signed "Lott". The book is in the collection of the Nottawa Township Library, Centreville, Michigan.

5. O.R., Vol 10, part 2, p. 161.

6. Diary of Ira Gillaspie, p. 27.

7. Rose Letters, 9 May 1862.

8. Diary of Ira Gillaspie, p. 28.

9. Ibid, p 28.

10. Ibid, p. 28.

11. *Western Chronicle*, 21 May 1862. Bennet wrote from Columbia on 9 May.

12. Rose Letters, 2 June 1862. Rose had just turned nineteen in May.

13. Diary of Ira Gillaspie, p. 29.

14. Stewart Diary. Stewart was a witty and keen observer of the war and his fellow man. The author felt as if he had lost a personal friend when he read the final entry in the diary.

15. Burke Foreman Letters, 21 June 1862, Regional History Collections, Western Michigan University, Kalamazoo, Michigan. Hereafter cited as Foreman Letters.

16. Diary of Ira Gillaspie, p. 29-30. See Wells Papers, 26 June 1862. Benjamin Wells had the Fifth Minnesota in place of the Twenty-eighth Kentucky. The author believes Wells to be correct as the 28th Kentucky was at this time in Gallatin. See O.R., Vol. 16, Part 1, p. 852.

17. Wells Papers, 26 June 1862.

18. Ibid.

19. Ibid.

20. Ibid, pp. 30-31.

21. Diary of Gillaspie, p. 30.

22. Bloom Diary, passim.

23. O.R., Vol. 16, Part 1, p. 738.

24. Diary of Ira Gillaspie, p. 31.

25. O.R., Vol 16, Part 2, pp. 132-133.

26. Ibid.

27. Diary of Ira Gillaspie, p. 31.

28. Ibid, p. 32.

29. Ibid.

30. Ibid.

31. Ibid.

32. Ibid.

33. O.R., Vol. 16, Part 1, p. 751.

34. O.R., Vol. 16, Part 1, p. 752. Smith was elected to Congress in the fall of 1862 and resigned his commision on December 4, 1863. *Generals In Blue*, p. 457.

35. Three of the writers of major letter collections were not present. King was with the Quartermaster in Nashville, Rose was in the hospital, and Wells was left behind as a nurse for his brother-in-law, Wallace Hoisington, and later went to Bowling Green. Gillaspie only said that Morgan was gone when they arrived.

36. *Journal*, 21 July 1862.

37. Cyrus Gilbert Letters, 30 July 1862, Burton Historical Collection, Detroit Public Library, Detroit. Author supplied the punctuation. The orginal letter is torn at the blanks. Hereafter cited as Gilbert Letters.

38. King Papers, 30 July 1862.

39. Wells Papers, 1 August 1862.

40. O.R., Vol. 16, Part 1, p. 770.

41. Ibid, p. 751.

42. O.R., Vol. 16, Part 2, p. 220.

Chapter Nine

"Your brigade...may soon succeed in either destroying or driving off the cavalry under Morgan and Forrest."

The Eleventh returned to Nashville on July 29 and set up camp on the Murfreesboro Pike without tents or other camp equipment, because all of the regimental property had gone with the detail to Bowling Green. That group arrived the following day, and the regiment prepared for a long stay. During the next two weeks the men were employed at guard duty or in building the fortifications in the Nashville area. A detail of sixty men under command of Lieutenant Patrick Keegan of Company K and Lieutenant Henry Platt of Company I went to Gallatin, Tennessee. This was a particularly vulnerable point on the Louisville and Nashville Railroad as there were a number of bridges and tunnels in that area. Colonel William P. Boone of the Twenty-eighth Kentucky Infantry was on duty there with his regiment. When Keegan and Platt arrived at Gallatin, they brought no tools. Since the first order of business was the construction of stockades at the bridgeheads and tunnel entrances, they had to press axes from the surrounding farms. Not surprisingly, in a community with strong Confederate sympathies, all of the axes needed new handles, sharpening or both.[1] After a few days the detail from the Eleventh returned to Nashville without finishing the stockades.

On August 12 John Hunt Morgan's cavalry captured Gallatin as the opening move of Braxton Bragg's invasion of Kentucky. Morgan took Boone and a few hundred of his men prisoners. The Con-

federates then burned one bridge, one tunnel lining, one train of
thirty-four cars and the fairground buildings which the Twenty-
eighth Kentucky Infantry had been using as barracks. In Bragg's
opinion the raid would close the railroad for a month.[2] Colonel
John F. Miller of the Twenty-ninth Indiana, commanding
Nashville, immediately organized an expedition to go to Gallatin.
He left just after midnight with the Eleventh Michigan, the Sixty-
ninth Ohio Infantry and four pieces of artillery from the Fourth Indiana Battery. The men carried only their haversacks filled with rations and their cartridge boxes with forty rounds. Undoubtedly every man took those things too precious to leave in camp. Gillaspie
put his "wifes with some other likenesses into my haversack and I
also put in my watch and flute..."[3] The train went very slowly during the night and arrived at a burnt bridge over Camp Creek at
daylight. Difficulties in unloading the horses and artillery delayed
the start towards Gallatin until seven o'clock in the morning. Just
south of town the advance guard of the Sixty-ninth ran into the
rearguard that Morgan had left behind to see that the fairground
buildings burned. Three of the raiders went down in the first exchange of shots. Sergeant Edward Frost of Company E reported
that:

> Col. Stoughton saw the men fall, when he turned in his saddle, took off his
> hat and waved it to us, at the same time saying, 'Come on boys - double
> quick!' and then if you ever heard loud cheering, you can just imagine what a
> noise our...regiment made...it was no double quick - it was double run...The
> way the canteens, haversacks and blankets flew was a caution.[4]

At last the Eleventh had caught up with the "oald bandit and
traiter," and there was no Colonel Maxwell nor Green Clay Smith
to stop them. Up the road they ran with the Ohio regiment in
front with the Eleventh right behind and the artillery coming pell
mell. When Sergeant Frost fell down, he was almost run over by a
cannon. But it was only Morgan's rearguard and the damage had
been done. They "put spurs to their horses and were soon out of
sight."[5]

Miller and his men stayed in Gallatin until four o'clock in the afternoon searching the "nearly deserted village."[6] Many of the residents had joined in the burning of Federal property and probably left with Morgan. "Stores were broken open [and] the boys helped themselves to whatever they wished."[7] As the infantry were boarding the train, "a party of Morgan's men fierd on the rear of our train killing one and a negro and wounding one of the railroad men. We run off our artillery and fierd on the rebils. We killed 25 of them and they took 2 of our men prisenors. A few round from Captl Bush's batry put the rebils to flite."[8] It was one of the men from the Sixty-Ninth Ohio who was killed. The Confederates saw it a bit differently. Basil W. Duke, Morgan's Adjutant and biographier, said a squad of fifteen men led by Sergeant Quirk attacked the train while it was loading and killed two or three and captured a few. "The artillery opened on him [Quirk] with canister but did little damage."[9] Leonard Carknard of Company A and Bryon J. Liddle of Company D were the men that were captured. Carknard died in a Confederate prison, but Liddle was eventually paroled.[10] Stoughton declared in an order to Company officers to prevent straggling that Liddle and Carknard had "straggled from their companies..." and had thereby "...rendered themselves little if anything less than deserters."[11]

The continual harassment of the Federal supply lines through Kentucky and Tennessee forced Buell and his staff to attempt to find some solution to the problem of Confederate cavalry superiority. The answer was to create a light brigade of hard marching, fast moving infantry and cavalry. There was a precedent for this type of unit from Washington's revolutionary army. Washington formed a light brigade in 1777 by drafting one hundred picked men from his other brigades. By 1779 he had a light brigade of 1300 men under the command of Anthony Wayne. This body "of picked men...would be distinguished by their special skills in swift movement and sharp striking power."[12] It would be hard to believe that the West Point graduates were not aware of the concept of light brigades which the British had continued to use. The basic idea was for the cavalry to hold the Confederate raiders until the infantry could arrive. The infantry would provide the punch to destroy the calvary. This solution was probably forced on Buell by the defeat of Brigadier General Richard W. Johnson's cavalry by a numerically inferior Morgan near Gallatin on August 22. Johnson was an experienced cavalry officer having served with the Second Cavalry in the prewar army. Buell reported to Halleck that "The disaster is most unfortunate..."[13] On August 26 Buell asked Major General George Thomas if he could recommend a Colonel "fit to command a light brigade of cavalry, infantry and artillery, to operate against Forrest?"[14] Without waiting for Thomas' reply Buell appointed Colonel Lovell H. Rousseau to replace Colonel John F. Miller as the commander of Nashville. Miller was given command of a light brigade consisting of the Eleventh Michigan and Nineteenth Illinois infantries and the First Kentucky, Second Indiana and part of the Fourth Kentucky cavalries. Stokes' Tennessee Cavalry were to act as guides for the brigade. Colonel Stoughton of the Eleventh was to command the infantry wing. The Eleventh had certainly made a mark for themselves as a hard marching regiment on the foray through Kentucky. Their behavior on the Gallatin operation must have added to their reputation for combativeness. The Nineteenth Illinois was a Zouave regiment. They had mustered into the service in June of 1861 under the command of John B. Turchin, a former Colonel in the Russian Imperial Guard. It was considered by many to be the best drill unit in the Army of the Ohio. The regiment was "notorious for the disregard of the persons and property . . . of enemy civilians."[15] The Nineteenth was with Turchin's brigade when they sacked Athens, Alabama. Turchin was courtmarshalled and relieved of duty for ordering the looting of the village, but his wife appealed to Lincoln. The President not only reinstated Turchin but promoted him to brigadier general. However, Turchin's brigade was broken up by General Buell, and the regiments sent to various railroad guard duties.[16]

Miller was told to keep the oraganization secret and to have it ready to move the next day. Buell's Chief of Staff, James B. Fry, wired Miller detailed instructions. He was to march to Murfreesboro which was to be his base to protect the supply lines south of

Nashville "paricularly against the cavalry force of the enemy under Forrest and Morgan."[17] Miller should not go north of the Cumberland River. The infantry was to be moved in wagons whenever it was possible. Men and officers were to carry only a blanket and never less than forty rounds. The entire command was to subsist off the land and the rations carried in their haversacks. Fry concluded,

> With activity, vigilance, and determination your brigade can render the most useful service, and it is hoped may soon succeed in either destroying or driving off the cavalry under Morgan and Forrest...You must chastise guerrillas and marauders, but do not make detachments such as would render you liable to be defeated by the Forrest or Morgan before you could concentrate."[18]

Considering that both the Nineteenth Illinois and the Eleventh Michigan had been involved in looting, did this "chastise guerrillas and marauders" represent a change in Buell's soft policy toward Confederate sympathizers? Whatever it meant in Buell's plans or thinking, Braxton Bragg quickly defeated this threat to his cavalry. Bragg started to swing his army out of Chattanooga towards Kentucky. Although the Eleventh and the Nineteenth Illinois got to Murfreesboro on September 1, Buell had no time to worry about minor distractions like cavalry raids. He had to find out where Bragg was going and catch up with him. Buell moved his army north using Murfreesboro as the first point of concentration. He then moved on into Kentucky to bring Bragg and Kirby Smith to battle at Perryville on October 8.

On September 4 the Eleventh and the Nineteenth marched back towards Nashville. The brief life of the light brigade was over. There is no evidence that it was ever used or that any attempt was ever made to recreate it. However, it did serve to bring the Nineteenth Illinois and the Eleventh Michigan together. They would be brigaded together until after the Battle of Missionary Ridge. By September 10 the Eleventh Michigan and the Nineteenth Illinois were combined with the Eighteenth and Sixty-ninth Ohio to form the Twenty-ninth Brigade under the command of Colonel Timothy R. Stanley of the Eighteenth Ohio. The Brigade was assigned to

Negley's Division of the Army of the Ohio. Gillaspie reported a strange run-in between Stoughton and the Nineteenth while they were waiting for the other regiments of the brigade to join them outside of Nashville. Gillaspie and two other men were on guard duty and were left behind. They were out all night and came back to the regiment about breakfast time.

> I made down my bunk after breckfast then took a good smoke and droped to sleep and was soon lost in plesant dreams of home. I slept about an hour when the Capt. come and asked the boys if I was asleep. I woke at the sound of his voice and in about five minutes I herd an aufull uprore at the guard lines. Presantly whang whang whang went some seven or eight guns. In the direction of the uprore the sound of the 19th Ill. Reg. could be herd shouting Zouave Zouave Zouave Turchin Turchin at the top of their voices. The next thing I herd was the well none vois of Capt. Hood crying Mutiny in camp, fall in evry man of Co. C come quick and in 3 minuets we to a man was in ranks. We was ordered to load which we done with all posable haste. We was marched whare the croud was, then Lieutenant Colonel Eldrige gave orders for the croud to go to their quarters. The onley answer he got was the cry of Give us Turchin Zouave. He told them he would give them hell if they did not dry up and go to their quarters. Co. C 11th Mich. Forward March cryed Eldridge Right Wheal Forward March. This brought us in the rear of the howling Zouaves. We marched steadely on and they began to fall back for they saw we was fully determined to fier. Finley we got them all into their regimental lines. Colonel Stoughton being in command of the Brigade he ordered the hole Brigade out under arms except the 19th. They were or-dered out without arms. They was formed into a square. Capt. Haden co-manded them. We the rest of the Brigade formed a line on each side of them and little Stoughton in their center he adresed them for about a half hour giveing them to understand that it was William L. Stoughton that they was dealing with and that oders they must obey. They gave him 3 hearty chears when they found that they had found an officer that they could not rule or scare and they then said that they would gladly dy for him if that was his orders. He thanked them and dismissed them and we was marched back to our quarters whare we was allso dismised. I went in and lite my pipe again.[19]

No doubt his hand shook a little as he "lite" his pipe. Stoughton would ask the Nineteenth to die at his orders on September 20, 1863, at Chickamauga, and they never hesitated.

The new brigade had one common characteristic: they had all been involved in the looting of civilian property. The Eighteenth Ohio was orginally a three months regiment that was reorganized as a three year one. They had been brigaded with the Nineteenth Illinois under Colonel Turchin and were with him at Athens. Stanley had been tried by the courtmartial that dismissed Turchin, but he was acquitted. The Sixty-ninth Ohio had been with the Eleventh at Gallatin. When Buell moved north, he left Major General George H. Thomas in command of Nashville with three divisions. However, he soon called for Thomas to march north with one or two divisions. Thomas decided that Nashville was in great enough danger of capture that he left two divisions and took only one. Negley was left in command of Nashville with his own division and that of Brigadier General John M. Palmer's First Division of the Army of the Mississippi on loan from Grant. Negley's Division had two brigades, Stanley's and John F. Miller's. Miller had ordered the Gallatin "search." It would appear that Buell and Thomas were trying to impress the Rebel sympathizers in Nashville as well as protect the military supplies stored there.

Once Thomas left to join Buell on September 15, Nashville was a city under seige, and it remained that way until November 6. For two months there was no mail in or out of the city and also no supplies. The men at Nashville knew that they were going to miss a big battle. After a full year in the army the Eleventh had not been able to strike a blow at the Rebellion. However, they also knew that their duty in Nashville was important, hard and dangerous. Buell told Negley that "He must defend his position to the last extremity."[20] Most of the time it was guard duty or working on the massive fortifications around Nashville. It was boring, hard work on short rations. Fortunately, Negley was active. He hit the Rebels time and again with small, fast moving columns. The Eleventh was not involved in any of these raids, but they took their turns on the foraging expeditions. On one of these Stoughton had command of three regiments of infantry, including the Eleventh, and a section of artillery. Going down the Cumberland River valley the column was hit twice by guerillas. On the way out there was no effect, but on the way back the guerillas had some Confederate help. There was a "brisk engagement" in which Stoughton brought up the cannons. The enemy had thirteen casualties and the Union force had no casualties. Stoughton succeeded in bringing in one hundred and fifty wagons full of forage that day.[21]

Notes

1. O.R., Vol. 16, Part 1, p. 854.

2. Ibid, p. 857.

3. Diary of Ira Gillaspie, p. 33.

4. *Western Chronicle*, 3 September 1862.

5. King Papers, 15 August 1862.

6. Ibid.

7. Ibid.

8. Diary of Ira Gillaspie, p. 34.

9. Basil W. Duke, *A History Of Morgan's Cavalry* (Bloomington: Indiana University Press, 1960) p. 203.

10. Michigan Volunteers, 1861-1865, Eleventh Infantry.

11. Regimental Order and Letter Book.

12. Russell F. Weigley, *History of the United States Army* (Bloomington, Indiana University Press, 1984) p. 66.

13. O.R., Vol. 16, Part 2, p.388.

14. Ibid, p. 426. Thomas recommended Colonel Charles G. Harker of the Sixty-fifth Ohio Infantry who was commanding a brigade in Thomas J. Wood's Division.

15. Generals in Blue, p. 511.

16. O.R., Vol. 16, Part 2, p. 87.

17. Ibid, pp. 431-32.

18. Ibid, pp. 431-432.

19. Diary of Ira Gillaspie, pp. 37-38.

20. O.R., Vol. 16, Part 2, p. 511.

21. Michigan in the War, p. 314.

Chapter Ten

"...our position is a responsible one."

When the army came back to Nashville on November 6, it was called the Army of the Cumberland, and Major General William S. Rosecrans was in command. Halleck had ordered Buell to turn over command to Major General George Thomas on September 30. Thomas refused the promotion on the grounds that Buell had made the troop dispositions to fight Bragg and he was not aware of all of Buell's plans. The Union victory at Perryville gave Buell a second chance, but his failure to pursue Bragg to the satisfaction of Washington lost him his command. Thomas was not asked a second time. Halleck wired Rosecrans the order to replace Buell on October 24. On October 30 he took command of the Army of the Ohio, which officially became the XIV Army Corps but was known as the Army of the Cumberland.[1]

It was generally said that few men and officers were sorry to see Buell go, and so it was with the Eleventh. James King wrote that "News has reached us today of the removal of Maj. General Buell and the gallant Rosecranze appointed in his stead. This is hailed with Joy by all the Officers and Soldiers in this Division. The men and Soldiers have had no confidence in General Buell as a Commander for a long time"[2] A month later he commented on the removal of McClellan and Buell" . . . we have tried such Generals too long. This stand still policy I do not believe in, never did. I hope our new leaders will not follow in the tracks of their predecessors."[3] If he had been near the White House, King might have heard an amen. Dan Rose was not greatly impressed by Rosecrans' appearance, but he made a shrewd guess about his character. Rosecrans "is a very common looking man and famillar with every one, he will

not leave the troops idle, I don't think."[4] However, General Rosecrans left his troops too idle for Halleck. The General in Chief
urged Rosecrans forward to attack Bragg who was concentrating
his army at Murfreesboro. At least, he started out urging but finally turned to threats. Early in December Halleck wrote Rosecrans that if he remained in Nashville one more week, "I cannot
prevent your removal."[5] The threats seemingly had little effect on
the commander of the Army of Cumberland. Rosecrans had some
major problems to contend with before he could move his army.
First and foremost was the reopening of the Louisville and
Nashville Railroad, so that he could feed his troops on a regular
basis and build a surplus to sustain an advance. Rosecrans wanted
two million rations on hand in Nashville. This would feed his army
only twenty days, if the railroad was broken by the Confederate
cavalry. The railroad opened to Nashville on November 27. Normally, Nashville could have been supplied by boats, but the unsea-
sonally dry weather made the Cumberland River impassable.
Rosecrans also had to reorganize and refit his army. Many of the
troops had just marched from northern Alabama to Louisville,
Kentucky, and back to Nashville. They needed shoes and uniforms. All of the troops had spent much of the last three months
without full rations. Rosecrans paid attention to his troops. He
began to inspect divisions, brigades, and even regiments, talking to
the men in ranks. The men knew that they had a commander who
cared about them. This quickly earned him a nickname "Old
Rosey." The army, being officially the XIV Army Corps, was divided into Right, Left and Center wings. In reality these were what
very shortly became army corps. Major General Thomas L. Crittenden had the Left Wing, Major General Alexander McCook
commanded the Right Wing and Major General George Thomas
was with the Center.

Rosecrans believed that time was on his side. The longer he
waited: the weaker Bragg would be. In this he was proven correct.
During Jefferson Davis's visit to Bragg in Murfreesboro, he ordered Bragg to send Major General Carter Stevenson's brigade of
seventy-five hundred men to reinforce Lieutenant General John

Pemberton's army in Mississippi.[6] More than the brigades of infantry, Rosecrans worried about the overwhelming cavalry superiority. Bragg lowered the odds on this. He sent Forrest to raid Grant's supply lines in western Tennessee and allowed Morgan to begin another raid into Kentucky. This was what Rosecrans was waiting for and was counting on Bragg doing. Even then Bragg still had Brigadier General Joseph Wheeler's four brigades of cavalry, which was more than a match for anything Rosecrans had, but it narrowed the odds. By mid-December Rosecrans felt that things were ready for an advance against Bragg. These Confederate moves that gave Rosecrans the edge that he needed were the result of one of the finest pieces of deception of the entire war. Rosecrans made Bragg believe that he was staying in the comfort of Nashville during the winter. Indeed, he had everyone fooled. James King, who almost always knew what was going on, wrote a letter on December 24 which had no mention of a possible move in the near future.[7] Just four days before the army moved, Dan Rose thought "there is not as much prospects for a fight here now as there was...."[8]

Rosecran's army began to move on December 26. Rosecrans was taking about 44,000 men out a total force of nearly 80,000. The necessity of leaving a strong garrison in Nashville and guarding the railroad supply line meant that he would have a small numerical superiorty on the field of about 7,000 men. Bragg's army was spread over forty miles with Hardee's corps at Triune and Eagleville, Polk at Murfreesboro, and a brigade at Readyville. Neither commander was quite sure where the other army was located. Rosecrans sent Crittenden down the Murfreesboro Pike towards LaVerge with 14,500 men. McCook's 16,000 men went down the McLensville Pike towards Nolensville and Triune. Thomas, with the smallest corps, was to go down the Franklin Pike to Brentwood and then swing east crossing McCook's rear at Nolensville to take a position on Crittenden's right at Steward's Creek.

Thomas's corps was reduced to about 11,700 troops as the march began. All but Walker's brigade of Fry's division and all of Reynold's division were left at Gallatin to guard the railroad.

Mitchell's division and Spears's brigade of Negley's division remained behind as the garrison for Nashville.[9] This left Thomas with the division of Major General Lovell Rousseau composed of four brigades, totaling 6,236 men, and the division of Brigadier General James Negley, composed of Colonel Timothy Stanley's and Colonel John F. Miller's brigades, totaling 4,623 men.[10] Negley's division was the vanguard of Thomas's line of march. Miller's brigade had been camped on the Franklin Pike during most of the forty-six days of waiting while Stanley's brigade stayed in Nashville until December 10.[11] Before beginning the march Rosecrans took twenty men from every regiment to form a Pioneer Brigade. This sort of primative engineering unit was organized into three battalions. Captain Calvin C. Hood of Company C was detailed to command the Second Battalion of the Pioneer Brigade.

Once the decision to march had been made, the rains began. Ira Gillaspie said, "The roads and fields are allmost unwalkable especial whare the wagons or horses have bin."[12] When Rosecrans announced the forward movement, he told his commanders that "We shall begin to skirmish probably as soon as we leave the outposts."[13] Negley's division proceeded down the Wilsonville Pike "about 2 or 3 miles when we bore off to the left towards Nolinsville."[14] The orginal plan called for Negley and Rousseau to camp at Owen's store on the Wilsonville Pike.[15] However, Negley heard the heavy firing from the direction of Nolinsville where McCook's leading division under the command of Jefferson C. Davis was hotly engaged with Hardee's skirmishers. Negley left his train with a guard and pushed his division to support Davis. They "got to Nolinsville just dark" on December 26, but the fighting had ended.[16] Somehow in the midst of the rain and mud and marching, the Illinois Zouaves had "presed a cople of barels of whiskey."[17] There is no record that they offered to share it with the rest of the brigade.

The next morning Negley brought up his baggage train and started to march eastward to join Crittenden's column on the Murfreesboro Pike. The route of the march was "over an exceedingly rough by-road."[18] Rose described it as "worst road I ever traveled slippery muddy and the most of it through a cedar swamp."[19] The regiment "reached the Murfreesboro pike just after dark 2 miles south of Lavergne whare we bunked down for the night on the coald and wett ground."[20] Thirty men from the Eleventh were detailed about midnight to return to Nolinsville and bring up the train. On December 28 Negley's division remained at Stewarts Creek waiting for the supply train and Rousseau's division, which had been delayed by the mud. For the men it was an opportunity to build fires and dry their blankets. Since they were carrying only their knapsacks, these were the only shelter that they had against the rain and cold. The men also had a chance to cook a hot meal. It was fresh beef without any salt, but they ate and called it "good anuff."[21] In the afternoon the train came up with hard tack and coffee, and they had their fill. In the evening the regiment sat around their fires "to talk of the hard march we had had and the probel fight we would have with oald Bragg at Murfreesboro til night when we bunked down to sleep and dream of our homes. As I lay thare I could not help but think that some who was in the talking tonight would not be able to talk ever agane maby in a few hours or days. It was a sad thought and I soon forgot it and went to sleep."[22]

On December 29 Negley's division started forward again, leaving Rousseau at the Stewart's Creek bridge. Rousseau detached one brigade at this point to guard the Jefferson pike crossing of Stones River. 23 Even the Murfreesboro Pike, which was macadamized, must have been in rough shape by the passage of Crittenden's corps, because the column went south of the Pike and crossed Stewart's Creek. All that day they had a heavy line of skirmishers supported by artillery out in front. Wheeler's cavalry was "contesting the ground obstinately."[24] About eight miles from Murfreesboro, the division returned to the Pike and came up behind Crittenden. Once again the men had a chance to build fires and cook. However, it was raining hard enough that the men stacked arms by putting the bayonets on and sticking them in the ground.[25]

On December 30 Thomas replaced Rousseau at Stewart's Creek
with Walker's brigade and brought the remaining three brigades up
to support Negley. Negley's division was "obliqued to the right and
took up a postion on the right of Palmer's division of Crittenden's
corps."[26] With Miller's brigade on the left and Stanley's on the
right the division advanced through a cedar woods to the Wilkinson
Turnpike. During the day the Pioneer Brigade cut roads through
the cedars to allow the ammunition train and artillery to come forward. About noon George Robert's brigade from Sherdian's division of McCook's corps came up to Stanley's brigade on Negley's
right. The skirmishing here was very heavy. Each brigade had a
full regiment out in front. The skirmish line was pushed forward
along the entire Union line in the afternoon. The Nineteenth Illinois had been in front of Stanley's brigade during the morning. It
was replaced by the Sixty-ninth Ohio about noon. "Thare was four
of our skermishers picked off from one post by the rebil sharp
shooters. The sharp shooter finley got a ball from one the 19th Ill.
Reg. The sharp shooter had a telascoped sited gun."[27] By this time
the artillery batteries had been brought up and were "sending their
death missles to the rebil ranks."[28] At three o'clock the Eleventh
was sent to the front. Companies A, D, F, and I were advanced to
the skirmish line while the rest of the regiment acted as the reserve. First Lieutenant Joseph Wilson, commanding Company F,
was killed shortly after the Eleventh went forward. He was the first
man of the regiment to die in combat. As his body was brought
back through the reserve, "we looked on his still form [and] we realized what war meant. Our cheeks paled as we viewed our first
sacrifice for our country."[29] Gillaspie thought that the Eleventh
did not shoot as much as the other regiments in the brigade, but
"they made every shot count."[30] The Eleventh remained on the
skirmish line all night. At dark some of the men started to built
fires, but Colonel Stoughton "came and told us that he was sorey
that it was so but the orders was such that we could not have any
fiers on the front for says he our posision is a responsible one. He
shoed much anciety about our comfort. We got a few tacks and lay
down to rest and sleep."[31]

That evening after the firing died down, one of the most famous incidents of the Battle of Stone's River occured.

Just before tattoo [the bands] they began to play their favorite tunes. The music carried clearly on the still wintry air. While the strains of *Yankee Doodle* and *Hail Columbia* drifted through the cedards from the Northern camps, the Confederate bands answered with *Dixie* and *The Bonnie Blue Flag.* After this exchange of musical bombardments had continued for a time, one of the bands struck up the air that was known and loved by all the soldiers, regardless of the color of their uniforms - *Home Sweet Home.* At once, as though by prearrangement, the tune was taken up by all the bands on both sides, and soon across the rocky glades for miles the simple melody rose in a great combined volume as Federals and Confederates joined in. The familiar and beloved words sprang to the lips of the soldiers, and the chorus of thousands of homesick voices almost drowned out the brassy blare of the instruments. The music swelled and died away, but that haunting last line - "There's no place like home" - chocked in the throats of bluecoat Yankees and butternut-clad Rebels alike as they huddled shivering in their blankets, and waited for the morning and its bloody work.[32]

Notes

1. O.R., Vol. 16, Part 2, pp. 642, 653.

2. King Papers, 29 October 1862.

3. Ibid, 29 November 1862.

4. Rose Papers, 14 November 1862.

5. O.R., Vol. 20, Part 2, p 117.

6. James Lee McDonough, *Stones River: Bloody Winter In Tennessee* (Knoxville: University of Tennessee Press, 1980) p. 37. Hereinafter cited as McDonough, Stones River.

7. King Letters, 24 December 1862.

8. Rose Letters, 22 December 1862.

9. Spears brought the supply column to the battlefield on January 2 and was immediately employed in the pursuit after the final day of fighting. Walker's brigade of S.S. Fry's division came up to the battlefield at Stones River on January 2 and were used to shore up the left flank of the army under the command of McCook.

10. O.R. Vol. 20, Part 2, p. 410.

11. King Letters, 24 December 1862.

12. Diary of Ira Gillaspie, pp. 40-41.

13. W.D. Bickman, *Rosecrans' Campaign With The Fourteen Army Corps* (Cincinnati, 1863) p. 135. Cited in Francis F. McKinney, *Education In Violence: The Life Of George H. Thomas And The History Of The Army Of The Cumberland* (Detroit, Wayne State University Press, 1961) p. 179.

14. Diary of Ira Gillaspie, p. 41.

15. O.R., Vol. 20, Part 1, p. 372.

16. Diary of Ira Gillaspie, p. 41.

17. Ibid.

18. O.R., op cit.

19. Rose Letters, 7 January 1862.

20. Diary of Ira Gillaspie, p. 41.

21. Ibid.

22. Ibid.

23. O.R., op cit.

24. Ibid.

25. Diary of Ira Gillaspie, p. 41.

26. O.R., op cit.

27. Diary of Ira Gillaspie, p. 41.

28. Ibid.

29. Hicks, Recollections, p. 525.

30. Diary of Ira Gillaspie, op cit.

31. Ibid, pp. 42-43.

32. Stanley F. Horn, *The Army of Tennessee.* (Norman, Oklahoma: University of Oklahoma Press, 1952) p. 199. No member of the Eleventh recorded this emotional moment. However, the battle line stretched over a great distance and possibly they could not hear the music.

Chapter Eleven

"The Eleventh Michigan and its gallant little colonel...behaved well."

Wherever Stoughton got his information, he was certainly correct. The position of Negley's division and, therefore, of the Eleventh Michigan was a responsible one. In Rosecran's plan of battle Negley's division was the hinge pin on which the entire attack would swing. Rosecrans planned to attack with his powerful left wing, driving into Murfreesboro to cut off Bragg's line of escape. McCook on the right was to engage the enemy hotly but not to bring on an all out battle. In order to fool Bragg into thinking that his right extended much farther than it did, Rosecrans ordered camp fires built to McCook's right. Bragg had the same plan: to attack with his left against the right of the Army of the Cumberland. Unfortunately, Bragg ordered Hardee to attack at dawn which was much earlier than Rosecran's order for Crittenden. Futhermore, Hardee moved far to his left because of the fake campfires, thereby seriously flanking the Army of the Cumberland.

The Eleventh came off the skirmish line at dawn with the fog still thick in front of the divisional position. The Eighteenth Ohio went forward. The Eleventh went back about three hundred yards and began to cook breakfast and dry their clothes and blankets. Before the men could finish their breakfast, heavy firing was heard from the far right of McCook's corps.[1] The divisions of Brigadier General Richard Johnson and Brigadier General Jefferson C. Davis were quickly broken and routed by the Confederates. Hardee had flanked Johnson to such an extent that the Union troops had no chance. In addition, the commanding officers on the right were not attentive to their potentially dangerous situation. As the disaster developed on the Federal right, Rosecrans did not understand its nature and believed that it was just McCook's troops making a demonstration. Fortunately, Brigadier General Philip Sheridan's division made a stand. Although they were driven back, they were not routed. Sheridan swung his division around to face west forming one half of a V. The other half of the salient was Negley's division. Colonel George Robert's brigade of Sheridan's division and Stanley's brigade of Negley's division forming the point of the salient. It was in this position that some of the bloodiest fighting of the Battle of Stones River occurred.

From nine until eleven o'clock this salient met every charge the Confederates could throw at it. This valiant stand gave Rosecrans the time to rally his broken army. Negley and Sheridan managed to mass five batteries of artillery to support their line. Negley's division had become the hinge on which the battle turned but from the opposite side. The fighting here was described by Sheridan as "one of the bitterest and most sanguinary contests of the day."[2] Colonel Stanley in a letter to Governor Blair called it, "that terrible carnage - death, bulldog fighting."[3] Negley referred to it as "a murderous storm of lead and iron."[4] It is probably impossible for anyone to describe the details of a battle. Sometimes, the uneducated do better than the generals. Ira Gillaspie said of this portion of the fighting:

We met the rebils and the fight comenced for certen. Boom Boom sounded the loud artilery. Crack Crack and a rattle went the musketry. Whew went the rebil shells over our heads. Whirr Whirr come the rifle bullets now and then laying low one of our brave fellows. Hear on this nole Schultzes batery was badly cut to peases the rebils haveing hit and eather killed and wounded a good many of the Shultzes men. The rebils kept coming and the 19th Ill. Reg. and ours charged on them poring a hole voley into them and then keeping up the fier we drove back a hole division of the gray backs. I notesed that the rebils had driven the wright wing of our armey clear back in the rear of us so as to give the rebils a raking fier across us just mowing our brave men down but our men stood the fier well and fought bravely under the destrucktive fier of three rebil baterys fiering one from the front and one on eather flank. Brigadeer Stanley and Gen. Negley seamed evry whare presant

chearing and encouraging the men and Colonel Stoughton won from his men
that esteem that will last while life lasts.[5]

In the cedars Stoughton and the Eleventh were called on by
General Rousseau to take the place of a regiment on the right of
the brigade position. Stoughton indicated that this move was made
at the request of General Rousseau and the order of Colonel
Stanley. Gillaspie recorded the moment with the drama of a dime
novel.

> Hear Gen. Russeaux rode up and said that a Reg. that was holding a point
> on our right was out of amanition and he wanted somebody to take their
> place. Colonel Stoughton told him he would take it and hold it. Your a
> gentlemen and by God you shall have it. Take it and hold it says Gen.
> Russeaux. We was then marched about 35 rods [a little less than two
> hundred yards] down to whare lay the Reg. that was out of amanition. They
> looked rather tierd out and bloody as they went to fill their cartrige boxes and
> we took their places. The rebils kept trying to drive this position but soon
> stoped . . . .[6]

Colonel Stoughton said the action lasted about half hour. Colonel
John Beatty, commanding Rousseau's left which had joined Stanley's right, recalled that he found a Michigan regiment to
strengthen his line when one of his regiments withdrew in disorder.
This could only have been the Eleventh.[7] Beatty's report in the
Official Records is very brief, and none of his regimental reports
are there, which makes his memoirs the only word on the behavior
of his troops. Beatty said that soon after this he found that all of
the other troops had fallen back and that he was unable to find
Rousseau. He therefore withdrew the remainer of his brigade
through the cedars without trouble. Beatty always seemed to have
a difficult time finding his commanding officer in battle. (See
Chapter 16 on the Battle of Chickamauga.) Stoughton said in his
offical report to Negley that after moving to the right the "heavy
roar of musketry and artillery indicated that the principal attack of
the enemy was being made immediately to our left and rear."[8]
Stoughton reversed the regiment under the fire and rushed back
towards Schultz's battery which was under "a galling fire." The
regiment delivered a volley directly into the enemy column and

"continued to load and fire with great coolness and bravery until orders came to fall back."[9] It was here that Major Sylvester Smith was shot in the face and Colonel Stoughton's horse was shot from under him. Lieutenant Matthew Faulker of Company C led Major Smith from the field. Adjutant Samuel Chadwick lost his horse and had his sword shot from his hand.[10] The Seventy-fourth Ohio of Miller's brigade came to the support of the Eleventh. "Colonel [Granville] Moody of the 74th Ohio marched his Reg. up in perfect order under a tremendious fier and comanded Halt Front Ready Fier poring a voley into the rebils."[11]

At eleven o'clock Sheridan announced that his division was out of ammunition and had to fall back. On his right Rousseau's division, which Thomas had placed there in hope of stopping the flanking attack of the Confederates, had already fallen back when it was flanked. On Negley's left Palmer's division of Crittenden's corps retreated to a new line that Thomas was attempting to form beyond the cedars in a depression in an open field. On high ground across the Murfreesboro Pike Thomas began to mass the artillery that would be the margin of success in stemming the rout. However, this left Negley's division nearly surrounded as a Confederate column was moving to cut off his avenue of retreat. Miller and Stanley drove the enemy back in their front, then quickly turned and charged the Confederate column crossing their rear, cutting their way out of the cedars.

The only description of the fight though the cedars was recorded by Gillaspie. He wrote:

Now men says Negley we are in a tight place and must retreat but if you will folow me I will take you out. We are allmost surrounded and we must cut our way with fier if nessary. We comenced our retreat in perfect order loading and fiering as we went thrue the ceeders which was very thick hear. Lieutenant [Ephriam] Hall of Co. I was wounded and Lieutenant [Thomas Flynn] Flinn of Co. E was killed. The rebils had to open for us and we pored out but they folowed us so clost in the rear that they was poring a deadly fier into our ranks. We loaded, fixed bayonets, about faced and pored a very destrucktive fier sending many of the trators to their mother earth and puting the rest to a halt and we thus got out of the ceeders very well but hear we had to cross a larg field to git to the railroad whare the rest of our right wing had falen back to and formed a line. The rebils had a raking fier on us while crosing the field.[12]

Gillaspie's company was left without a single commissioned officer by the end of the day. Lieutenant Thomas Flynn, commanding Company E, was one of the First Michigan Infantry men. He had become a hero at the First Battle of Bull Run by saving the regimental colors.

Once out of the cedars the division had to cross the open field to reach Thomas's new line of defense. Although they were fighting all the way, the two brigades were in serious trouble. At this point they were saved by the regular army brigade of Rousseau's division who charged back across the open field into the cedars. The regulars suffered "severe loss in officers and men in the effort."[13] Thomas reported that the regulars "came under murderous fire, losing 22 officers and 508 men in killed and wounded."[14] Thomas does not indicate if this was in the charge to aid Negley's withdrawl. However, just after Stanley's brigade reached the crest of the hill, both the Eighteenth Ohio and the Eleventh Michigan charged back into the cedars.

The reason for this foolhardy but gallant move has been clouded by reports in the official records. Colonel Stanley's report to General Negley gave the following account:

> After we [his brigade] had formed in line behind the crest of a hill an officer from another division rode to the front of the Eighteenth Ohio and ordered them forward, himself leading the way, and made the charge upon the enemy in the woods; but the enemy was so strong there that the regiment was compelled to fall back with heavy loss. As soon, however, as I saw the move, I called the Eleventh Michigan to follow me to their support, which they did most gallantly; but I soon called them off, as they had no support and the fire was murderous. I exceedingly regretted this order from an officer not having command over me, and without consulting yourself or me. Many of my men were left on the field.[15]

Stanley was the Colonel of the Eighteenth and had recruited the regiment in the early days of the war. Lieutenant Colonel Josiah Given, who was commanding the Eighteenth, in his report named the "officer of another division" as General Rousseau. Given had just rallied and reformed his ranks after the final dash across the open field when:

> ...General Rousseau ordered me to charge the woods again, encouraging the men to charge by taking the lead in person. The men, already breathless from fatigue, approached the close woods, but slowly, yet perfect order, notwithstanding the enemy from the cover of the woods met us with a withering fire. My men bravely charged upon the hidden enemy and drove them back into the woods, where they held them a bay for some twenty minutes. Seeing that I was unsupported and standing against a much stronger force, and that some 50 of my command had already fallen, I ordered a retreat, returning to the same place from which I had started with General Rousseau.[16]

The Michigan Eleventh had made a stand at the edge of the cedars for twenty or thrity minutes and was the last of Stanley's brigade to cross the open field. No one recorded the time of the charge of the Eighteenth, but it must have been between twelve and one o'clock in the afternoon. Stoughton was bringing the regiment off in good order because he reported that:

> [The regiment] was then marched about half way across the open field to the pike, when orders came to charge back into the cedars. My regiment promply obeyed my orders, rallied on their colors, and charged back into the woods with great gallantry, checking the enemy by their sudden and impetuous charge. After delivering our fire, orders came from the brigade commander to retire, and the regiment fell back, in good order, to the left of the Murfreesborough pike.[17]

Major General Rousseau did not recall the event in the same way. Reporting to Thomas on the action of his division on December 31, he said:

> I fell in with many gallant regiments and officers on the field not of my command....The Eighteenth Ohio, I think it was, though I do not know any of it officers, faced about and charged the enemy in my presence, and I went along with it. The Eleventh Michigan and its gallant little colonel (I do not know his name certainly, but believe it to be Stoddart) [Stoughton] behaved well....[18]

The results of this charge can be seen in the casualties of the Eighteenth Ohio which were the highest in the brigade. There was no military necessity for the charge. The artillery was massed on the high ground beyond the railroad and the troops were basically in position behind the crest of the hill. Indeed, Bragg had shot his bolt. His men were winded and tired and had taken heavy losses. He did not have any reserves to renew the assault.

James King, with the regimental Quartermaster staff, had helped to bring up the train to the rear of the brigade the night of December 30. When the heavy firing began on the right, the train was pulled back about two miles. King and William Davis, also of Company A and detailed to the Quartermaster, "borrowed guns and went back to the field. At first we tried to find the regiment but twas all in vain."[19] The train returned to the front that night and the men were resupplied with food and ammunition. Then the train left for Nashville. Wheeler's cavalry destroyed a great part of the wagon train the next day, but the wagons of the Eleventh were in the rear and arrived safe in Nashville. It was news of this wagon train that led Bragg to believe that Rosecrans was retreating after the battle on December 31.

Captain Calvin Hood of Company C was in command of the Second Battalion of the Pioneer Brigade. On the morning of December 31 his men were improving a ford across Stones River until they were driven off by heavy enemy fire. This ford was intended to be used in the attack by Rosecran's left. As the battle developed on the right, the Pioneer Brigade was brought back to the right with Van Cleve's and Wood's divisions. These latter two were to be part of Rosecran's assault on Bragg's right in the original plans. Now they were used to stop the rout of McCook's troops on the Union right. As the brigades of Harker, Fyffe and Samuel Beatty were thrown against the attacking Confederates, they stopped the charge and advanced. Hood described the subsequent action:

> We moved forward in line with the brigade, my battalion was on the right, and took position about midway of the woods, and about a 100 rods from the field. The troops in front of us there gave way, and regiment after regiment came through our lines entirely broken up. We here received orders from Captain Morton [commanding the Pioneer Brigade] to fix bayonets and allow no stragglers to pass our lines, and to hold fire and give the enemy cold steel. The retreating troops passed on our right, except the Seventy-ninth Indiana

[S. Beatty's brigade] whose commander rallied them on my right and rear. The Eleventh and Fourteenth Texas [Ector's brigade of McCown's Division] came on at a charge, and tried to flank my right, when my battalion changed positions by the right flank and fronted toward them. General Van Cleve here rode up from my right, and asked what troops we were and said we must fall back. I here learned that a small part of his command was on my right and near the pike. I replied that I was ordered to hold this position at all hazards. I then ordered my men to lie down and wait until the enemy were well upon us. They then rose, gave them a volley, and charged with the Seventy-ninth Indiana, and drove them from the woods.[20]

Hood's battalion, drawn from forty different regiments, behaved like veterans and were to a large degree responsible for stopping the advance of the Confederate left to the pike. The Pioneers had forty-eight casualties including Hood's orderly, Benneth Smetts of Company C of the Eleventh Michigan among the killed. By the next day Hood was so hoarse that he could not speak aloud.

Notes

1. Gillaspie, p. 43.

2. O.R., op cit, p. 349.

3. Ibid, p. 424.

4. Ibid p. 407.

5. Gillaspie, p. 43.

6. Ibid, p. 44.

7. John Beatty, *Memoirs of a Volunteer, 1861-1863* (New York: N. W. Norton & Co., 1946) p. 153.

8. O.R., op cit, p. 426.

9. Ibid.

10. Chadwick to *Reporter*, 17 January 1863.

11. Gillaspie, op cit.

12. Gillaspie, p. 44.

13. O.R., op cit, p. 408.

14. Ibid, p. 373.

15. O.R., op cit, p. 421.

16. Ibid, p. 429.

17. Ibid, p. 427.

18. Ibid, p. 380.

19. King Letters, 3 January 1863.

20. O.R., op cit, pp. 247-248.

Chapter Twelve

"The boys have always expressed great anxiety to be in a battle. Today none wish to see another."

After the Confederate assault of December 31 died under the massed artillery and infantry on the Murfreesboro Pike, Negley's division was ordered to the extreme right to help guard the wagons. The focus of the fighting had shifted to the Round Forest on the left where Hazen held against Bragg's final charges of the day.

There was very little fighting on the first day of 1863. Bragg seemed to be at a loss about the next step. Rosecrans, determined not to retreat, finally fell back on his original plan to turn Bragg's right by attacking with his left. To set this plan in motion, he ordered Colonel Samuel Beatty, commanding Van Cleve's division, to cross Stones River on the morning of January 1. During the day Rosecrans supported Beatty by sending more brigades across the river and he massed the artillery on high ground to the left of his line in order to command the immediate front across Stones River. Bragg, realizing the threat of these movements, massed Major General John C. Beckinridge's division to meet it.

At one o'clock on January 2 Rosecrans brought Negley's division from the extreme right to support General Crittenden on the left. The division took a position in the rear of the batteries on the west bank of Stone's River.[1] James Fenton of the Nineteenth Illinois recorded that shortly before three o'clock in the afternoon "a large crowd of soldiers were grouped around a number of Company A boys, who were among the best singers in the whole army. There were thousands of soldiers listening to all the war songs. 'Rally Round the Flag' was just out, and they gave that. The crowd joined in the chorus."[2] At the same time that the Union boys were listening to the singing, General Breckinridge used the smoke of some burning buildings to cover his troops for the charge against the Federal right.

At four o'clock the five thousand men in the Confederate division poured down on Beatty's badly outnumbered men. The Union forces were quickly routed and fled towards the river and the main body of the Army of the Cumberland. Once the fleeing Federals were out of the way, the fifty eight massed guns under the direction of Crittenden's chief of artillery, Captain John Mendenhall of the Fourth U.S. Artillery, delivered a salvo of solid shot, grape and spherical case.[3] The artillery staggered the Confederates, but they continued to pursue Beatty's fleeing division.

Rosecrans and Negley were both sitting on their horses on the crest of the hill watching Breckenridge's attack. According to poetry and legend, Negley cried out, "Who will save the left?" and Colonel Joseph R. Scott of the Nineteenth Illinois Infantry shouted, "The Nineteenth!"[4] James Fenton recorded that Colonel Scott asked Rosecrans for permission to lead a charge into the Confederates and that Rosecrans personally ordered the countercharge that broke Bragg's attack and won the Battle of Stones River.[5] Stanley said in his report that "General Rosecrans and General Negley were both on the ground occupied by the Eighth Division [Negley's] and ordered my brigade forward across Stone's River to stay the advancing forces."[6] Colonel John F. Miller, commanding another of Negley's brigades, did not mention receiving any orders to cross the river. There is folklore about his attack across Stones River that fateful afternoon. Wilson Vance wrote:

> Miller sent his staff officers and orderlies, Lieutenant (afterward Brigadier General) Henry Chiney, Lieutenant Ayers, and Major A.B. Bonnaffin (I repeat that I am writing now what I saw with my own eyes and heard with my own ears) to scour the field and ask permission to cross the stream to Van Cleve's relief. Only one such officer could be found, General John M. Palmer (of Illinois) and from him came instead of the desired permission a positive prohibition - an order not to cross. The other two brigade comman-

ders, belonging to the division, General Spear of Tennessee and Colonel T. R. Stanley of the Eighteenth Ohio, were not present. General Negley was not to be found....

Miller found himself the ranking officer present with the division and realized that the decision fraught with so much importance lay with him. He was surrounded by a group of regiment commanders who alternately studied the field and his face . . . .He turned to the officers around him saying quietly: 'I will charge them.'

'And I'll follow you,' exclaimed the gallant Scott, wheeling and plunging his spurs into his steed to hasten back to his regiment [the Nineteenth Illinois]. Colonel Stoughton of the Eleventh Michigan and other regimental commanders belonging to the Twenty-ninth brigade {Stanley's}, echoed Scott's enthusiastic adherence and they, too, started for their troops. [7]

What seems to have occurred was that Rosecrans ordered Negley to move his division to the river bank to support Beatty. Negley ordered his brigade commanders to carry out Rosecran's order. However, neither Rosecrans nor Negley went forward with the division. The next question was how the division would support Beatty. It is very possible that the decision to charge across the river was made by Miller and the regimental commanders at the river bank.

Regardless of who made the decision, when the troops got to the river bank, they laid down and allowed Beatty's broken division to pass over them. Stoughton reported that one of the fleeing regiments "crossed the river in great disorder, many without arms . . . ."[8] When the charging Confederates were in range of the Union rifles, the entire division rose from the grass and delivered a volley. Many of the Confederates had reached the river, and the volley was extremely destructive. The Union troops charged across the river in pursuit of the now fleeing Rebels. From the evidence, it would appear that the Nineteenth Illinois was the first to cross. In crossing the river the regiments became mixed, and Stoughton led the Eleventh to a fence to dress his line. The Confederates had retreated into a woods. The Eleventh "immediately opened an effective fire on the enemy, who, in a short time, retreated through the woods."[9] The regiment now advanced to the edge of the wood and, firing as rapidly as possible, chased the Confederates across an open field. Of course the regiment was not alone in this. They were very close to the Nineteenth Illinois, when that regiment reached the battery of four guns which the Confederates had abandoned in their flight. Stoughton said that the regiment aided in the capture of the guns. With their ammunition nearly exhausted, Stoughton formed the brigade into line of battle to hold what had been won and to wait for reinforcements. Stanley commended Stoughton for his actions in rallying the brigade after the guns had been taken. There was a stand of regimental colors taken in this charge and credit was claimed by several regiments. Stanley said some of his men claimed it for the Nineteenth, but some of Miller's brigade also claimed it.[10] Fenton said one of his company stepped on the flag on the way to the guns, and that it was picked up by a straggler.[11] What was more important was the fact that Breckinridge's division had been badly handled by the Union boys. He suffered seventeen hundred casualities out of the five thousand troops engaged.[12] Indeed, what was lost by the Confederates on January 2 was any possibility of winning the battle. Just before midnight on January 3, Bragg retreated in a heavy rain, withdrawing through Murfreesboro to the hills about thirty or forty miles southeast of town. Stones River was a Union victory.

The Eleventh had done well in its first battle. Colonel Stoughton was favorably mentioned in the offical reports of Rousseau, Stanley, and Miller. Stanley felt compelled to write Governor Blair a letter to commend Stoughton and the Eleventh. Stanley asked Blair to use his influence in Washington to get Stoughton promoted to brigadier general.[13] Even Stoughton's longtime opponent, Samuel Chadwick, wrote of his outstanding gallantry during the battle. Since Stoughton was not mentioned by name in Negley's report, it would appear that he had little influence or standing in Negley's eyes.

Stanley's brigade had suffered heavy losses in the campaign. The Eighteenth Ohio had casualities of thirty-nine percent, the Nineteenth Illinois had twenty-eight percent, the Eleventh Michigan lost thirty-one percent, and the Sixty-ninth Ohio had seventeen percent in dead, wounded and missing.[14] The lighter losses for the Sixty-ninth were in part the result of Colonel Cassilly being so drunk during the battle on December 31 that the regiment apparently broke and ran. Stanley removed him from the battlefield under arrest and personally reformed the regiment. The heavier losses of the Eighteenth probably resulted from the charge that was ordered by Rousseau. The Eleventh had the most men killed in the division, and indeed suffered only one less death than the highest figure for Rousseau's regulars. The high casualties for the Eighteenth were in the thirty one more wounded than the Eleventh had. The total casualities for the Eighteenth ranked among the heaviest in the Army of the Cumberland.

	Present		Killed		Wounded		Missing		Total
	Officers	Men	Officers	Men	Officers	Men	Officers	Men	
18th Ohio	23	423	1	25	8	107	0	26	167
19th Ill.	23	350	1	13	8	75	0	11	108
11th Mich	17	423	2	28	6	78	0	25	139
69th Ohio	23	523	1	4	6	47	0	38	96
Totals	86	1719	5	70	28	307	0	100	510

15

A chart shows some aspects of the total losses suffered in battle but not all of them. Major Smith never returned to the regiment. Smith and Lieutenant Faulker were captured, and Smith was later found in a Confederate hospital in Murfreesboro with his wounds untended. Indeed, by March the only remaining original captain was Bennet. Adjutant Chadwick had his horse shot from under him on December 31 and soon resigned his position. There were many men who had close calls. Daniel Rose wrote that "a ball struck my canteen, haversack and through my clothes and just drew blood a little."[16] Many men were hit by pieces of shell or spent Minie balls. In the battle in the cedars men were hurt by falling trees that were cut down by the heavy firing. Years later Stoughton would recall that among the greatest achievements of the regiment were the two charges made on December 31; the one in the cedars in the morning and the one back into the cedars in the early afternoon.[17] Four days after the battle, Chadwick reflected on it in a letter to the Three Rivers *Reporter* saying, "The boys have always expressed great anxiety to be in a battle. Today none wish to see another."[18]

Notes

1. O.R., op cit, p. 408.

2. Mesha Fenton Hanson, "A Civil War Diary" (Unpublished typescipt of James Fenton's Diary, Illinois State Historical Library, Springfield, Illinois. n/d) p. 58. Fenton was a member of Company K, Nineteenth Illinois Infantry. Hereafter cited as Fenton's Diary.

3. William M. Lamers, *The Edge of Glory: A Biography Of General William S. Rosecrans, U.S.A.* (New York, Harcourt, Brace and World, 1961.) p. 240

4. J. Henry Hayne, ed. *The Nineteenth Illinois* (Chicago: M. A. Donohue & Co., 1912), pp. 11-12.

5. Fenton Diary, p. 59.

6. O.R., opcit, p. 422.

7. Wilson Vance, *God's War* (London, New York: F. Tennyson Neely, 1899) no page quoted in Wilson J. Vance, *Stone's River: The Turning Point Of The Civil War* (West Orange, New Jersey: Albert Saiffer Publisher, 1914) p. 72.

8. O.R., op cit, p. 427.

9. Ibid.

10. O.R., Vol. 20, Part 1, p 423.

11. Fenton Diary, p. 61.

12. McDonough, Stones River, p. 202.

13. O.R., op cit, p. 424.

14. O.R., op cit, p. 211.

15. O.R., op cit, pp. 211-423.

16. Rose Papers, 7 January 1863.

17. Stoughton to Robertson, 20 December 1879, Regimental Records. The Colonel also held that the charge to relieve the left at Chickamauga and the charge up Missionary Ridge ranked with the work at Stones River.

18. Reporter, 17 January 1863.

Chapter Thirteen

"...Stoughton is a bully colonel and leads the bulliest regiment."

The two wrecked armies stumbled away from the battlefield at Stones River. Bragg retreated southeast to a defensive line between McMinnsville and Tullahoma. Rosecrans dug in south of Murfreesboro to protect the thirty miles that he had won. Both armies were weakened by the loss of thirty-three percent of their personnel and heavy losses of transportation animals.

On January 4, 1863 Negley's division, including the Eleventh Michigan, moved to the north side of the railroad as an advance force. The following day the division moved in pursuit of the retreating Confederates and marched into Murfreesboro without incident.[1] Rosecrans stopped just south of town and began a six month process of rebuilding the Army of the Cumberland and its transportation, not advancing against Bragg until June 24.

January 5 was a day that was etched into the memories of the men of the Army of the Cumberland and the Eleventh Michigan. That day the army issued half-shelter tents to replace the big Sibley tents. These "dog kennels" were pronounced "miserable" by Ira Gillespie of Company C.[2] Daniel D. Rose of Company A wrote home that the tents were "the poorest things that ever soldiers stayed in."[3] The half-shelter tents quickly became known as pup-tents.

On January 10 the Eleventh moved into Murfreesboro as provost guard. Colonel William Stoughton of the Eleventh Michigan had been appointed provost marshal two days earlier. A provost marshall prosecuted soldiers and civilians charged with mi-

nor offenses in occupied territory. Stoughton had served as the
prosecuting attorney for St. Joseph County, Michigan, from 1856
to 1860 and was at the time of his enlistment the United States District Attorney for the District of Michigan.[4] The regiment remained in Murfreesboro for six months except for a brief expedition to Columbia, Tennessee. The provost guard duty was a pleasant interlude for the Eleventh. Although the duties were constant,
they were not hard. Most of the men were quartered in buildings
which gave greater protection and warmth than tents. This was a
great advantage since the winter and spring were unusually rainy.

As comfortable as life was in Murfreesboro, it was still the dull
routine of camp. In the first weeks everyone was busy with the aftermath of the Battle of Stones River. Ira Gillaspie recorded that
he was corporal of the burial guard on January 31. "We buried 27
dead bodeys an extra leg and three arms. The wounded men are
dieing off very fast now." On February 10 he wrote, "I was agane of
the buryal party. Buryed 48 bodeys. The wounded dies very fast
now, but it seams thare is more of the rebils that dies than of our
men."[5] However, the primary duty was guarding prisoners and
buildings. This was done by the men on an every-other-day schedule.

Camp life brought out the business instincts of the soldiers.
Trading in stamps, stationery, and food, and loaning money were
the major activities. Daniel Rose did business in writing paper
which he had his mother send him.[6] Benjamin F. Bordner of Company D reported "Some of the boys are getting rich pedling and
buying and selling. They buy apples at twenty-five to thirty dollars
per barrel and retail them out for forty....I and one of the boys went
and bought a barrel of apples at twenty-five dollars and a half barrel of flour and some sugar. Then took some of our extra sowbelly
and fried it out for shortening. Then we went to making pies (and
they were good). In five days we had all worked up and how much
do you suppose we cleared. Well I will tell we made just forty dollars clear of all in five days."[7]

On February 25, the regiment was paid four months pay but still
had two months backpay coming. For the privates this was fifty-

two dollars. Ira Gillaspie sent twenty dollars to his wife, loaned eighteen dollars, and kept the rest for himself.[8] Daniel Rose, who was worried about his widowed mother, sent seventy-five dollars home; his fifty-two dollars of pay, some money that was repaid to him, and twenty dollars that he borrowed made up the sum.[9] However, he did keep some money for himself. He wrote to his friend Mark Richards of the Nineteenth Michigan, "By the by we have received our little 'Nine Cents' you know how good it makes a man feel to have a 'grccn back' or two in his pocket even if it is at about sixty percent discount for gold, but alas how it vanishs."[10]

One day that did not pass unnoted by the regiment was February 24, 1863. This was the halfway mark in their enlistment. Gillaspie came to the end of his journal four days later and expressed the feeling of many in the regiment. "February the last-I must now finish up this book. I have now been a soldier just 18 monthes and four days. One half of the time I enlisted for but I am willing to quit soldiering as soon as our Union is restored but should it, the South continue to defy the athoratys of the United States I am willing to remain in the armey for years yet. Thus endth the first year and a half of my life as a soldier. My energy is with my country heart with my friends."[11]

During the first weeks of March both James King and Daniel Rose denounced the Copperheads and peace men in the North. Apparently, this was a reaction to the Michigan Democratic Party Convention held in Detroit and reported in the *Western Chronicle* on February 18. The *Western Chronicle* also reported the results of some St. Joseph County elections which the Democrats won. James King, after reviewing the prospects for a victory by General Grant at Vicksburg, said, "The prospect looks more cheering....than it ever did before. All there is to cloud or shadow is the sympathy shown these black hearted traitors by a few, No I will not say a few, But by some of the northern Peace Men....They find fault with Proclamation of the President and in every act of the Administration. Why don't they find fault with the Southern Confederacy who have trampled all rights and Liberties under foot."[12] The day before King wrote, Daniel Rose said, "The Copperheads of the north are hurting us as much as the rebels for they are a regular stimulant (so to speak) to the rebels. They look to them for succor before long." On March 12 he wrote, "I wish that I was at home for a while. Some of them traitors would keep quiet or else I would get most mightily thrashed (which I flatter myself is not apt to be done). I would as soon fight traitors at home as here. I think I would flatten out a few copper heads or at least silence their hissing tungs."[13]

On March 12, T. Buchanan Reed spoke at the court house in Murfreesboro. Reed was a well known poet and painter and was serving as a major on the staff of Major General Lewis "Lew" Wallace. His greatest service was on the lecture platform. Rose referred to the speech as spirited, but James King wrote home a long, detailed description of the event. He repeated this in a letter to the *Three Rivers Reporter*. For the men of the Eleventh who were concerned about the actions of the Copperheads at home, Reed's message was that "the masses of people at home would stand by the army."[14] It must have been enough to convince King and Rose since neither of them mentioned the Copperheads again.

Later, in early June, the Eleventh had an opportunity to meet the nation's leading Copperhead, Clement L. Vallandigham. Vallandigham was arrested in Dayton, Ohio, on May 5 by orders of General Ambrose E. Burnside commanding the Military District of Ohio. He was tried by a military court and sentenced to Fort Warren in Boston Harbor. Vallandigham became a national figure as a martyr for the peace movement. President Lincoln was embarrasssed by the affair. He defused the issue by commuting the sentence and banishing Vallandigham to the Confederacy. According to Lieutenant Borden M. Hicks, of Company E, it was the Eleventh that "had the pleasure, as well as the duty, of escorting Vallandigham through our lines, and turning him over to his avowed friends, our enemy."[15]

On April 6 the regiment presented Colonel Stoughton with a six hundred dollar sword. The men subscribed the money to buy the sword. Considering that the privates only received thirteen dollars per month, it was a princely gift. Captain Benjamin Bennet of

Company D, who was commanding while Stoughton acted as provost marshal, took the regiment to the parade ground, and the Colonel was invited to come and drill them. When he arrived, there was a large crowd on hand to watch the ceremony, including the brigade commander, Colonel Timothy R. Stanley, and the division commander, Brigadier-General James Negley. Captain Melvin Mudge, of Company B, presented the sword to Stoughton. Negley told Stoughton that "it was a great honor to receive so magnificent a present, but the greatest honor of all was to be the leader of such men as the noble Eleventh."[16] These were the kind of words that volunteer units remembered all their lives. When James King reported the incident to the *Three Rivers Reporter*, he concluded: "Our regiment has never been praised as highly as some, but for all that Stoughton is a bully Colonel, and leads the bulliest Regiment that ever went into a fight."[17]

Notes

1. U.S. Congress, Joint Committee on Conduct of the War, *Report of Major General George H. Thomas* (Washington, D.C.: 1866; reprint ed., Millwood, N.Y.: Kraus Reprint, 1977), p. 32. (Hereafter cited as *Report of Thomas*).

2. Diary of Ira Gillaspie, p. 46.

3. Rose Papers, 18 January 1863.

4. William L. Stoughton to Charles Lanman, 18 November 1868, Charles Lanman Papers, Burton Historical Collection, Detroit Public Library, Detroit, Michigan.

5. Diary of Ira Gillaspie, pp. 46-47.

6. Rose Papers, 29 January 1863, 13 February 1863.

7. Bordner Letters, 2 April 1863.

8. Diary of Ira Gillaspie, p. 48.

9. Rose Papers, 28 February 1863.

10. Ibid, 1 March 1863.

11. Diary of Ira Gillaspie, p. 48.

12. King Papers, 3 March 1863.

13. Rose Papers, 2 March 1863 and 12 March 1863.

14. James W. King, "Letter from the Eleventh," *Reporter*, 28 March 1863.

15. Hicks, "Personal Recollections."

16. James W. King, "Letter from the Eleventh," *Reporter*, 6 April 1863.

17. Ibid.

Chapter Fourteen

"...the rebels left and we had a Good Time to see them run."

On June 24, 1863, Rosecrans finally moved against Bragg. Secretary of War Stanton, Major-General Henry Halleck, and President Lincoln had all been pressuring Rosecrans to move. On June 16 Lincoln had Halleck ask, "Is it your intention to make an immediate movement forward?   A definite answer, yes or no, is required." Rosecrans replied with both yes and no: "In reply to your inquiry if immediate means tonight or tomorrow, no. If it means as soon as things are ready, say five days, yes."[1]

Everything about this campaign is controversial: the delay in starting, the nature of the objective, and, in particular, the Battle of Chickamauga. The only agreement is that Rosecrans's tactics in Tennessee were brilliant. The six months delay in moving against the Army of Tennessee tried the patience of everyone. Washington wanted Rosecrans to engage Bragg in order to make sure that Johnston could not be reinforced against Grant in Mississippi. However, Rosecrans thought that if Bragg was driven from Tennessee he would surely join Johnston to overwhelm Grant.[2]

Major-General George Thomas, commander of the Fourteenth Corps, later testified that "The apparent inactivity of the army of the Cumberland during its stay in Murfreesboro was due really to the severity of the winter, which rendered it almost impossible to move large bodies of men on the ordinary roads of the county, and to the difficulty of procuring animals to refit the transportation and equip the cavalry and artillery."[3] During their first three months at Murfreesboro the men of the Eleventh confirmed the heavy rains.

Gillaspie noted in his diary on February 1, "It rained all day hard I tell you. I never have seen it rain so much and so long and so hard as it rains hear."[4] James King mentioned hard rains and impassable roads on February 28, March 13, and March 23, but on April 7 he wrote, "The roads are in good (he crossed out 'splendid') condition and everything in readiness to make a forward move."[5] He also cited a rumor which he discredited, but which might provide an insight into Rosecrans's delay. "Yet we may not leave here for many weeks if Bragg is receiving the reinforcements they say he is, our General may await his coming and be glad to receive him behind our own fortifications. They could not whip us...with five times our force. Let us fight them from the position we now occupy. But I hardly think they will venture back here again...."[6]

When the Army of the Cumberland finally began its march, it rained hard for two weeks, turning the roads and countryside into a quagmire. As late as June 30, Daniel Rose, writing from the convalescent camp in Murfreesboro, said, "It has been raining ever since the troops commenced moving. They seem to always move in a storm...."[7] On July 5 he added, "The water in the river is so high that we can with difficullty get some to drink for it has drowned out our springs. We have had a great deal of rain lately...."[8] On August 16, when Rosecrans began to move his army across the Tennessee River, King wrote, "Now that we have orders to move the rain begins to fall in torrents."[9] If the Army of the Cumberland had waited for good weather and roads, they would not have moved until 1864.

The Army of the Cumberland's campaign to secure Middle Tennessee and Chattanooga during 1863 can be divided into three major parts. The first, from June 24 to July 16, consisted of Rosecrans's movements to the Tennessee River which forced Bragg back into Chattanooga. The second, from August 16 to September 20, was the series of movements which resulted in Bragg's evacuation of Chattanooga and culminated in the Battle of Chickamauga. The third phase was the Federal victory at Missionary Ridge on November 25 which broke the Confederate siege of Chattanooga. Rosecrans commanded the first two stages of the operation but was relieved of command as a result of Chickamauga. U.S. Grant directed the final phase as the commanding general of the western theater with General George Thomas in charge of the Army of the Cumberland. In the final part of the campaign the Army of the Cumberland was heavily reinforced by Brigadier General Joseph Hooker, commanding the Eleventh and Twelfth Corps of the Army of the Potomac, and General William T. Sherman, commanding the Fifteenth and Seventeenth Corps of the Army of the Tennessee. Hooker brought 20,000 men plus transportation, and Sherman added 17,000 to the forces in and around Chattanooga.

Bragg's Army of the Tennessee was heavily reinforced prior to the Battle of Chickamauga. General Simon Bolivar Buckner brought Bragg his corps of 8,000, which had held Knoxville until Rosecrans's movement began, and General Ambrose Burnside moved against the city from Kentucky. General Joseph Johnston sent two divisions and two separate brigades for a total of 11,500 men from Mississippi. And, in the greatest transportation achievement of the Confederate government in the entire war, General James Longstreet brought 15,000 men from the Army of Northern Virginia. These reinforcements at Chickamauga gave Bragg a rare edge for a Confederate commander, numerical superiority.

When Rosecrans began the army's forward movement on June 24, the orders came so suddenly that even the rumor mill was caught off guard. James King's letter of June 21 gave no hint of a move. "There is nothing new in regard to war news in the Army."[10] Then on June 23 he wrote a hasty note saying, "Orders have been received to march tomorrow morning. In what direction I am unable to state." He added a line the next day, "The Army is moving South."[11] John T. Bloom noted in his diary, "We got orders to march but where I daunt no."[12]

Alexander McCook's Twentieth Corps and George Thomas's Fourteenth Corps were to carry the main attack against Bragg by moving down the macadamized Manchester Pike through Hoover's Gap. Hoover's Gap was one of four openings through the hills that had separated Bragg and Rosecrans armies for six months.

Hoover's Gap was a "narrow valley about three miles long, surrounded by high hills covered with a dense, heavy growth of timber."[13] Colonel John T. Wilder's brigade of mounted infantry seized control of the Gap on the first day and held it until the infantry moved up. The Eleventh stopped a few miles short of the gap since Negley's division was acting as the reserve. Although heavy rains on the twenty-fifth slowed the movement, Negley's division moved into the gap in support of Thomas's other divisions. There was continual skirmishing, but the Confederates did not make a concerted defense of their lines in Tennessee. On the morning of June 27 Thomas's advance units entered Manchester without resistance. Negley's division, still acting as support, was the last to arrive at about eight o'clock in the evening.

On the twenty-eighth Thomas sent Wilder's mounted brigade on a raid behind the Confederate lines to disrupt their rail connection with Chattanooga, the main supply base for Bragg's army. The bulk of the Fourteenth Corps was rushed south toward Tullahoma to support Major General Philip Sheridan's division of Major General Alexander McCook's Twentieth Corps. Negley's division remained in Manchester and made a small demonstration to the east toward Hillsboro. No Confederate forces were encountered to the east.

On June 29, Negley started his division south towards Tullahoma. The Eleventh acted as guard for the division ammunition train. On July 1 Negley's division was engaged in a sharp skirmish at Elk River, south of Tullahoma. John J. Bloom of Company E described the action in his diary, "we marched about 3 miles south of the Tolihoma Road and at 4 PM we formed our skirmish line and we skirmish threw the woods and picking hucklebery & we walk wright in the rebel skirmish line and they opened on us and we fought 2 hrs and the Rebels fell back across Elk River and it got dark and we fell back about 1/2 mile and we got our supper and staid the night. Rain and Mud."[14] He added on the following day that "at 10 AM the Dutch battery opend on them and noct down there brest works at Elk River and the Rebels left and we had a Good Time to see them run."[15] The temperature must have been very high during this march as several of the Eleventh passed out with heat strokes.

On July 8 the Eleventh went into camp near Dechard Station at the foot of the Cumberland Mountains. Rosecrans halted the whole advance to repair the railroad between Bridgeport and Murfreesboro. The forward movement would not start again until August 16. Bragg retreated to Chattanooga, fifty miles up the Tennessee River from Bridgeport.

Daniel Rose wrote his mother from the convalescent camp in Murfreesboro on July 18 and expressed a general optimism about the campaign.

> Our rgiment hasn't been in any fight (except for a little skirmish) since they left here. The railroad is repaired as far south as Elk River. The Rebels have possession of Chattanooga yet but I don't think they will much longer for "Old Rosey" is bound to advance as fast as he can have the railroad repaired. He will soon have the "rebs" out of this state. At the rate of our present success it will not take many months more to crush the rebellion entirely.[16]

Rosecrans's six-week delay troubled not only the Washington officials but also the men behind the lines. Rose wrote again August 4 that "our grand army seems to have stoped again probably to let the rebs get organized."[17] He was to get a closer look as he was sent forward to join the regiment at Cowan on August 15.

Rosecrans now faced the second phase of his campaign to drive Bragg out of Tennessee. He began the campaign with a marked numerical superiority but ended on the battlefield at Chickamauga badly outnumbered. The cautious, brilliant moves that characterized the earlier parts of the campaign were lost in the final aspects. Rosecrans became an opportunist after the beginning of this phase. His original goal was to flank Bragg out of his defensive works at Chattanooga, but it changed into a campaign either to destroy Bragg or to strike deep into Georgia. Rosecrans was handicapped by a lack of cavalry which could have provided him with intelligence on his immediate front. He was, moreover, badly misled by the information that he received from Washington about the Confederate reinforcement of Bragg, especially from the Army of Northern Virginia. Only a week before the Battle of

Chickamauga, Halleck told Rosecrans that Bragg was reinforcing Robert E. Lee when exactly the opposite was true.[18]

Rosecrans planned to take his army across the Tennessee River at a number of crossings downriver from Chattanooga while demonstrating with cavalry and mounted infantry units at crossings north of the city. Once across the river Major General Thomas Crittenden's Twenty-first Corps would move northeast against Chattanooga, and Major General George Thomas and the Fourteenth Corps would move southeast over the mountains towards LaFayette and Dalton, Georgia. Finally, Major General Alexander McCook's Twentieth Corps would go still farther south crossing the mountains at Alpine and Summerville, arriving just north of Rome, Georgia. Part of Rosecrans's overall planning was Ambrose Burnside's projected move against Knoxville, Tennessee.

On August 16 Rosecrans began to move his troops closer to the Tennessee River. Thomas's huge Fourteenth Corps, which made up almost half of the 57,000 man Army of the Cumberland, was to cross at four different places. Negley's division was scheduled to cross the pontoon bridge at Caperton's Ferry. The Eleventh marched over the Cumberland Mountains to Stevenson, Alabama on August 17. Daniel Rose reached the regiment from the convalescent camp at Murfreesboro on August 16.

Notes

1. O.R., vol 23, pt 1, p.10.

2. Bruce Catton, *Never Call Retreat* (New York: Doubleday, 1965), p. 309.

3. *Report of Thomas*, p. 39.

4. Diary of Ira Gillaspie, p. 47.

5. King Letters, 7 April 1863.

6. Ibid.

7. Rose Letters, 28 June 1863.

8. Ibid, 5 July 1863.

9. King Letters, 16 August 1863.

10. King Letters, 21 June 1863.

11. Ibid, 23 June 1863.

12. Bloom Diary, 23 June 1863.

13. King Letters, 19 July 1863.

14. Bloom Diary, 1 July 1863.

15. Ibid, 2 July 1863.

16. Rose Letters, 18 July 1863.

17. Ibid, 4 August 1863.

18. Freeman Cleaves, *Rock of Chickamauga: The Life of General George H. Thomas* (Norman, Oklahoma: University of Oklahoma Press, 1948) pp. 154-155.

Chapter Fifteen

"Now that we have orders to march the rains fall in torrents."

Rose wrote home that "Monday morning early we started over the mountains on a march with our knapsacks on. We marched slow but our load and hot weather gave us considerable fatigue."[1] King pointed out that "Now that we have orders to march the rain begins to fall in torrents."[2] Both Rose and King commented on the fertileness of the valley north of Stevenson. King said it was one vast cornfield.[3]

Although the Eleventh did not cross the Tennessee River until September 1, preparations were under way much earlier. King reported on August 23, "Pontoons have been moving all day and without a doubt by the last of the week the main body of the army will be across the river. The Railroad is in use between here and Murfreesboro. Trains of cars loaded with provisions and supplies for the army is constantly arriving and the greatest activity prevails."[4]

On August 24 the regiment celebrated two years of service in the army. In a letter to the *Western Chronicle*, Frank H. Love of Company D described the scene. The officers had contributed thirty dollars "to buy a barrel of beer for the boys." After a parade and the manual of arms, "the boys 'tipped the tickler' to the tune of two years in the service of Uncle Sam." After speeches by Colonel Stoughton and others, "the boys marched to their quarters, singing the 'Battle Cry of Freedom.' "[5] At this time the regiment had 415 present for duty out of 565 enrolled.[6]

On September 1, the Eleventh marched through Stevenson towards the pontoon bridge at Caperton's Ferry and crossed the Tennessee River during the night. According to James King the regiment had to wait for the moon to rise before crossing the pontoons.[7] Daniel Rose wrote, "We crossed the river in the night so we had a poor chance to see it. It is quite a large river about forty rods across. It took fifty-nine boats to make a pontoon bridge across it. It is more than three times as large as the St. Jo."[8] Most of the regiment's supply train carrying twelve-days rations went upstream on the north side of the river in order to cross at Bridgeport.

Once across the river, Thomas planned to concentrate his corps at Trenton, Georgia on Sand Mountain. Between the Tennessee River and LaFayette, Georgia, there are three mountain chains standing parallel to the river. Sand Mountain, next to the river, is divided from Lookout Mountain by Lookout Valley. Lookout Mountain is separated from Pigeon Mountain by a cul-de-sac called McLemore's Cove that is open at the northeast end. Chickamauga Creek runs through McLemore's Cove to enter the Tennessee River near Chatanooga.

On September 2 Negley's division turned northeast and marched along the river towards the Bridgeport crossing. The following day the division moved south across Sand Mountain to Trenton, Georgia for the corps. Rose wrote that "we had to repair the road so it took until afternoon to get up the train. We stayed on top of the mountain that night. There is a table land on top of about ten miles in extent and quite level for this country. There is considerable pine, chestnut and a little hemlock. It is very thinly settled...."[9] Apparently even with the road repaired it was a difficult ascent as Bloom noted "We helpt the Teems over Coon Mountain."[10]

Negley's division now became the advance unit of the Fourteenth Corps. On September 8 the Eleventh had been given the duty of clearing Stevens Gap of fallen trees and other obstructions. Lieutenant Stephen Marsh of Company A headed the detail that cleared the gap, and by two o'clock in the afternoon the regiment was in McLemore's Cove. The regiment had a sharp skirmish with the Confederates when it reached the east end of Stevens Gap. When the Eleventh had driven them back about a mile, Stoughton took a defensive position around the gap. Negley apparently thought the regiment was too isolated and exposed, because he ordered the Eleventh back to the top of the mountain at approximately midnight. Stoughton protested the withdrawal, but the orders stood, and the regiment reached the top about two o'clock in the morning.

The following day the Second Brigade (Stanley) and the Third Brigade (Sirwell) went down Stevens Gap into McLemore's Cove. The First Brigade (John Beatty) went down through Cooper's Gap just to the north. On reaching McLemore's Cove, Negley sent Stanley's brigade on reconnaissance toward Dug Gap in the Pigeon Mountains. Opposed by only a small force of cavalry, the brigade pushed them across the cove toward Dug Gap. The Eleventh succeeded in capturing a few prisoners including a lieutenant.[11]

As early as September 5, the regiment had heard that Bragg was evacuating Chattanooga. On the day that the Eleventh came down into McLemore's Cove, the last of Bragg's forces left Chattanooga to concentrate at LaFayette, Georgia, on the south side of the Pigeon Mountains. The main route to LaFayette from McLemore's Cove was through Dug Gap. At this point Stanley's brigade was facing Bragg's entire army.

Rosecrans was urging Thomas to attack Bragg with his leading units. The commanding general was, of course, being pushed by Washington, but he was also not informed that Bragg was receiving heavy reinforcements. Indeed, Rosecrans was being misled. Halleck notified him on September 11 that "a portion of Bragg's army was reinforcing Robert E. Lee in Virginia."[12] Rosecrans without any encouragement believed that Bragg was in head-long retreat, and Bragg was doing everything possible to maintain this illusion. At this time the Union army was in three columns spread over seventy miles of mountainous roads. Bragg had an opportunity to destroy the three corps of the Army of the Cumberland individually.

On September 10, with two divisions still crossing Lookout Mountain and one still farther behind in Lookout Valley, Thomas moved Negley across McLemore's Cove toward Dug Gap. The skirmishing was heavy from Chickamauga Creek to the gap. By early afternoon, Negley discovered that he was in serious trouble. To his north in McLemore's Cove was Confederate Major General Thomas C. Hindman's division of Polk's corps, and Lieutenant General D. H. Hills's entire corps was moving through the passes of the Pigeon Mountains. Bragg had tried to get his unwieldly army to attack Negley from the moment his division came into McLemore's Cove. Negley made strong demonstrations against the forces that opposed him in the late afternoon. However, he became increasingly convinced that his position was too exposed in front of Dug Gap and at nine o'clock in the evening withdrew Stanley's and Sirwell's brigades towards Chickamauga Creek.

Thomas was in the cove on the afternoon of September 10. He decided that although Bragg was retreating there were still strong Confederate forces between Negley's position and Chattanooga. As a result, he hurried General Absalom Baird's First Division to Negley's support.

On September 11, at eight o'clock in the morning, Baird's two leading brigades (Starkweather's and Scribner's) reached Negley. Heavy skirmishing began across the front as General Simon Bolivar Buckner's corps moved to support Hindman and prevent Negley's withdrawal to Stevens Gap. In the early afternoon Lieutenant Stephen Marsh of the Eleventh climbed a tall tree to observe the movement of the enemy forces and report it to General Negley and his staff, who were at the base of the tree. Marsh was under Confederate fire during the entire time. He reported to Negley that the Union position was being flanked on the left by a large force of cavalry.[13]

Realizing that they were heavily outnumbered, Negley began his withdrawal towards the high ground around the mouth of Stevens Gap. When Baird had come up in the morning, Negley had placed his two brigades at Davis Crossroads where the road from Crawfish Springs crossed the road leading from Stevens Gap to LaFayette. Negley's command was at this time directly in front of Dug Gap south of the crossroads. The first problem was to secure a line of withdrawal and the mouth of Stevens Gap. Beatty's brigade was ordered to send one regiment to Bailey's Crossroads near Stevens Gap and to hold it against the cavalry. Once the divisional train was moving Beatty's, Scribner's and possibly Sirwell's brigades were ordered back across Chickamauga Creek to protect the train and to secure the left flank.[14] Starkweather's brigade of Baird's division was withdrawn and placed on a high ridge with ten pieces of artillery. To protect these moves Stanley's brigade was skirmishing heavily. When all was ready, Stanley crossed Chickamauga Creek withdrawing to a ridge about one thousand feet from the Creek. Here the men quickly prepared breastworks. The regiment was positioned with the Eighteenth Ohio on the right facing a cornfield, the Eleventh Michigan in the center, and Nineteenth Illinois on the left. Directly in front of the Nineteenth was a stone wall which flanked the route of the Confederate attack. Parts of the Fourth Indiana Battery of Starkweather's brigade were placed on the flanks and in the center of Stanley's men. The Confederate infantry moved through the cornfield in front of the Eleventh Michigan and the Eighteenth Ohio, and a cavalry unit came through a woods on the left. The Nineteenth advanced along the stone wall and poured a destructive volley into the flank of the cavalry, driving them from the field. The entire brigade then concentrated on the cornfield, but the Confederates kept coming, finally moving some artillery into the cornfield. At that point the brigade hastily withdrew over the ridge, many of the Eleventh leaving their knapsacks which had been taken off to build the breastwork. Daniel Rose wrote "we had to withdraw in a hurry and left our knapsacks with them [the Confederates] so I lost neary everything I had paper, envelopes, and stamps and my pictures...."[15] Borden M. Hicks of Company E recalled in later years, "I had hung my haversack on the limb of a tree, we were ordered to fall back and take position behind one of the other brigades. The enemy were so close on us that the boys left their knapsacks....I had gotten back about two or three rods when I realized I had deserted my base of supplies, so back I charged in the teeth of the enemy, and snatched my haversack....."[16]

When the Confederates topped the just vacated ridge they were struck by the combined volley of Negley's rear guard. The Confederates withdrew, Negley and Baird were safe, and the next day Thomas brought the remainder of his corps through Stevens Gap into McLemore's Cove.

The fight of September 11 was called the Battle of Davis Crossroads, but in the minds of the men it was only a skirmish. Daniel Rose wrote on September 13, "our division had a small engagement."[17] However, the losses of the Eleventh were heavy; three killed and thirteen wounded. Sergeant James T. Lovette of Company A was among the dead.

On September 12 the regiment remained in camp and rested. In the late evening a heavy picket line was established about a mile and a half in front of the divisional lines. A detail of sixty men from the Eleventh under the command of Lieutenant James M. Whallon of Company C was part of this force. "Just before dark the officer in charge of the pickets received notice from the field officer of the day that the enemy was massing heavily in front of the line held by guards from the Eleventh, and that indications were that he would attack in force at that point about daybreak the next morning."[18] About midnight the entire division was called up but nothing happened. In fact, Thomas's corps combed the area from Stevens Gap to Dug Gap the next day without finding any Confederates. General Bragg had turned his attention to Crittenden's corps to the north.

Notes

1. Rose Letters, 21 August 1863.

2. King Letters, 21 August 1863.

3. Ibid., 23 August 1863.

4. Ibid.

5. *Western Chronicle*, 9 September 1863.

6. Consolidated Descriptive and Morning Report Book, Regimental Papers, Michigan Eleven;th Infantry, Record Group 94, Box 1999, National Archives, Washington, D.C. (Hereafter cited as *Report Book.*)

7. King Letters, 5 September 1863.

8. Rose Letters, 5 September 1863.

9. Ibid.

10. Bloom Diary, 3 September 1863.

11. Charles E. Belknap, *The History of the Michigan Organizations at Chickamauga, Chattanooga, and Missionary Ridge* (Lansing, Michigan: R. Smith Printing Co., 1897), p. 244. (Hereafter cited as Belknap, *Michigan Organizations.*)

12. Freeman Cleaves, *Rock of Chickamauga: The Life of General George H. Thomas* (Norman, Oklahoma: University of Oklahoma Press, 1948), pp. 154-5.

13. *Report of Thomas*, pp. 66-67. See also Belknap, *Michigan Organizations*, p. 111. Negley's report on the action at Davis Crossroad, which is in *Thomas' Report*, states that that this event happened at 1:00 p.m., but in Belknap it was reported to have to have happened at 4:00 p.m.

14. The whereabouts of Sirwell's brigade is a bit of a mystery. Belknap, *Michigan Organizations*, p. 111, placed it with Beatty, but Negley does not mention it in his report.

15. Rose Letters, 13 September 1863.

16. Hicks, Personal Recollections, pp. 527-528.

17. Rose Letters, 13 September 1863.

18. Belknap, *Michigan Organizations*, p. 112.

Chapter Sixteen

"We have passed through another heavy fight...we was a little worsted."

From September 13 to September 16 Thomas's corps remained at Stevens Gap, patrolling and searching the south end of McLemore's Cove while they waited for McCook to join them. On September 17 the Fourteenth Corps began to move northeast on the LaFayette Road to join with Crittenden. By the end of the day Rosecrans had managed to reunite his army. Negley's division led the corps, halting when he met with Van Cleve's division of Crittenden's Twenty-first Corps. Negley was followed by Baird and then Brannan. Reynold's division was divided with one brigade guarding the passes through Pigeon Mountain on the right flank of the march and Wilder's mounted brigade scouting ahead of the corps. Thomas ordered his division commanders to have each man carry twenty rounds in his pockets as well as a full cartridge box. That evening McCook's leading units connected with Thomas's right.

On September 18 Thomas's corps, following Dry Valley Road, passed in the rear of Crittenden's corps. Baird's division led the corps northeasterly toward the Widow Glenn's house with Brannan following. Negley's division had relieved Palmer's division of Crittenden's corps to the north of Lee and Gordon's Mill during the night. When McCook relieved Reynolds from guarding the passes in McLemore's Cove, his remaining brigades (Wilder was already on the field) hurried forward but were now behind Johnston's division of McCook's corps and Palmer's division of Crittenden's corps on the road to Glenn's. The route of march mixed the divisions and left Thomas in command of troops from all the corps.

Negley's division skirmished with the Confederate forces from early morning until the afternoon of September 19. That morning he sent the division's wagon train, except for ammunition and ambulances, to Chattanooga by Dry Valley Road. James King of the Quartermaster staff for the Eleventh was with this group. He wrote, "The next morning [September 19] we received orders to move the train to the city. This was Saturday. We could feel the throb of cannons and hear the roar of musketry as we left."[1] Negley reported on his division's actions of the morning and early afternoon of September 19 as follows:

> Very early in the morning the enemy advanced a heavy line of skirmishers upon Beatty's front, which was a very exposed position, and engaged his pickets sharply for some hours. 11:30-Enemy appeared in force flanking two batteries within 400 yards of Beatty's position, which was followed by a fierce cannonading, during which Bridge's battery of Beatty's brigade, sustained a loss in men and horses. A part of Beatty's line being gradually driven back (but soon re-established). I sent one regiment (Eighteenth Ohio volunteer infantry and a section of Schultz's battery), of Stanley's brigade, to his support. 12:30 p.m.-Beatty repulsed the enemy. 2:30 p.m.-General McCook's corps had passed to the left of my position, leaving me on the extreme right; General McCook assuming command.[2]

John M. Bloom of Company E summed it up better; "and at 8 AM a gen engagement commance and a heavy firing was kept up all day."[3]

To the north, near Reed's Bridge, the Battle of Chickamauga had begun. As the battle swung south paralleling the LaFayette Road, Rosecrans gave Thomas, commanding the left, the divisions as they came on the field. A division was committed to battle and would drive the Confederates back only to be flanked when the next Confederate unit was committed. In this manner Brannan was supported by Baird, and in their turn, Johnston, Palmer, Reynolds, and Van Cleve were committed to the battle. The command was hopelessly confused. Thomas commanded two of Crittenden's divisions and one of McCook's. McCook had two of his own divisions, Davis and Sheridan, plus Wood's division of Crittenden's corps and

Negley from Thomas's Fourteenth Corps. Crittenden was a corps commander without a corps.

At 3:30 in the afternoon Rosecrans pulled Negley's division from the extreme right to his headquarters at the Widow Glenn's house. Thomas was calling in his remaining division. Negley apparently only took Sirwell's and Stanley's brigades, leaving Beatty with Mc-Cook. The brigades quickly marched the three miles to Glenn's arriving about 4:00 p.m. They were just in time. Major General Alexander P. Stewart's "Little Giant" division of Buckner's corps had broken through the center of Rosecrans's line. Stewart's leading units caught Van Cleve before he could close on Reynolds. This was a dangerous moment for the Union as a gap had existed all day between Thomas's right and McCook's left. Bragg had been so intent on flanking the Union left and driving the Army of the Cumberland back down into McLemore's Cove that he never exploited this weakness. Thomas also realized the danger to his right, and to help check it he brought Brannan's division off the left flank to shore up the rapidly crumbling center.

Negley's men came up the Dry Valley to Rosecrans's Headquarters and turned down the slope toward the battle.

> At about 4 o'clock p.m. the Brigade with their arms at support, led by the band to the tune of the "Red, White and Blue" passed down this road towards the point of tumult and strife. About half way down the slope General Rosecrans was seen standing on a rise in the ground at the left of the road, as each company gained his front, arms were brought to the shoulder as a salute, which in each case was returned by the General. As the colors passed by him they were dipped in his honor and on returning the salute, he said: "Make it warm for them, Michigan boys." This was answered by a cheer from the men and the General added: "I know you will."[4]

As Negley's two brigades came down the slope and headed northeast from the Widow Glenn's toward Brotherton field, Brannan was moving southwest. The two Union divisions struck the Confederates on both sides, "driving the rebels before them like chaff before the wind."[5] John J. Bloom recorded, "at 5 p.m. we maid a charge and drove them back 1/2 mile and stoped and gave them about 60 rounds a peace...."[6] Stewart's penetration of the

Union line was turned back. Brannan and Negley remained in the line where Van Cleve had been.

After driving the Confederates back, Negley's command withdrew from the LaFayette Road to a woods where they built a barricade of rails and logs. The regiments of Stanley's brigade detached one company for picket duty during the night. John J. Bloom of Company E recorded, "we fell back to fense and a continuel firing was kept up all night and we was on Picket and we almost Frose to Death."[7] Years later Lieutenant Borden M. Hicks recalled, "At dusk we threw up a line of works, and sent one Company out as skirmishers, then the balance layed down on their arms for rest, it was so cold that it was impossible to sleep and we got very little rest. I was informed by one of the residents of the battlefield, that ice formed that night, this was told me some thirty years after the war, and his memory might not have been good, but it certainly was very cold, especially for men who had just loaned their blankets to Longstreet's men."[8] (Hicks was referring to the loss of the knapsacks at Davis Crossroads.) Negley reported on the last part of the fight of September 19 as "6 p.m.-Stanley and Sirwell were ordered to push the enemy back vigorously, so as to connect our line with the troops on the left. A sharp engagement with the enemy immediately followed, lasting until 7:30 p.m., during which time our line was pushed forward from one-half to three-quarters of a mile, but I was unable to connect with any of our forces on my right or left."[9] Apparently Negley did not meet with Brannan on the field.

Stanley's and Sirwell's men fortified a line just west of the LaFayette Road and spent a cold night with a cold supper and no fires. Company E of the Eleventh spent that night on the picket line. John Beatty brought his brigade up during the evening. He was ordered off the picket line near Crawfish Springs about five o'clock. This was the same hour that Stanley and Sirwell were "double-quicking" towards the rebels northeast of Widow Glenn's. "Arriving at the springs, the boys were allowed time to fill their canteens with water, when we pushed on the Chattanooga road to a ridge near Osborn's, where we bivouacked for the night ... While the boys were preparing supper, a very considerable engagement was occurring not far distant to the east and south of us."[10] This must have been the attack of the Confederates on the extreme right of Rosecrans's army, the repulse of which ended the fighting in that section for the day. This would mean that Beatty stopped before dark.

Rosecrans met with his corps commanders after the fighting died down. There were adjustments to be made in the line. McCook's corps was moved to the left or north to contact with Thomas's right or southern flank. Crittenden's command was re-established by pulling Wood's and Van Cleve's divisions out of the line to act as the reserve just behind the junction of Thomas and McCook.

Before attending the meeting with Rosecrans, Thomas had left orders for the construction of strong fortifications made of logs all along his front. His concern with the necessity of strengthening the left was apparent from the beginning. Baird's division on the extreme left of the army was ordered to bend his line back to the LaFayette Road. At two o'clock in the morning of September 20, Baird reported to Thomas that he could not do this as he would have too few men to defend the center and right of his position. Sometime between this report and six o'clock, Thomas requested that Rosecrans send Negley to hold the extreme left next to Baird.

Glenn Tucker, the author of *Chickamauga: Bloody Battle of the West*, implies that Thomas made the request immediately upon getting Baird's report although he says "consequently."

> Rosecrans replied that Negley's division would be sent immediately. The movement of this division and its consequent replacement in the line by Wood's division would come to have a decisive bearing on the battle of the twentieth, but its progress toward the left was slow indeed for such an officer as Thomas, who as he catnapped that night seems to have had his subconscious mind on a watch for the arrival of Negley. Dawn came, then 7 a.m., but not Negley.[11]

However, Freeman Cleaves in his biography of Thomas says,

> At two o'clock that morning, Sunday, September 20, Thomas received a message from General Baird reporting that his left did not quite extend to the road and that he could not reach it without weakening his line. Thomas then went back to sleep but aroused himself at six o'clock when he sent a note to

Rosecrans asking that Negley take position on Baird's left and rear. Negley, who was in poor physical shape, had been consistently behind schedule during the movements of the last two days, and unfortunately for all concerned he was to prove late again.[12]

General Thomas said in his own report on the battle that when he received Baird's report, "I immediately addressed a note to the general commanding requesting General Negley be sent me to take position on General Baird's left and rear, and thus secure our left from assault."[13] Whenever the order was first given to Negley to move left, he had not done so when Rosecrans began his inspection early in the morning of the twentieth. Tucker says that Rosecrans now personally ordered him to the left, "and the commanding general directed him (Negley) to go to Thomas at once."[14] This was about 6 a.m. Negley in his report said, "Military operations were suspended until 8 o"clock a.m. in consequence of a dense fog."[15] For whatever reasons, when Rosecrans returned to the center after inspecting the left with Thomas, Negley had not moved, and McCook had not closed in to the left to replace Negley. Rosecrans took matters into his own hands and ordered Crittenden to replace Negley with Wood's reserve division. Rosecrans continued to the right where he consulted McCook. When he returned to the center, Negley was still in the line. Negley told Rosecrans that Wood had not moved up to replace his division. At this point John Beatty's brigade arrived, and Rosecrans ordered him to report to Thomas on the left. General Beatty reported to Thomas at 8:00 a.m. Thomas ordered that Beatty's brigade be placed perpendicular to the rear left of Baird's line. Beatty later described the situation: "Baird's line appeared to run parallel with the road (LaFayette Road) and mine running to the rear crossed the road."[16] Rosecrans then found Wood and, after severely upbraiding him in front of his staff for his failure to move earlier, ordered him to replace Negley.

Negley began to withdraw his command after Rosecrans's last visit. All of the accounts from the Eleventh tell how they began to leave and were then ordered back to prevent the Confederates from seizing their previous fortifications. Stanley's brigade had begun to move to the left. Hicks remembered that, "Our Colonel noticing that no troops had occupied our place and that the Johnnies were making for the works that we had just left, ordered us about, and it was a foot race for twenty of thirty rods, to see which would get there first, whether we were nearest or the swiftest sprinters, I do not know, but we got there."[17] When the Eleventh reached the line the Confederates were about fifty feet away, and the regiment got in a volley to stop them. The Nineteenth Illinois and the Eighteenth Ohio then reached the line to drive them back.[18] The brigade was brought off the line again as soon as the Confederates were driven back. Sirwell's brigade apparently had not yet left the line.

Negley's story is at variance with that of the Eleventh.

> ...the remaining two brigades of my command were not relieved until 9:30 when one brigade was sent from Gen. Wood's division for that purpose. In withdrawing these two brigades the enemy availed himself of the change, and pressed so hard upon the relieving force that I was compelled to halt, and *send one* [underlining is the author's] of the brigades back to assist in re-establishing my former line, also to protect my ammunition train which was passing at the time. Those serious detentions had the effect of separating my division, and destroying the unity of action in my command, which I was unable to restore during the day.
>
> I deeply regret the circumstances which rendered this subdivision necessary, actually placing two of my brigades beyond my personal supervision. 10 AM-On being informed that General Thomas's left was being turned I left Sirwell's brigade to follow with the artillery, and pushed Stanley's brigade forward under a heavy fire to the left of General Thomas's line, where Stanley met the enemy in heavy force.[19]

Negley's story breaks down at this point. He begins his excuse and apology too soon. Until ten o'clock he had the same two brigades that he had had under his direct supervision since the afternoon of the nineteenth. There is no record that Stanley moved forward under heavy fire. For whatever reason, once the Second Brigade moved towards the left, they never saw Negley again on the field at Chickamauga. According to his later report, Negley was ordered by Captain W. B. Gaw of Thomas's staff to take charge of all artillery and point it south, although he also took credit for the placing of Bridge's battery of Beatty's brigade and Smith's Fourth Regular Battery which helped save Thomas's extreme left that morning.

However, General Thomas was not interested in cannons aimed south. He was concerned about his left being turned from the north. Thomas said in his report, "This order General Negley, in his official report, mentions having received through Captain Gaw, but from his description of the position he assumed, he must have misunderstood my order, and instead of massing the artillery near Baird's left, it was posted on the right of Brannan's division nearly in the rear of Reynold's right."[20]

Fortunately for the Union army, Bragg's early morning attack had been delayed, but when it came at 10:00 a.m., it was almost too much for Thomas's extreme left. The danger to the left was greatly increased by a last minute change in the position of John Beatty's brigade by Captain Gaw, the same member of Thomas's staff who, according to Negley, had ordered the massing of artillery in the wrong direction. Beatty wrote,

> Fifteen minutes after this line was formed [this was the line that ran perpendicular to Baird's], Captain Gaw of General Thomas's staff, brought me a verbal order to advance my line to a ridge or low hill, fully one-fourth of a mile distant. I represented to him that in advancing I would necessarily leave a long interval between my right and Baird's left, and that I was in the position that General Thomas himself told me to occupy. He replied that the order to move forward was imperative and that it was to be supported by Negley with the other two brigades of his division. I could object no further, although the movement seemed exceeding unwise....[21]

Beatty was caught by the rebel attack before he established the new position and was driven back along the LaFayette Road.

Beatty started a desperate search for help. "On the way before proceeding far, I met the Second Brigade of our division, Colonel Stanley, advancing to my support."[22] Indeed, anyone who could be spared from other duty was being rushed to Baird's left. Thomas sent several regiments of Palmer's reserve and Van Der Veer's brigade of Brannan's reserve. These were placed between Baird's division and the LaFayette Road. Next to them across the LaFayette Road was Stanley's brigade with Stanley still commanding. He was wounded about noon and command passed to Colonel Stoughton of the Eleventh Michigan. Finally, on the extreme left was Beatty's brigade.

The story of what Stanley's brigade did on the Federal left was remembered consistently. Belknap wrote:

Soon the Brigade again started for the left. It marched off at quick time for about a mile and a quarter, passing along the rear of the line where the battle was raging fiercely. On reaching the left of Baird's Division, who were fighting desperately from behind log works which they had built during the night before, the command took a position in the edge of the woods at the north end of Kelly's field. Its line was formed at right angles to the general line of battle and facing north; the Eighteenth Ohio being on the right of the Eleventh and extended nearly to the LaFayette Road. The Nineteenth Illinois was posted a few rods in the rear of the other two regiments as a support. In front of the line was quite a dense thicket of grubs and underbrush, beyond which was an open woods of heavy timber. For a few minutes all was quiet in front, during which time the low underbrush for a few rods in advance of the line was cut down and carried back and piled in front of the Brigade to more effectually screen its position. This gave the men who lay behind this screen a clear view out into the open woods in front while they were entirely out of sight of those advancing from that direction. General John Beatty now came up with a part of his Brigade and formed on the right, extending the line across the LaFayette Road to the east. While waiting in this position Colonel Stoughton passed along the line and ordered the colors dropped upon the ground to the rear, and after ordering several soldiers to keep their heads down, said: 'Boys, we've got them. Let every man take aim as if he were shooting at a target, and be sure and not waste a bullet. Aim at their legs and you will drop their front rank. No troops in the world will stand and have their front rank shot down. As soon as you fire we will charge and capture the balance.' About that time the 'Rebel Yell' was heard, and the Colonel said, 'Pay strict attention to orders and we will make those fellows sing a different song.'

In the meantime the enemy had driven the skirmish line and were coming on at a double quick, unconscious of what awaited them. On arriving within twenty feet of Stoughton's line his flag was raised abruptly in their front as he gave the command, 'Aim, fire, charge.' There was a simultaneous report from every gun in the two regiments and the enemy's front line instantly dropped to the ground and were placed hors de combat; and the survivors broke to the rear in the wildest confusion. The Brigade instantly charged and passed over a windrow of dead and wounded at the point where they received the Federal fire. The enemy fled, precipitately throwing away everything that impeded them in their flight. The Brigade pursued them through the woods for over sixty rods and across McDonald's field capturing hundreds of prisoners. Among those captured by the Eleventh was Brigadier General Daniel W. Adams, commanding the leading Brigade, whose sword and field glasses were brought to Michigan by members of the regiment. To the Eleventh therefore, belongs the honor of capturing the only rebel general officer taken in that battle.[23]

Lieutenant Borden M. Hicks later recalled,

We took up ap new position in Kelley's field, just to the left of the road, where we concealed ourselves in the underbrush, and awaited the oncoming Confederates, who were now flushed with victories. When within two or three rods of our line, we opened fire on them, their front rank went down, the rear rank was nearly put out of business, and we captured nearly all of the balance, including General D. W. Adams who was in command of the rebel forces making this charge-our regiment captured General Adams, yet there are no less than six regiments who claim the honor of having captured him, but as the best proof would say that I had his sword, others members of our regiment had his field glasses and revolvers, belt and so forth. I carried his sword on the charge we now made to the McDonald field, going into the charge with a sword in each hand, and looking as savage as a meat ax. Here we took many more prisoners.[24]

A detail from the Eleventh conducted these prisoners to Chattanooga. John Bloom noted in his diary "a general egagement commance and our Regiment was ordered to make a charge and we gave them a voley and then charge them double quick and drove them 1/2 mile and we took one hundred prisoners and captured a General out of Longstreet Division...."[25] Bloom believed the Eleventh was fighting Longstreet's troops ever since Davis Crossroads. There can be little doubt that Beatty and Stanley broke Adams's advance, and it is very probable that they also put the finishing touches on the efforts of Helm's division to take Baird. Stovall's advance in the same area was undoubtedly stopped by Van Der Veer and Barnes.

Although the left of the Army of the Cumberland was temporarily secured, Longstreet, commanding the left wing of Bragg's Army of Tennessee, took advantage of an opening in the center of the Union army. This gap in the line occurred when General Thomas

J. Wood, who had replaced Negley in that section, was ordered by Rosecrans to support Reynolds by withdrawing behind Brannan. Rosecrans's order to Wood was received at 10:55 a.m. At the same time, directly across from the resulting gap, Longstreet ordered 23,000 Confederates towards the Federal lines at 11:00 a.m.[26]

Wood met Thomas as he was executing this order, and Thomas reported "I ordered General Wood, who had reported to me in person, to send one of his brigades of his division to General Baird."[27] This was the Third Brigade of Van Cleve's division, commanded by Colonel Sidney M. Barnes, and it helped to reinforce the left.

By the time Stanley had things sorted out on the left, it was apparent to Thomas that he would have to establish a new line on his right along the ridge of the Missionary Mountains known as Horseshoe Hill and Snodgrass Hill. This was where he had suggested relocating the federal right wing to Rosecrans the night before.[28] The Eighty-second Indiana Infantry under Colonel Morton C. Hunter of Brannan's division, retreating from the Confederate breakthrough, refused to retreat farther than Snodgrass Hill and became the first unit to take a position on the new right.

Thomas began sending units to Snodgrass Hill from his extreme left. It was a short march. When Stanley was ordered to fall back to the right and rear, the brigade changed direction, and as they began to move,

(Brigadier General Marcellus) Stovall's brigade of Breckenridge's division opened a heavy fire on its left flank and rear from the direction of the Lafayette road. The brigade immediately changed front, facing east, and a terrific fire was kept up for some time, the contending forces moving slowly to the south, the enemy apparently trying to outflank Stanley's brigade. On reaching a point in the woods west of the north end of the Kelley field, and about due east of the Snodgrass house, the enemy disappeared. In this movement to the right the regiment lost more men than at any other point during the two days' battle.[29]

Stovall's Confederates proceeded on behind the Union left.

Stanley, now freed, once again turned the brigade toward the sound of firing from the army's right. However, he was now much farther south. The brigade reached Snodgrass Hill near Snodgrass House about noon.

Northeast of the Snodgrass house one of the ridges—the only one cleared of timber—trails off and descends to the more gently rolling Snodgrass farmlands. On this cleared ridge, where the brigades of Harker and later Hazen joined Stoughton, some of the early and late desperate actions of the Snodgrass Hill battle were fought. Here Kershaw unloosed the initial bolt of Longstreet's assault on Thomas's position, and here the Alabama brigade led by the New York City-bred Archibald Gracie delivered its bloody attack as the battle neared its close.[30]

It was at this time that Colonel Stanley left the field wounded, and Colonel William Stoughton took command of the brigade. Lt. Colonel Melvin Mudge took charge of the Eleventh.

After Stoughton cleared the ridge of Confederate skirmishers, he, placed the 11th Michigan and the 19th Illinois Volunteers in line of battle in a strong position under cover of the hill, leaving the 18th Ohio to support a section of the 4th U.S. artillery....Soon after the Brigade had taken this position the enemy hade a spirited attack on a hill to my right occupied by the left of Brannon's Division apparently driving our troops back. I at once ordered the 11th Michigan and 19th Illinois Volunteers to their support, these Regiments advanced at a double quick and charged upon the enemy driving him from the hill.[31]

Stoughton took command of the troops between Brannan on the right and Wood on the left. He continued in his report of the battle,

I... placed my forces [this is after the above described action] along the crest of the hill, the 19th Illinois on the right and the 11th Michigan Volunteers on the left and constructed a rude breastworks. My Brigade was by far the largest if not the only organized force on the hill and I accordingly assumed command [of] the fragments of the Regiments on the hill and all men found in the rear were placed in the most available positions.[32]

In his analysis of the Battle of Chickamauga, Glenn Tucker said of the Confederate attack on Snodgrass Hill, "When he was recalling the battle in later years, Longstreet said he made twenty-five assaults in all on Snodgrass Hill. However he may have broken them down, they continued all afternoon and each seemed desperate and protracted. Instead of twenty-five, it was really one of sustained duration."[33] The first of the great concentrated assaults was Kershaw's attack on Harker, Hazen and Stoughton. Kershaw began a series of attacks against the eastern slope of Snodgrass Hill that were repulsed each time. Borden Hicks recalled, "The slope in our front was strewn with the enemy's dead, so thick that you could almost walk on them...."[34] Lieutenant Colonel Alexander W. Raffen of the Nineteenth Illinois wrote his wife that, "At the place where we made our last stand the ground is covered with cartridge papers which in itself shows how desparate the struggle must have been".[35]

The constant firing of the guns with their black powder charges was beginning to foul them. By 3:00 in the afternoon the Eleventh was short of ammunition, and the men were hungry and thirsty. Most of them had last filled their canteens on the day before at Crawfish Springs. Some had begun to replenish their supply from the dead Confederates on the slope. At one point the whole regiment was waiting for the next attack and a chance for pursuit that would give them an opportunity to get the cartridge boxes, canteens and knapsacks of the dead. Shortly after 3:00 they had their opportunity. Using the same tactic that worked so well against Adams earlier in the day, Stoughton allowed the Confederates to charge closer and closer. At a hundred yards they began their rebel yell, and at ten yards the entire command fired a volley into the charging ranks and instantly counter-charged with fixed bayonets. Stoughton's men followed the Confederates for about two hundred yards. As they returned to their positions on the hill, the Eleventh cut the canteens and cartridge boxes off the enemy dead. The Confederates used fifty-seven caliber Enfield rifles, and the Union was supplied with fifty-eight caliber Springfields. Indeed, it was easier to load the smaller Confederate ammunition into their own fouled rifles.

The laconic John Bloom noted in his diary, "We fell back to the hill and a contiluel firing kept up till 4 PM and then the Rebels made a charge on our Brestwork and they got repulse...."[36] This was the last great assault of the day. The attack of Archibald Gra-

cie's and John H. Kelley's brigades was the last assault against the
Union lines at Chickamauga.

Colonel Stoughton in his official report, said:

At 4 o'clock the enemy made a vigorous attack upon our position and a conflict ensued, which in its fierceness and duration had few parallels. Our
troops, without exception, maintained their ground with unfaltering ocurage,
and the few who recoiled from the storm of bullets were rallied and returned
with renewed ardor. The enemy was in heavy force and fought with the most
determined obstinacy. As fast as their ranks were thinned by our fire they
were filled up with fresh troops. They pressed forward and charged up to our
line, firing across our breastwork, and planting their colors within one hundred feet of our own. A dense cloud of smoke enveloped our lines, and in
some places the position of the foe could only be known by the flash of his
guns. At 6 o'clock the enemy still held his position, and as a last resort I ordered up the Eighteenth Ohio, and rallying every man that could be got,
charged forward with a cheer upon his colors.[37] His flag went down and his
line broke and he fell back from the hill.

Captain Brenner of the Nineteenth Illinois wrote,

The assault by the rebels between four and five o'clock was most desperate.
The foe succeeding in forcing back a part of the left of the Nineteenth and
the right of the Eleventh, advancing to the rail breastworks. There was no
confusion in the ranks of the troops forced back, however, nor did they retire
over one hundred and fifty feet. The Eighteenth Ohio immediately advanced, and with its help we soon regained the line, which the Confederates
had held not to exceed twenty minutes, if that long. Nor did they at any time
advance beyond the rails. We maintained this recovered position until after
dark, and there we repulsed all the numerous assaults made by the enemy.[38]

The historian of the Eigteenth Ohio recalled in later years,

At 5 p.m. Gen. Preston's division joined Kershaw's in a final effort to capture
the ridge. Gen. Gracie's brigade, moving directly toward the front of Stanley's brigade, pushed up to the crest, and for a time the confederates held the
works. This was the crisis. Gen. Beatty, coming from the right of the line,
called upon Col. Grosvenor to move the 18th double quick to the works,
about 300 feet away. The Colonel promptly ordered the regiment forward,
& himself and Gen. Beatty charged with it. The barricade was retaken, and
several Confederates captured. The enemy now retired in haste to the base[39]
of the hill, and the battle was at an end.

Gracie's losses in his attack on Stoughton's brigade have been compared with those of Pickett at Gettysburg. He lost over seven hundred men. "Nothing in this battle, marked with gallantry so frequent that it becomes commonplace, surpassed the courage of these two brigades (Gracie and Kelley) as they watched their ranks thin minute by minute and still doggedly refused to yield an inch of ground."[40] Yet they were repulsed by a make-shift command led by Colonel Stoughton of the Eleventh Michigan.

No one can follow the fortunes and actions of the Eleventh Michigan and the Second Brigade without feeling a need to refute the later reports by John Beatty. Beatty managed to somehow lose an entire brigade between the morning action against Adams and the move to Snodgrass Hill. Beatty wrote his memoirs in 1879 and has been quoted ever since. This is his description of the afternoon on Snodgrass Hill from his *Memoirs*:

Supposing my regiments and General Negley to be still on the field, I again dispatched Captain Wilson in search of them, and in the meantime stationed myself near a fragment of the Second Brigade of our division, and gave such general directions to the troops about me as under the circumstances I felt warranted in doing. I found abundant opportunity to make myself useful. Gathering up scattered detachments of a dozen different commands, I filled up an unoccupied space on the ridge between Harker, or Wood's division, on the left, and Brannan, on the right, and this point we held obstinately until sunset. Colonel Stoughton, Eleventh Michigan, Lieutenant Colonel Raffin, Nineteenth Illinois, Lieutenant Colonel Grosvenor, Eighteenth Ohio, Colonel Hunter, Eighty-second Indiana, Colonel Hays and Lieutenant Colonel Wharton, Tenth Kentucky, Captain Stinchcomb, Seventeenth Ohio, and Captain Kendricks, Seventy-ninth Pennsylvania, were there, each having a few men of their respective commands; and they and their men fought and struggled and clung to that ridge with an obstinate, persistent, desperate courage, unsurpassed, I believe, on any field. I robbed the dead of cartridges and distributed them to the men; and once when, after a desperate struggle, our troops were driven from the crest and the enemy's flag waved above it, the men were rallied, and I rode up the hill with them, waving my hat and shouting like a madman. Thus we charged, and the enemy only saved his colors by throwing them down the hill. However much we may say of those who held command, justice compels the acknowledgment that no officer exhibited more courage on that occasion than the humblest private in the ranks.[41]

In his official report to Thomas after the battle he was less presumptuous. "Supposing them (his brigade) to be near I made every effort to find them and find my division commander. Failing in this, I stationed myself near the 2nd Brigade of our division then commanded by Colonel Stoughton of the 11th Michigan and gave such general directions to him and the troops about me as under the circumstances I felt warranted in doing."[42] This is not to demean his courage or usefulness. He stayed and served well. It is meant rather to put his role at Snodgrass Hill in perspective. Stoughton in his report said, "During the fight Brig. General John Beatty rode up the hill and assisted materially in sustaining and inspiring the men, his assistance there and also in sending men forward was timely and very valuable."[43]

Thomas began to withdraw his left at about 5:30 p.m. with Reynold's division. Stoughton's brigade was one of the last Union units to leave the Chickamauga battlefield if not the very last. Beatty went to tell Stoughton to withdraw "near eight o'clock", but he was already moving. Stoughton in his report said, "About 8 o'clock orders came from Genl Brannan to retire, and the Brigade quietly formed and marched in good order to Rossville. About half an hour before we left, a raking fire was poured into our ranks by the enemy from a hill to our right which had been occupied and as we supposed was still held by Genl Granger's Reserve Corps."[44] One of the men from the Eleventh was sent to inform the commander of the unit to the rear that they were firing into a Federal brigade. The soldier returned to report the Confederates had captured the Twenty-second Michigan and the Eighty-ninth Ohio. A half an hour later two of the men of the Eleventh went to the top of the hill to the right and returned to report that there were no Union troops along the hill in that direction. John Bloom of Company C recorded, "9 PM fell back 3 mile toward Chattanooga and got three days racient and stop fore the night. We left our kild and wounded on the Battle Field."[45] A member of Stanley's brigade wrote the Nashville *Union* on October 15 that, "about 8 o'clock orders came to retire and this brigade was the last to leave the field."[46] Subsequent memoirs remembered the hour somewhat later. Borden Hicks recalled, "About ten p.m. we received word to quietly leave the battlefield and fall back to Chattanooga this was the first intimation that we had received that the battle had gone against us."[47] The Eleventh Michigan was, indeed, one of the last Union units to leave the field.

Back in Chattanooga, Quartermaster James King loaded a wagon with rations for the Eleventh and started for the battlefield on Sunday, September 20. Three miles out of Chattanooga he began to run into stragglers who told him about the retreat of the right of Rosecrans's army. The supply train was ordered to stop. "We lay here from noon until dark while down the valley came the boom of cannon and the roar of musketry. It was Stone River enacted again. Just as darkness set in we received orders to move forward. I reached the Regiment about 9 or Ten o'clock. They had fought all day against appalling odds and had held their ground...They were in the best of Spirits and had lost lightly considering the desparate fighting which had taken place."[48]

For all the fighting, the Eleventh Michigan did not suffer heavy losses at Chickamauga. The regiment had 5 killed, 42 wounded, and 19 missing, for a total of 66. These were small losses for a regiment that was engaged on both days. Indeed, the losses of the Second Brigade of Negley's division were not heavy: 20 killed, 146 wounded, and 49 missing, for a total of 215. In Negley's division the heaviest losses were suffered by the Twenty-first Ohio of Sirwell's brigade that Negley sent to Brannan on September 20. This regiment lost 243 men with 147 missing. One of the reasons the brigade's losses and those of the Eleventh were light was the small number of men who were missing and probably captured.[49]

In later years the actions that had seemed commonplace on the battlefield came to appear greater and greater. On October 21, 1895, William G. Whitney of Allen, Michigan, was awarded the Congressional Medal of Honor for acts of heroism under fire on September 20, 1863 at Chickamauga. At the battle, Whitney was the sergeant of Company B of the Eleventh. One of the affidavits used in his application was from private James Rayner. "In 1863, September 20, while in the line of battle at Chickamauga, Ga. at

Snodgrass Hill, late Sunday afternoon and after the rebels had made several charges and had as many times been repulsed, the ammunition of our company became exhausted. The rebels were about to charge again when William G. Whitney went outside our temporary works, went among the dead and dying rebels outside, and at great exposure to himself, cut off and removed cartridge boxes from the rebels and brought them within our own lines for our own use and which were used to good effect in again repulsing the enemy."[50]

As Thomas's command moved toward Rossville on the evening of September 20, he met Sheridan and Negley, who had organized parts of the retreating wing of the Army of the Cumberland around Rossville. Once the troops were fed and rested, Thomas deployed his command and returned units to their original corps commanders. In his report of the battle it appears that Thomas kept the overall command, placing the corps and division to suit his own plans. This would have been possible as Rosecrans did not leave Chattanooga.

Negley's division had the responsibility of holding the Rossville Gap. Sometime between three and four o'clock on the morning of September 21, the Eleventh and the other regiments of Stoughton's brigade were called out to help hold the Rossville Gap. The brigade was placed directly across the LaFayette Road which the retreating Union army had followed toward Chattanooga. John Bloom in his diary always referred to the Rossville Gap as "Skidatle Gap."

On the afternoon of September 21 the Confederate cavalry of Nathan Bedford Forest made a concentrated attack on Negley's division in the Rossville Gap. Negley reported, "2p.m.-The enemy advanced a heavy force, with artillery on Lafayette road, and on the crest of the mountain. After a brisk engagement with artillery and musketry, he was checked in the gap by Stanley's brigade and driven from the mountain crest by a gallant charge of the Fifteenth Kentucky, General Beatty's brigade."[51] John Bloom wrote, "and at 3 p.m. the Rebel got there Jackass battery on the mountain and give us grape and canister and our regiment run the rebels the other way and our cornal raley the Regiment and we stopt till 10 p.m."[52]

At nine o'clock in the evening the last units of the army began to withdraw into Chattanooga. Thomas had prepared for this by sending back the wagons, ambulances, and artillery before dark. Negley's division started back about 10 P.M. Thomas covered this final movement with a very heavy screen of skirmishers. Stoughton had command of the skirmish line that covered the final withdrawal from the Battle of Chickamauga. He had the Fifteenth Kentucky from Beatty, the Thirty-seventh Indiana from Sirwell, and the Sixty-ninth Ohio from Stanley. The Sixty-ninth Ohio had come up from Cowan, Tennessee, with McCook's division of the Reserve Corps but was not engaged at Chickamauga. Stoughton also kept two companies of the Eleventh. The picket line withdrew at four o'clock on the morning of September 22 and marched into Chattanooga.

Daniel Rose wrote his mother from Chattanooga on September 27 and said, "we have passed through another heavy fight our loss was heavy but no greater than the enemies. Our regiment lost 7 killed, 41 wounded and about 20 missing. We was a little worsted."[53] It is a laconic summary of one of the hardest fought and bloodiest battles of the war. The Army of the Cumberland and the Confederates each lost twenty-eight percent of their men in the two days at Chickamauga.

Notes

1. King Letters, 4 October 1863.

2. *Report of Thomas*, p. 68.

3. Bloom Diary, 19 September 1863.

4. Belknap, *Michigan Organizations*, p. 113.

5. Ibid., p. 113.

6. Bloom Diary, 19 September 1863.

7. Ibid., 20 September 1864.

8. Hicks, Personal Recollections, p. 528.

9. *Report of Thomas*, p. 68.

10. John Beatty, *Memoirs*, pp. 245-246.

11. Tucker, *Chickamauga*, p. 202.

12. Cleaves, *Thomas*, p. 164. Negley cannot be faulted for his behavior up to this point, and he had not been late. As to him being "in poor physical shape", Cleaves does not give his sources for this information.

13. *Report of Thomas*, p. 46.

14. Tucker, *Chickamauga*, p. 204.

15. *Report of Thomas*, p. 68.

16. *Memoirs*, p. 246.

17. Hicks, Personal Recollections, p. 529.

18. Belknap, *Michigan Organizations*, p. 114.

19. *Report of Thomas*, p. 68-69. Negley said he sent back one of his brigades which would indicate that it was Sirwell's since it was left behind. However, at the end of this section of his report, Negley spoke of two brigades.

20. Ibid., p. 47. The final words on Negley's conduct on September 20 at Chickamauga were written by Ambrose Bierce, "A Little of Chickamauga" *Ambrose Bierce's Civil War*, ed. by William McCann, (Chicago: Gateway, 1956), p. 35. Bierce recalling the events later in the afternoon after the retreat of the right wing of the Army of the Cumberland stated that, "On my way [to Thomas] I met General Negley and, my duties as topographical engineer having given me some knowledge of the lay of the land, offered to pilot him back to glory or the grave. I am sorry to say my good offices were rejected a little uncivilly, which I charitably attributed to the general's obvious absence of mind. His mind, I think, was in Nashville behind a breastwork."

21. Beatty, *Memoirs*, p. 246.

22. Ibid., p. 248.

23. Belknap, *Michigan Organizations*, pp. 114-115.

24. Hicks, Personal Recollections, p. 539.

25. Bloom Diary, 20 September 1863.

26. Tucker, *Chickamauga*, p. 258.

27. *Report of Thomas*, p. 47.

28. Cleaves, *Thomas*, p. 163

29. Belknap, *Michigan Organizations*, p. 249. This is a quote from "The Oration of Sergeant James W. King" on the dedication of the Michigan Eleventh monument at Chickamauga Battlefield.

30. Tucker, *Chickamauga*, p. 330.

31. Col. William L. Stoughton, Report on Battle of Chickamauga, Michigan Eleventh Infantry, Regimental Papers, Record Group 94, Box 1999, National Archives, Washington, D.C. (Hereafter cited at Stoughton's Report.)

32. Ibid.

33. Tucker, *Chickamauga*, p. 356.

34. Hicks, Personal Recollections, p. 530.

35. Letter of Alexander W. Raffen, 22 March 1864, Illinois Historical Library, Springfield, Illinois. This letter was written after Raffen and his fellow officers visited the battlefield the following spring.

36. Bloom Diary, 20 September 1863.

37. Stoughton's Report. Also quoted in Belknap, *Michigan Organizations*, p. 118.

38. J. Henry Hayne, ed., *The Nineteenth Illinois* (Chicago: M. A. Donohue & Co., 1912), p. 241.

39. Joseph C. McElroy, *Record of the Ohio Chickamauga and Chattanooga National Park Commission* (Cincinnati: Earhart & Richardson, 1896), p. 43.

40. Tucker, *Chickamauga*, p. 355. On Gracie's brigade's losses, see O.R., Vol. 30, pt. 2, p. 420.

41. Beatty, *Memoirs*, p. 250.

42. O.R., Vol. 30, pt. 1, p. 380.

43. Stoughton, Report.

44. Ibid.

45. Bloom Diary, 20 September 1863.

46. *Journal*, 19 November 1863. The Sturgis *Journal* reprinted the letter from the Nashville *Union*, 15 October 1863. The letter was signed J.V.G.

47. Hicks, Personal Recollections, p. 530.

48. King Papers, 4 October 1863.

49. O.R., Vol. 30, pt. 1, p. 172.

50. Minnie Dubbs Millbrook, *A Study in Valor: Michigan Medal of Honor Winner in the Civil War* (Lansing: Michigan Civil War Centennial Commission, 1966), pp. 118-119.

51. *Report of Thomas*, p. 70.

52. Bloom Diary, 21 September 1863.

53. Rose Papers, 20 September 1863.

Chapter Seventeen

"A lot of us will die tomorrow on that ridge."

When the Eleventh reached Chattanooga, the orders were to fortify. Work began immediately on Fort Negley. Rose wrote his mother on September 27: "Since we came here, we have been fortifying night and day, incesently."[1] John Bloom recorded in his diary that the Eleventh worked day and night on September 22, but that the work was completed by the twenty-fifth. On September 23 Rosecrans gave the troops a ration of whiskey. Many of the men of the Eleventh did not drink and probably sold or gave their share to others because Bloom reported "some of the boys got tite."[2]

One week after the battle of Chickamauga the Confederates allowed Rosecrans to send ambulances to the battlefield for the dead and wounded. Chattanooga was well supplied with military hospitals that had been built by the Confederates. The major problem was to transport the wounded. Most of the dead were left to the Confederates. Many of them were still unburied months later. The ambulance train left on September 28 and returned the next day. Bloom said, "our Train of Ambulances came in from Chickamauga with our wounded. It was an awfull sight."[3]

When the army of Braxton Bragg occupied the south side of the Tennessee River, it controlled the river route for supplies for the Army of the Cumberland. The Confederates quickly closed the water route and disrupted the land routes. Chattanooga was under siege.

By September 27 the realities of the siege condition of the Union army became apparent. Bloom described it as, "Tuff time

on quarter ration."[4]   The Eleventh had been under siege at
Nashville in 1862 and had experienced reduced rations. However,
there had only been two divisions in Nashville, and the surrounding
countryside was rich and productive. On October 2 a supply train
including the wagons of the Eleventh was caught in a Confederate
raid. James King wrote, "The worst blow which we have received is
the burning of a train of supplies between here and Bridgeport.
Our regimental Teams were among them. Billy Davis was in
charge of our train but made his escape. I should have went with
them but it being the end of the month, the Quarter Master said I
had better remain and make out the reports. Many of the Team-
sters were taken prisoners and some of them killed. Billy was back
to day at the spot where they were captured and everything is a
perfect mass of ruins."[5] From the ninth to the thirteenth of October the Eleventh was foraging in Washington Valley, thirty miles
northwest of Chattanooga. According to John Bloom the expedition was successful. "We went up the valey 10 miles and loted up
our Teems and came back 10 miles."[6] However, foraging would
not keep Rosecrans's huge army supplied, and things got worse.

In Washington the War Department was finally taking measures
to reinforce the Army of the Cumberland. Indeed, the entire western theater of the war was being reevaluated. As early as September 25 General Joseph Hooker became commander of a relief
force from the Army of the Potomac composed of General O. O.
Howard's Eleventh Corps and General Henry Slocum's Twelfth
Corps. Hooker's force had twenty thousand men and ten batteries
of artillery. In one of the great logistical feats of the war Hooker's
army traveled to Bridgeport, Tennessee, from Virginia with a hundred train cars of baggage in just twelve days.

On October 3 General William T. Sherman's Army of the Tennessee left Vicksburg with seventeen thousand men. Sherman's
army went by water to Memphis, and then overland along the
Memphis and Charleston Railroad line, rebuilding it as they went.
They would take six weeks to reach Bridgeport. By then the crisis
was over.

Secretary of War Stanton had more on his mind than the reinforcement of the Army of the Cumberland. He was planning to replace Rosecrans. On October 3 General Grant was ordered north to meet with an "officer of the War Department" at Louisville, Kentucky. On October 16 Grant and Stanton met in Indianapolis as they were making connections for Louisville. Once there, Stanton handed Grant two sets of orders; both created a Military Division of the Mississippi with Grant as commander. One order left the department commanders as they were, and the other removed Rosecrans from command of the Army of the Cumberland. In the other General George Thomas, commander of the Fourteenth Corps, was to be given the Army of the Cumberland. Grant was told to choose which set of orders he wanted. Grant chose Thomas.

On October 19 Rosecrans was informed of the change. It was exactly one month from the start of the Battle of Chickamauga. Thomas was ordered to take command of the Army of the Cumberland and to "hold Chattanooga at all hazards." Thomas immediately wired his new commander, "We will hold the town until we starve."[7] Interestingly, although Rosecrans and Thomas were both much respected by the men of the Eleventh, there is no mention of the change in command in any of their letters or diaries.

Grant arrived in Chattanooga on October 23 and personally approved a plan which Thomas and his staff had developed to open a supply line to Bridgeport. The situation must have been desperate as Bloom recorded in his diary on October 26, 27 and 28, "Nothing to eat."[8] On the twenty-eighth the "Cracker Line" was opened, and on the twenty-ninth there were quarter rations. The following day there was mail. The siege was over.

During October and November, as the two armies lay face to face, there developed a kind of truce and camaraderie between the Union and Confederate enlisted men. Bloom recorded on October 3, "I was on Picket at the Rolling Mill and Alferd G. Wright went out with a Flag of Truth and exchanged papers and got a corect account of there kild and wounted."[9] Rose wrote his mother on October 4 that,

The "rebs" pickets are in sight of ours. I should think about eighty rods apart but there is no shooting between them and ours. They stood in plain sight and so did we. Both pickets had orders not to fire unless the others advanced. One of the "Co. E" boys of our regiment held up a paper and then he saw a "reb" do the same. They both advanced and met about half way between the lines, shook hands, talked a short time, exchanged papers then each returned to his respective post, so you can see how much the "reb" soldiers and ours hate each other. There is another place where both pickets get water out of the same creek, they on one side and ours on the other. At night we could plainly see their camp fires on the side hills in front. Their army and ours are not over three miles apart. We could plainly hear their brass band nearly as plane as our own. They played well but we couldn't hear what tunes they played.[10]

There were less pleasant duties than listening to "reb" brass bands and digging rifle pits. Rose wrote "Old Mr. [Oliver W.] Wilcox from near Centerville came here after his boy [Abner V.Wilcox] but he was buried the day before he arrived. He died on the 29th from wounds received in the battle of Chickamauga on the 20th of Sept. He was a noble young man and a good soldier. His loss is felt by all of his fellow soldiers. The old man felt very bad about him. He took all of his things home with him."[11] Bloom also noted a death in his company: "at 2 PM we buried Irvin Snyder from his wound recived from Chickamauga."[12] Snyder had joined Company E in its original enlistment as a corporal. He was a Sergeant Major when he accepted the surrender of Brigadier General D. W. Adams, the only Confederate officer of that rank to be captured at Chickamauga. Snyder must have loaned Adam's sword to his Lieutenant, Borden Hicks, who returned it to Snyder's family. He was twenty years old when he died.

During the siege of Chattanooga the entire Army of the Cumberland was reorganized. The Eleventh Michigan became a part of the Second Brigade of the First Division of the Fourteenth Corps. Brigadier General Richard W. Johnson commanded this division. He had led the Second Division of McCook's Twentieth Corps at Chickamauga but had fought under Thomas's command. Brigadier General John H. King was in command of the Second Brigade which consisted of Fifteenth, Sixteenth and Nineteenth United States Infantry, the Nineteenth Illinois, the Sixty-ninth Ohio and the Eleventh Michigan. Colonel Stoughton of the Eleventh was the senior officer under General King and led the brigade at Missionary Ridge. The brigade took 1,541 men and officers into that battle.[13]

Once the problem of supply had been solved Grant considered taking the offensive. This was forced on Grant in part by the concern of the War Department for Burnside at Knoxville. On November 4, Bragg sent Longstreet and his command of fourteen thousand troops to drive the Union forces out of eastern Tennessee, an area that was dear to Lincoln's heart. Grant attempted to use the badly supplied Army of the Cumberland to prevent this.

> On the 7th [November], before Longstreet could possibly have reached Knoxville, I [Grant] ordered Thomas, peremptorily to attack the enemy's right, so as to force the return of the troops that had gone up the valley. I directed him [Thomas] to take mules, officers' horses, or animals wherever he could get them, to move the necessary artillery. But he [Thomas] persisted in the declaration the he could not move a single piece of artillery and could not see how he could possibly comply with the order. Nothing could be done but to answer Washington dispatched as best I could; urge Sherman forward, and encourage Burnside to hold on....[14]

Thomas's lack of transport animals was very serious. As late as November 23, when Grant had the Chief of Artillery, General J. M. Brannan, move forty pieces of artillery from the Army of the Cumberland to support Sherman on the left, "he [Brannan] had to use Sherman's artillery horses for this purpose, Thomas having none."[15] The implication that Thomas did not move against Bragg on November 7 because he was afraid or reluctant was contradicted by Grant's own words.

The head of Sherman's column reached Bridgeport on November 14, and the general hurried ahead to Chattanooga to meet Grant. During the morning of November 16 Grant, Sherman and Thomas inspected the entire front at Chattanooga and developed a general plan of battle. Sherman would cross behind Thomas and take the left wing of the line. He would then start to attack attempting to roll up the Confederates on Missionary Ridge, or at least cut off Bragg's communications by seizing the rail lines south of the ridge. Hooker would move around Lookout Mountain in order to attack the right end of the ridge. Thomas, occupying the center, "was to assault while the enemy was engaged with most of his forces on his two flanks."[16]

Grant wanted Sherman to begin the attack on the 21st, but bad weather and bad roads delayed the Army of the Tennessee. Grant then ordered an attack for November 22, but again there were delays. On the following day without Sherman, Grant moved Thomas into action on the left center. Grant was forced to move in hopes of relieving some of the pressure on Burnside in Knoxville or at least preventing Bragg from moving in that direction. The object of Thomas's attack was a hundred-foot-high hill called Orchard Knob. This hill was about a mile from the Union defensive works. Johnson's division did not participate in the attack of the twenty-third. The Eleventh Michigan was on picket duty along with most of the division. John Bloom thought the fighting was farther northeast where Sherman was to assault the Confederate line for he recorded in his diary: "Gen. Sherman is driving the Rebels & captured 6 hundred prisoners. Good news."[17]

On November 24 Sherman crossed the South Chickamauga Creek and began his assault on the left (northern) end of Missionary Ridge. Although he made some headway, the country was broken and heavily fortified. Thomas's Army of the Cumberland had already taken the object of their planned assault for the first day on the twenty-third and therefore did not go into action on the twenty-fourth. They were spectators for one of the most memorable events of the war. The Eleventh was on picket on the extreme right of the forces facing Missionary Ridge, and were in an excellent position to watch the Battle of Lookout Mountain. John Bloom wrote, "I was on picket at the foot of Lookout Mountain and at 8 AM the fight commance and Gen Hooker drove the Rebels off the Mountain and he captured about 2 thousand prisoners. This charge I have witness with my own eyes and was a beautiful sight to see...."[18]   Rose wrote, "Wednesday morning Hooker's men wave their flag on the peek of Lookout, it was a glorious sight. When we were on picket we could see all of the fighting."[19]

Grant set the twenty-fifth as the day for a concerted push by the combined forces of Sherman, Thomas and Hooker. Sherman, who was not as far along the Ridge as Grant thought, was to attack at sunrise. Thomas was informed that "your attack which will be simultaneous, will be in co-operation. Your command will either carry the rifle pits and the ridge directly in front of them or move to the left, as the presence of the enemy may require."[20] Hooker was to consolidate his victory of the twenty-fourth and to assault the right flank of Bragg's army. Grant watched the battle from Orchard Knob and, when Sherman's drive failed, Thomas's assault was tied to Hooker. However, when Hooker was delayed, Grant had to relieve the pressure on the left with a frontal assault by the Army of the Cumberland. The movement of the troops had resulted in some mixing of the commands, but Thomas had four divisions arranged from right to left: Johnson, Sheridan, Wood and Baird.

Johnson placed his two attacking brigades with Brigadier General William Carlin's First Brigade on the right and Colonel William Stougton's Second Brigade on the left. Stoughton in turn divided his brigade into two wings for the assault. The left wing, consisting of the regular United States Infantry units, was under the command of Major John R. Edie of the Fifteenth Infantry. Colonel M. F. Moore of the Sixty-ninth Ohio commanded the right wing which was composed of the volunteer units. Moore had commanded the Brigade during the absence of King and Stoughton. The Eleventh was led by Major Benjamin Bennet of Burr Oak. Lt. Colonel Melvin Mudge had been wounded at Chickamauga and was not with the regiment.

The Eleventh was called back from picket duty about eight o'clock in the morning and issued three days rations. The brigade assembled in line of battle in a wooded area that was behind their assigned position in the coming attack. They waited there until nearly four o'clock in the afternoon, looking at the imposing heights of Missionary Ridge. The Confederates had not been idle during their two month occupation of the ridge. A line of rifle pits stretched along the base, a line of breastworks had been constructed about half-way to the top, and another with artillery redoubts went the length of the top. During the day the troops listened to the guns on the left where Sherman had bogged down.

The object for Thomas's four divisions was the line of rifle pits at the base of the ridge, and the signal to advance was to be the rapid, successive firing of the six 10-pound Parrott rifled cannons at Orchard Knob. Finally at 3:45 the guns were fired and the entire line began to move. In front of the wooded area where the men had waited was an open field of a half mile and then the ridge. It was another three-quarters of a mile at about a forty-five degree angle to the top.[21]

When the line emerged from the woods, the men immediately came under fire from the Confederate cannons at the top of the ridge and the rifles from the base. The Confederate rifles were very accurate at 800 yards. The Eleventh started at the double-quick but broke into a flat-out dash at top speed for the rifle pits. This willingness to break ranks and run probably saved many from the terrible fire that was directed at them. Daniel Rose wrote soon after the battle that, "the top of the ridge seems a perfect blaze."[22] Hicks recalled "a blinding storm of shot and shell."[23]

When the racing Union troops reached the rifle pits, there was a confused hand-to-hand struggle between the opposing forces, but many of the surprised Confederates just surrendered. The men of the Eleventh remembered the following minutes as a time of catching their breath. However, it was apparent as the artillery on the crest was redirected that the rifle pits could not be held. It was either on up the ridge or back to their original position. Quartermaster Sergeant James King, who was among the attacking troops, later recalled that someone yelled, "On up the ridge....the man who gave that order was within a few yards of us but whose voice it was has never been known by the men of the 11th, yet no comrade in that regiment of that brigade will ever forget it."[24] The call was repeated all along the base of Missionary Ridge. Others were shouting, "Remember Chickamauga! Remember Chickamauga!"[25]

The entire line of Union troops surged up the steep face of Missionary Ridge.

Probably the only people more surprised than the Confederates by the charge up Missionary Ridge were Grant and Thomas. Grant turned to Thomas and demanded, "Thomas, who ordered those men up the ridge? I don't know; I did not," was the reply. But Thomas asked Major General Gordon Granger, commander of the Fourth Corps and in charge of the assault, if he had ordered the move. "No," said Granger, "they started up without orders. When those fellows get started all hell can't stop them." Grant then muttered that someone would pay if the assault was a failure.[26]

As the Union line swept up the ridge, it became a series of "regimental flying wedges, with their colors forming and leading the apex."[27] Color-Sergeants had a high casualty rate that day. The colors of the Nineteenth Illinois went down three times. Color-Sergeant John M. Day of the Eleventh, who had carried the colors at Chickamauga, was killed. The flags of the Eleventh went down twice and were finally carried to the top by Second Lieutenant Borden Hicks of Company E and First Lieutenant Charles Coddington of Company A.

When the fleeing Confederates reached the top, the firing grew more intense as the artillery firing down the hill on the oblique did not have to worry about hitting their own troops. The Union artillery did their part; King said, "the Union siege guns in Fort Wood could readily be distinguished as they sent their huge projectiles shrieking over the heads of the Union forces into the rebel positions, exploding caissons, tearing to pieces men and horses and causing terrifying havoc."[28]

In Stoughton's brigade, Colonel Moore's wing of volunteer units reached the top before the regulars. Just before the leading members of the brigade reached the top, the Confederate defenders fled down the other side. Indeed, all along the crest of the ridge the Confederate line was crumbling. However, here and there pockets of defenders kept up the fight. One such unit of about four hundred infantry and a battery of six guns was still in action just to the right of the brigade's position on the top of the ridge. It was in the fight against this position that James King was wounded. His right arm was broken just above the elbow, "by a Minie ball fired by a Confederate soldier not six rods away."[29] Borden Hicks later told a story about this part of the attack.

> I placed myself behind a tree about six inches in diameter, kindly remember that I was not as fleshy then as now, and besides we had a knack of shrinking ourselves to about the size of a match when exposed to fire. As I stood behind this tree facing to our right, watching a battery of six guns, whose position projected to our front, with my sword hanging in my left hand, a Johnnie up in front thought it would be well to pick off an officer, so he blazed away at me, his bullet struck my sword, the sword struck me on the leg, making a black & blue spot for a few days, and this was the only wound I received while in the service.[30]

As more rifles were brought to bear on the Confederate position they also broke and ran. After a short chase, the Union troops began cheering. Bloom recorded it as, "three cheers for Gen. Sherman and three grone for Gen. Bragg."[31]

James King walked from the top of Missionary Ridge into Chattanooga to the hospital. He had received special permission from Stoughton to join in the attack. When he told Major Bennet, Bennet "said James, you are a little fool. A lot of us will die tomorrow on that ridge. I shall not come out of battle alive."[32] Bennet was killed about half-way up the front of the ridge. In general, however, the losses of the Eleventh were not heavy; six killed and twenty eight wounded or about thirteen per cent.[33]

The Eleventh and the rest of the Second Brigade spent the night on Missionary Ridge, and early the next morning they joined in the pursuit of the retreating Confederates. The Second Brigade led the division as it went southeast, accompanied by Major General John M. Palmer, the Fourteenth Corps commander. As the Confederates retreated they destroyed the bridges slowing the pursuit. However, between eight and nine o'clock in the evening of the twenty-sixth, the division caught up with them just south of Graysville. Palmer stayed with Stoughton and the Second Brigade. Johnson in his report of the action said, "Colonel Stoughton's brigade was, by the direction of the corps commander, directed to advance on the Ringgold [road] and to its crossing with the Lafayette road, and to attack the enemy vigorously. This movement was made in gallant style, and about 9 o'clock a volley was fired into Stewart's rebel division, the men of which scattered in all directions, throwing away their arms, abandoning their colors, and leaving in our possession three Napoleon guns, two caissons, with horses, harness, &C., and quite a number of prisoners."[34] Rose put the number of prisoners at two hundred.[35] Bloom recorded that after the fighting the Eleventh built a big camp fire and "stait till morning."[36] The Eleventh was sent back to Chattanooga the next morning with the prisoners and captured artillery. On the twenty-eighth Bloom said, "I was in camp and took a good rest."[37]

Daniel Rose summed up the Battle of Missionary Ridge: "it pays us well for Chickamauga. We captured near a hundred pieces of artillery. Bragg has been thouroughly routed from as strong a position as he ever had and it is a complete victory."[38]

Notes

1. Rose Papers, 27 September 1863.

2. Bloom Diary, 23 September 1863.

3. Ibid., 29 September 1863.

4. Ibid., 27 September 1863.

5. King Papers, 4 October 1863.

6. Bloom Diary, 11 October 1863.

7. E. B. Long, ed., *Personal Memoirs of U.S. Grant* (New York: Gossett Dunlap, 1962), p. 312. Hereafter cited as Memoirs.

8. Bloom Diary, 26-27 October 1863.

9. Ibid., 3 October 1863.

10. Rose Papers, 4 October 1863.

11. Ibid., 5 November 1863.

12. Bloom Diary, 6 October 1863.

13. O. R., Vol. 31, pt. 2, p. 481.

14. U. S. Grant, *Memoirs*, p. 324.

15. Ibid., p. 333

16. Ibid., p. 327.

17. Bloom Diary, 23 November 1863. Bloom often had the names of officers and units wrong.

18. Ibid., 24 November 1863.

19. Rose Papers, 28 November 1863.

20. *Report of Thomas*, p. 131.

21. Hicks, Personal Recollections, p. 532.

22. Rose Papers, 28 November 1863.

23. Hicks, Personal Recollections, p. 533.

24. James King, "History of the Eleventh Michigan Infantry", James W. King Papers, Regional History Collection, Western Michigan University, Kalamazoo, Michigan, n.d. (Hereafter cited as King Papers.)

25. Glenn Tucker, *The Battles for Chattanooga* (Philadelphia: Eastern Acorn Press, 1981), p. 39.

26. Joseph S. Fullerton, "The Army of the Cumberland", *Battles and Leaders of the Civil War*, 4 Vols., ed. Robert U. Johnson and Clarence C. Buel (New York: The Century Co., 1884; reprint ed., New York: Castle Books, 1956) Vol. 3, p. 725.

27. Hicks, Personal Recollections, p. 533.

28. King, "History".

29. Ibid.

30. Hicks, Personal Recollections, p. 534.

31. Bloom Diary, 25 November 1863.

32. King Papers, 17 February 1902.

33. O. R. , Vol. 31, pt. 2, p. 481.

34. *Report of Thomas*, p. 159.

35. Rose Papers, 1 December 1863.

36. Bloom Diary, 27 November 1863.

37. Ibid., 28 November 1863.

38. Rose Papers, 1 December 1863.

Chapter Eighteen

"Mother, you must know that it has been hard for me to be a slave for nearly three years but I know that it is serving my country."

On December 2 the Eleventh Michigan went into winter quarters at Rossville, Georgia. "Rossville existed in location, and name only, it being the home of a Mr. Ross, who had quite a palatial house which was made use of for a Hospital."[1] Guarding the Rossville Gap or, according to Bloom, "Skidatle Gap" was the only responsibility of the regiment for the next three months.

This was an interlude from the war that was badly needed by the regiment. After nearly thirty months of service and five months of marching and fighting, the Eleventh Michigan needed to rest, heal, and reorganize. The command structure was once again depleted. Lieutenant Colonel Melvin Mudge, who was wounded in the left arm at Chickamauga and was for a brief time a prisoner, spent two and half months in the Officers' Hospital at Chattanooga. When he returned to the regiment in February, it was for light duties only. He never regained the use of his left hand. Major Benjamin Bennet was killed leading the charge at Missionary Ridge. His successor, Patrick Keegan, who had been the Captain of Company K, was also seriously wounded in the same charge. Keegan had been shot through the chest, seriously damaging one lung. Captain Charles Newberry of Company E was killed at Chickamauga, and Captains Thomas Briggs of Company G and Henry Fisher of Company A were wounded so seriously that they were soon discharged for disability. Captain Lewis Childs of Company H was wounded and taken prisoner at Chicamauga. He did not return to the regiment until August 7, 1864. In the case of Captain Loren Howard of Company C, a wounded knee from the Battle of Stone River became so painful that he could no longer perform field duty. The command problem in Company D, Major Bennet's original company, is difficult to unravel. Frank Lane became the Captain when Bennet was promoted to Major. However, Colonel Stoughton later said that he given the regimental color bearer, Benjamin Hart, a sword at Missionary Ridge and ordered him to lead Company D in the charge. Hart became the First Lieutenant of the company in January of 1864.[2] Lane was ultimately cashiered from the service.

Early in 1864, the organization of the regiment was as follows:

Colonel - William L. Stoughton
Lt. Colonel - Melvin Mudge
Major - Patrick Keegan
Company A - Captain Charles Coddington
Company B - Captain Francis Bissell
        Captain Chauncey Koon (after June 17, 1864)
Company C - Captain Loren Howard
        First Lieutenant John Graham, commanding
Company D - Captain Frank Lane
        Captain Henry Platt (after June 13, 1864)
Company E - Captain Borden Hicks
Company F - Captain John Birdsall
Company G - Captain Albert Rossiter
Company H - Captain Lewis Childs
        First Lieutenant Edward Catlin, commanding
Company I - Captain Ephraim G. Hall
Company K - Captain Addision Drake, after June 17, 1864
        First Lieutenant Joseph R. Carpenter, commanding.

Two other absent regimental officers were Quartermaster Addison Drake and Chaplain Holmes A. Pattison. Drake served as Assistant Divisional Quartermaster during 1863 and in February 1864 was serving as Assistant Quartermaster for the Fourteenth Corps. In this position he supervised the operation of four saw mills in the Chattanooga area.[3] Chaplain Pattison, who was injured dismounting his horse at the Battle of Stones Rivers, never rejoined the regiment.[4] Pattison was fighting his own Civil War with the secessionists of the Methodist Episcopal Church, South. He was the first chaplain to enter Murfreesboro after the Battle of Stones River, and he took possession of a Methodist Church building that the Confederates had used as a hospital. With orders from General Thomas, Pattison restored the building for worship services for the Union Army. When the members of the former congregation petitioned General Rosecrans for the return of the building, Rosecrans referred the matter to Thomas. Pattison wrote Bishop Matthew Simpson that,

> General Thomas replied that he [Pattison] had applied for it for the use of the Army - that he was a Methodist preacher, and if the rebel Methodist would not worship with me they could go without worship and returned the petition. . . .[5]

Pattison told the Bishop in the same letter that he thought a loyal congregation of eight to ten people could be formed in Murfreesboro. According to Chaplain Israel Cogshall of the Nineteenth Michigan Infantry, Pattison served the occupied church as its preacher but inferred that he was not serving as a chaplain in any of the military hospitals.[6]

The regiment probably missed the Chaplain more than the Quartermaster. The members of the regiment not only had to attend services with other units but had to use the chaplains of other units for counsel and other religious services.[7] On February 21, Richard Brayman of Company E married one of the local girls, Miss A.G. Wright. The ceremony was conducted by Rev. William H. Weeks, Chaplain of the 101st Indiana Regiment.[8] Richard Hemenway, one of the new recruits from Leonidas, wrote his wife on April 23 that, "This Reg. has not had any preaching for a year."[9]

The other great need of the regiment was men. In the fighting during the Chattanooga campaign the Eleventh had lost one hundred and twenty-five men and officers killed, wounded or missing. The Eleventh was fairly successful in recruiting new soldiers. Hicks recalled that the regiment received 150 to 175 recruits from the North.[10] This was especially true of Company A which was from the Mendon-Leonidas area. Rose told his mother, "Last night twenty-eight more recruits arrived. Making in all sixty for our Co. but we can't keep them all for it would make our Co. more than full".[11] John F. Downey of Three Rivers was typical of the new recruits. He was only fifteen or sixteen when the war began. Boys like him had followed the war news, they had heard the speeches that recruited the original regiments, and many of them were in school where the patriotic spirit of the times was reinforced by memorizing the great speeches of American History. These boys organized little paramilitary units with uniforms and mock guns. They held parades and drilled "by tactics that were partly Hardee's, partly Scott's, and partly original and wholly different from any laid down in the books."[12] When the veterans began to return on thirty day furloughs granted for reenlisting and the new young captains returned home to recruit, the boys left behind were now eighteen and nineteen.

John Downey had his eighteenth birthday while boarding at the Colon Seminary, a near-by college preparatory school. He and two friends joined the Michigan Eleventh Infantry at the recruiting station in Colon. Upon, returning to school, they in turn recruited all but two from the senior class. Returning to Three Rivers, they recruited many of the other eighteen and nineteen year olds.[13] Of course, it did not hurt to have nineteen year old Captain Borden Hicks and twenty year old Captain Charles Coddington as examples.

If Downey was a typical recruit of 1864, Felix Balderry must have been one of the most unusual. He was probably the only Philippine national to fight in the American Civil War. As a sixteen year old stowaway, he had hidden on the American whaling ship "Milton" in 1858. He was found by the crew and allowed to continue to New Bedford, Massachusetts. In 1860, when the ship landed in America, Balderry accompanied the first mate, Joseph Foster, and his family to Leonidas Township, St. Joseph County, Michigan.[14]

Rose wrote to his brother " . . .we had to turn over about a doz to other Co's that enlisted for our Co and there is more yet in Mich. that enlisted for our Co but we can't take them. You can see by this what a reputation our Co has at home . . .All that didn't live at Leonidas had to go to other Co. Our commissioned officers are all from Leonidas so you can see that Leonidas just about runs this Co. now"[15] This hint of village and township rivalry does not appear any other place in the sources about the Eleventh. However, Rose noted in his diary on April 28, 1864 that he had preferred charges against Captain Charles Coddington.[16] The following day he wrote his only bitter, complaining letter.

> My stay is perceptably growing shorter and every day makes it shorter. It makes me bouyant with hope thinking of my return but I may hope in vain for there is time and chances enough yet to make my stay enternal [sic]. I would not think of returning while my country needs me but for you . . .If Charles or Joel was at home then I could shape my course as best suited me but now I have to submit to circumstances that can't control. But in the army as a private soldier is a poor place to plan, we are governed entirely by circumstances and officers, when and where they say go or what they say do that is our duty as we are sworn to obey our officers not matter how unjust. Mother, you must know that it has been hard for me to be a slave for nearly three years but I know that is serving my country.[17]

Richard Hemenway wrote that a complaint has been "entered against Charles [Coddington] by the Co. [company] for carrying off 76 dollars of Co. funds."[18]

The bounty for enlisting was a sore point with many of the men, and Dan Rose was representative. "I blame our government for giving much large bounties to new recruits. They ought to enlist for the same that we did. If they would not, then the draft should take place. I wish I could be there to tend some of the war meetings for they are taxing us to pay recruits and we do the fighting."[19]

On February 28, 1864, seventy-four enlisted men from the Ninth Michigan were transferred to the Eleventh.[20] These were the men who did not reenlist when that regiment signed for the veteran service. The Ninth had spent most of its enlistment as the provost guard of the Fourteenth Corps under Colonel John G. Parkhurst. Once they were transferred to the Eleventh, most of them were detailed to jobs at corps headquarters. John O. Rossetter, for example, was detailed as a saddler and harness maker. John C. Love and Hugh Anderson were detailed to General Palmer's escort. Love was apparently glad for the change. "I am heartily glad that I have got out of that regiment."[21] John Bloom noted on February 12 that, "we got 30 new recruits from the 9th Mich. fore our Regiment."[22] This was probably the number that was actually incorporated into the Eleventh, until the Ninth returned from veteran's leave.

The government made a major effort during the winter of 1863-64 to reenlist the three-year regiments as veterans. The bonus was three hundred dollars and a thirty-day furlough. "A small effort was made a few days ago to reenlist our regiment in the veteran service but there was only a few felt enclined [sic] to try the service for three years longer."[23] There was great concern from the folks at home over this question. Dan Rose wrote his mother as early as February 3, "I know that it panes [sic] you to think that I comtemplate reenlisting and I hasten to ease your mind on that point. Large inducments are offered now-the largest that ever had been offered. Never the less for your sake I will not reenlist yet, at least, but I would if one of the other boys was at home but as it is I will wait until I get home and stay awhile if I live long enough. Although I like the service well enough to serve another term but you can rest assured that I will not enlist again while circumstances are as they are at home."[24] When Daniel Rose had enlisted in the summer of 1861, he left three brothers home with his widowed mother. All of them enlisted in other Michigan regiments. James King was trying to assure his sweetheart that he was not going to reenlist. He returned to camp after a furlough for the wound that he received at Missionary Ridge. Finally on April 12 he wrote, "Now, Dear Jenny, I will answer the question you asked of me at home. Whether I intended reenlisting in the Army. I can say

Jenny that I shall not stay longer than my period of enlistment which expires the 24th day of August 1864. Now that is plainly answered is it not."[25] He had to reassure her again two weeks later, "You wished me to write and tell you whether I intended reenlisting or not. I think I can answer you to a certainity Jenny that I shall not."[26] In the end not many in the Eleventh chose to reenlist.

The reasons for not reenlisting were given occasionally but often changed. King felt his broken arm was not strong enough for another three years. Indeed, he was almost discharged for disability. Rose said he would return to care for his mother but later added that he thought the fighting would end in 1864. Although he noted, "Soldiers will be needed for a long time yet and have enough to do to."[27] Rose wrote to his brother, "I think there will be no need of our reenlisting to keep up the regiment."[28]

The only duty besides routine camp chores was guarding the Rossville Gap, yet there was none of the complaints that had marked the time in Bardstown in 1862. Many of the men made handicrafts. John Bloom made pipes, rings, and other things from laurel root. He also did much of the sewing for his company and for the regiment. Cooking, baking, gathering wood and washing clothes took a good deal of the time. Not all these activities produced successful results. John Bloom cooked a "mess of dumplings" and reported "we had a joley time of eating our wet-sones."[29] However, Dan Rose wrote his mother, "We are living first rate now since we draw flour and do our own baking and cooking. We are all or nearly all good cooks by experience. I spent my Christmas and New Years as all other days; the duties to do and no excitment but had a good chicken pot pie new years."[30] James King, the quartermaster sergeant, was eating well also. He wrote, "...I visited the city of Chattanooga today and made the Colonel and [Daniel] Holbrook a visit and had good time generally. Staid to dinner and returned just in time to take supper with the Boys. We did not have hard Tack for supper as you would suppose but our very intelligent *American* of *African descent* made us some warm biscuit which would have been called eatable in a land where people pretend to live. The other articles I will not name but consider them *to numerous to enumerate.*"[31]

During off-duty times the men visited Chattanooga and the surrounding battlefields. Both Rose and Bloom had their pictures taken in Chattanooga. Rose was quite taken with the realism of one of his portraits. He wrote, "Mother, that picture I did not send as a present but for myself if I should live to get home. It looks very Natural. The scene is as familar to me as home and its memories I will always cherish. I can tell you more about it if I get home. I want to have a heavy curly black walnut frame put on it and a good thick clear glass. I dont care if it costs five dollars. It is a very choice picture."[32] Rose noted that "a detachment went out on the battlefield of Chickamauga."[33] Lieutenant Stephen Marsh of Company A also "went to Chickamauga Battlefield."[34] Neither of them recorded any details of these trips. However, Lieutenant Colonel Alexander Raffen of the Nineteenth Illinois wrote his wife that:

> Last Sunday myself and several officers of the regiment took a ride over [the] battlefield of Chickamauga. We went over the whole field and of course took special interest in the parts where our regiment fought. The trees in some places are cut down so much by the Artilery [sic] that it looks as if a tornado had swept over the field, all the trees and stumps are plugged all over with bullets it is astonishing to think that any one could have come off safe without being hit.[35]

John Bloom wrote, "Jan. 20 2 P M a detail went out on Chickamauga Battle field to take Captain C.W. Newbury body up and bought it to camp. Jan. 21 I was in camp and at 10 A M we went to the burial sesion and buried Captain C.W. Newbury at the Solgers Grave Yard. Solem Day to Co. E."[36] Trips to Missionary Ridge are recorded in more detail. Rose wrote home that, "One of the boys got a bush from the ridge where our regiment charged up in the last fight we had. It was about six feet long and the branches spread between four and five feet. It had twenty-six bullet markes on it so you can imagine how the missells [sic] of death flew around us. Another little tree has thirty-one bullet marks."[37] Rose went for a "stroll on Missionary Ridge" on March third and saw a "dead Rebel."[38]

There were also camp diversions. According to Bloom, "the Boys are enjoying them self. Riding each other on a Pole and throwing each other in the ditch. Soloman Shirey is the Capt of the Pole Riding."[39] Rose told his mother, "... nothing to break the montony of camp life except on occasional game of ball or slag taner as we call it."[40] However, Rose wrote to his brother, "There was a dance out about three miles last night but I was on guard I didn't attend but I was told that there was about sixty boys and only eight girls so they had to frequently hang the girls up to drean [sic]. There is some very nice and decent girls near here and I think that we will some day have a civil country dance."[41] Some enterprising showman must have brought a diorama to Rossville. Bloom said, "I went to the painting show or eye meusium. It was a good show."[42]

On March 15, 1864, the Eleventh left Rossville for Graysville, which was about twelve miles east. At this time the regiment was carrying 600 men on its rolls.[43] At Graysville they rejoined the Second Brigade of the First Division of the Fourteenth Corps. The brigade consisted of the Fifteenth, Sixteenth, Eighteenth and Nineteenth United States Infantry Regiments and the Sixty-ninth Ohio, Nineteenth Illinois and Eleventh Michigan volunteer regiments. Just prior to the move, Company A received twenty more recruits from the training barracks in Grand Rapids. Most of these men had been recruited in the Mendon-Leonidas area. Since the first of the year the regiment had received sixty-eight recruits, and fifty-nine of them were for Company A.

The march to Graysville was uneventful and Dan Rose referred to it as "short but tiresome."[44] The Eleventh set up camp only to move the whole thing on March 19 in order to be closer to the rest of the brigade. On that day they began target practice. This was a regular activity of the regiment until the beginning of the Atlanta Campaign. John Bloom recorded the best shot each time. There was some horse-play on the rifle range. On April 15 Bloom notes that, "Solomon Shirey poot a double load in his gun and it noct him over."[45] There was also regimental and brigade drill at Graysville.

General Thomas was preparing the Army of the Cumberland for the campaign.

The weather in northern Georgia was as varied as it was in Tennessee and constantly shocked the Michigan boys. On March 6, James King sent peach blossoms home in his letter, and on March 22-23 it snowed ten inches. Many of the regiment were on picket duty during the heavy snowfall and suffered severely.[46]

Between March 31 and April 5 the regiment was on picket duty at Parker's Gap in Tennessee about five miles from Graysville. Except for the rain it was not difficult duty. Rose wrote, "We would have a good time while there but it was bad weather nearly all of the time. Still I went visiting in the valley among the Union citizens and had a good time."[47] He also drew a sketch of the Gap which he sent home.

Toward the end of April the regiment began the final preparation for the Atlanta Campaign. Grant in the east and Sherman in the west were to move against the Confederates at the same time. Sherman began stripping the army of extra baggage. James King wrote, "Preparations have been going busily forward for an early move. All our surplus baggage has been sent to the rear and the army put in trim for a long march. The weather is splended and the roads in good condition. The amount of luggage that is now allowed the officers and men is very limited. A half a shelter tent to a man and one of the same to an officer constitues their habitations. The transportation allowed to a Regiment when we came into the service 14 teams. Now they talk of cutting it down to one. We have six teams at present and I cannot see but what we get along as well as when we had the 14 and, if they make it one, I am sure we can get along."[48]

On May 2 the brigade moved to Ringgold, the concentration point for the Fourteenth Corps. On May 6 the day before the start of the Atlanta campaign, the Nineteenth Illinois Infantry was transferred to General Turchin's brigade (First Brigade, Third Division, Fourteen Corps.) The Nineteenth Illinois and the Eleventh Michigan had been brigaded together since 1862. That night there was a "grand camp illumination."

On the eve of the grand march some soldier, who though the occasion worthy of some sort of demonstration, concluded that he would illuminate; so he lighted all his candles and stuck them on top of his tent. The next soldier liked the spirit of that and put his candles out, and then the next and the next, until all the tents in the company had lighted candles upon them. The other companies of the regiment followed. It went from regiment to regiment, from brigade to brigade, from corps to corps, until that whole great army was brilliantly illuminated. We were encamped on an eminence where we could over-look nearly the entire valley where the Army of the Cumberland lay, and it was a magnificent sight. There were thousands of tents in view and each had upon it from two a dozen candles. There were that broad valley and those hill tops and those gentle slopes, stretching away in the distance as far as the eye could reach, all brilliantly decked with those twinkling lights. Why, it looked as if the stars had been translated from the heavens to the earth.[49]

The laconic John Bloom noted in his diary that, "our 14 Army Corps was all lit up with candles and it was one of the best sight I ever saw. A scare for the Rebels."[50] At sunrise on May 7, 1864, the final march into war began for the Eleventh.

Notes

1. Hicks, Personal Recollections, p. 536.

2. Records of the Department of the Interior, Pension Office, Various files, National Archives, Washington, D.C.

3. History of Officers, Regimental Records, State Archives of Michigan, Lansing, Michigan.

4. Records of Department of Interior, op. cit., Pension file of Holmes A. Pattison.

5. Holmes A. Pattison to Bishop Matthew Simpson, Simpson Papers, op. cit., 8 February 1864.

6. Cecil K. Byrd, ed., "Journal of Israel Cogshall, 1862-1863", *Indiana Magazine of History*, vol. 42, no. 1, Marc, 1946, pp. 84-87.

7. See Bloom Diary, passim, on this problem.

8. Three Rivers Reporter, 19 March 1864.

9. Richard Hemenway Letters, Burton Historical Collection, Detroit Public Library, Detroit, Michigan, 23 April 1864. Hereafter cited as Hemenway Letters.

10. Hicks, Personal Recollections, p. 536.

11. Rose Letters, 17 March 1864.

12. "Decoration Day Address," John Florian Downey Papers, University of Minnesota Archives, Minneapolis, Minnesota, n.d. (Hereafter cited as Downey Papers.)

13. Ibid., passim.

14. Undated Newspaper Clipping, Wayne C. Mann Collection (A999), Regional History Collections, Western Michigan University, Kalamazoo, Michigan.

15. Rose Letters, 12 March 1864.

16. Diary of Daniel D. Rose, 28 April 1864. The diary of Private Rose is in the possession of Leland W. Thornton, Centreville, Michigan. (Hereafter cited as Rose Diary.)

17. Rose Letters, 29 April 1864.

18. Hemenway Letters, op. cit.

19. Rose Letters, 28 February 1864.

20. Report Book, February, 1864.

21. John C. Love Letters, 4 March 1864, Ness Collection, University of Michigan, Michigan Historical Collections, Bentley Historical Library, Ann Arbor, Michigan.

22. Bloom Diary, 12 February 1864.

23. Rose Letters, 28 March 1864.

24. Ibid., 3 February 1864.

25. King Letters, 12 April 1864.

26. Ibid., 26 April 1864.

27. Rose Letters, 28 February 1864.

28. Ibid., 17 March 1864.

29. Bloom Diary, 19 January 1864.

30. Rose Letters, 4 January 1864.

31. King Letters, 9 March 1864. (Underlining is King's.)

32. Rose Letters, 15 January 1864.

33. Diary of Daniel D. Rose, 24 February 1864.

34. Diary of Stephen P. Marsh, Lieutenant, Company A Eleventh Michigan Infantry, January 1864 to September 1864 (typed copy of original made by Wayne Mann, Guy Marsh Collections (A485), Regional History Collections, Western Michigan Archives, Kalamazoo, Michigan) 3 March 1864. (Hereafter cited as Marsh Diary.)

35. Alexander Raffen Letters, op. cit.

36. Bloom Diary, 20-21 January 1864.

37. Rose Letters, 1 February 1864.

38. Rose Diary, 3 March 1864.

39. Bloom Diary, 8 February 1864.

40. Rose Letters, 1 February 1864.

41. Rose Letters, 12 March 1864.

42. Bloom Diary, 18 Februry 1864.

43. Report Book, May, 1864.

44. Rose Diary, 15 March 1864.

45. Bloom Diary, 15 April 1864.

46. Ibid., 22 March 1864.

47. Rose Letters, 1 May 1864.

48. King Letters, 1 May 1864.

49. "Atlanta Campaign", Downey Papers, n.d., pp. 4-5.

50. Bloom Diary, 6 May 1863.

Chapter Nineteen

"Oh, misery, where is thy end."

Sherman began the Atlanta campaign with nearly 100,000 men and 254 pieces of artillery. More than half of these were assigned to Major General George Thomas's Army of the Cumberland. Thomas's task was to hold Joseph Johnston's Confederate army while the smaller armies of the Ohio and the Tennessee attempted to turn the enemy's flanks and to break the Confederate supply line to Atlanta. The first objective was Johnston's stronghold at Dalton, Georgia. The Confederates had been fortifying the mountainous terrrain in front of Dalton since their retreat from Chattanooga the previous November. In order to prevent Lee and Johnston from reinforcing one another, Sherman's move in the West was to begin simultaneously with Grant's advance in the East.[1]

The Eleventh Michigan was part of the Second Brigade (John H. King) of the First Division (Richard Johnson) of the Fourteenth Corps (John Palmer). At the beginning of the campaign the Second Brigade had a total of 2,590 men and officers, and when the Sixty-ninth Ohio returned from veterans leave on May 11, the number rose to 2,937. The Eleventh Michigan was the largest unit in the brigade with sixteen officers and 428 men present. The regiment was carrying six hundred men on its muster books, but many were in hospitals or convalescent camps, and some were detailed for special duty.[2] William Iddings of Company A was detailed as one of General Thomas's highly regarded scouts, and Addison Drake, who was serving as a divisional quartermaster, are examples of this latter group.

On Saturday, May 7, 1864, Sherman's armies began the series of movements which resulted ultimately in the capture of Altanta four months later. The combined forces of the Armies of the Ohio and the Cumberland were to attack the Confederate fortifications in front of Dalton while the Army of the Tennessee under the command of Major General James B. McPherson slipped south through Snake Creek Gap to break the Confederate rail connection at Resaca. This maneuver was designed to force Johnston out of his fortifications at Dalton.

The Eleventh had roll call at 3:30 a.m. on May 7 and marched at sunrise through Ringgold and Tunnel HIll toward the Confederate fortifications on Rocky Face. At the beginning of the march it was easy to tell the new men from the old hands although there was practically no difference in their ages. The recruits had yet to learn the great truth about the backpack: the longer you carry it, the heavier it gets. Many things that were useful and valuable in camp were only weight on the march. At the first rest the overcoats were thrown away. They were after all in Georgia in May. At the second rest several more items would be discovered that were unnecessary. After three hours on the march the road was lined with overcoats, extra blankets, tents, vests and even knapsacks.

The experienced soldier knew how to pack at the beginning of the march, but the new ones caught on fast.

> After the first day's march a soldier's baggage consisted of the following: one rubber poncho, one woolen blanket, one towel, a small piece of soap, and a euchre deck - not even a knapsack in which to carry these things. The rubber poncho, the blanket and the towel were twisted into a rope, the ends tied together, and it was worn over the shoulder and obliquely across the body after the manner of a scarf. The cake of soap was carried in the haversack with the hard tack, and the euchre deck was carried in the side pocket - where it would do the most good in case a bullet should be seeking the region of the heart. Of course, those boys who had any poetry in their souls, and most of us had more or less of it, kept the girl's photograph. This was carried with the euchre deck - somewhat suggestively perhaps, next to the queen of hearts.[3]

The First Division came up to the Confederate defenses along Rocky Face ridge at Buzzard's Roost Gap. This natural cleft in the bare rocky precipice was in more peaceful times the route of the

Chattanooga and Atlanta railroad. However, on May 9, 1864 it was the most heavily defended portion of Johnston's line. He had artillery placed on both sides of the gap and had diverted a small steam to flood the gap itself. The Division was to probe the center of the gap to test the Confederate defenses. When they were about half way across the cleared area in front of the gap, the Confederate artillery began firing on them. At first the shells were going over the advancing Union lines, but it didn't take the artillerymen long to correct their range. In that first brief moment it must have been a thrilling sight for the new men: the long lines of infantry moving forward with their battle flags in front, the white puffs of smoke from the cannons along the top of Rocky Face, the whistle of the shells as they passed overhead, and the explosions far to the rear. But the veterans knew, it was just a matter of time before the shells would start to land among those long marching lines. The new men expected to hear the order to halt and take cover. The old hands knew that the order wouldn't come until Sherman and Thomas were satisfied that the guns had been located. Then and only then were the brigades of the division allowed to split right and left to seek shelter along the base of the cliffs. Now the new men felt safe again because the muzzles of the cannons could not be lowered enough to bring them into range. But they soon found, it was not necessary to lower the muzzles of the cannons. The Confederate gunners put a "squib load" into their pieces. This was just enough powder to light the fuses and push the shells out of the cannons. John Downey was almost indignant when he recalled that "those things dropped right down there where we were stopping."[4] The division was soon called back and, while not out of the range of the artillery, they were no longer in the open. For the next two days the regiment took its turn in the front line under heavy artillery fire. At night they lay in line of battle with all their equipment on. Although Johnston was kept busy with the attack on Dalton, McPherson failed to break the Confederate supply line in Resaca.

The Confederates began to move south to meet the flanking movement at Resaca on May 11. Sherman moved the Fourteenth

Corps through Snake Creek Gap, and the battle begun at Buzzard's Roost and Rocky Face was continued at Resaca. On May 12 the Eleventh moved about fourteen miles to the right, camping in Snake Creek Gap. On May 13 the regiment left their knapsacks under guard and moved toward the fighting. Having lost their "home away from home" once, they were not going to do it again. Rose wrote that they were "keeping nothing for shelter but our rubbers."[5] On the fourteenth, the regiment moved forward to the front line of the battle and received its first casualties of the campaign.

The diary entry of Stephen Marsh gave a tense record of the Eleventh at Resaca.

> 7 get rations, form lines move forward on left wheel one line in front 9 sharp skg [skirmishing] in front one man wounded chance shot 12 ben heavy work some charge drove rebs bak 5 up in site of rebs breast work fire keep us brisk and heavy we keep them down in their works drove them back 2 miles work heavy on their flanks 5 [?] still rages heavy each holds line with desperation keeps up till dark I goe on line from 11 to one[6]

Charles Powers of Company A was the wounded man.[7] On the next day the fighting was heavy. That night Johnston withdrew across the Oostanaula River.

The morning of May 16 the regiment "fell in ready for a fight," but it was "very quiet."[8] At nine o'clock the Fourteenth Corps entered Resaca. The houses, barns, stores, church and other buildings in Resaca were riddled by bullets and artillery shot. The Confederate evacuation was so rapid that the dead were left unburied and "the ghastly, mutilated corpses lay everywere."[9] By ten the railroad cars with supplies and mail were coming into Resaca from Chattanooga. Throughout the campaign Sherman's engineers and pioneer departments kept the railroad repaired and operating throughout the campaign. They rebuilt the burnt railroad bridge across the Oostanaula River in only three days.

The pursuit of the retreating Confederate army began on May 16 with the Fourth Corps (Howard) and the Twentieth Corps (Hooker) of the Army of the Cumberland crossing the Oostanaula River on pontoon bridges.[10] The Fourteenth Corps followed them, keeping close to the railroad route. King's brigade with the Eleventh passed through Calhoun, Adairsville, Kingston, and Cass Station without incident.[11] Daniel Rose was impressed with the countryside. He wrote, "Passed through the best looking and most level country that we have seen since leaving Murfreesboro, Tenn."[12] The next day he added, "Country level and fertile like my own native home. Considerable wheat sown."[13] On the 21st of May the last regimental wagon and team was turned over to the division. Marsh recorded, "send all our trunks to rear and get ready for 20 days hard fiting."[14] On May 25, Hooker's lead division ran into Joe Johnston's army near Dallas, Georgia. Hooker committed his divisions as they came up, and the Battle of New Hope Church was the result. Palmer's corps was in the rear of the Army of the Cumberland and was further delayed on May 26, and it was placed in reserve. As the Eleventh Infantry came up they passed a hospital with the wounded of the Nineteenth Michigan. Daniel Rose found his brother: "Saw Charles. he was wounded in the left hand and had had one finger taken off. Saw several more of the 19th slightly wounded."[15] He wrote to his mother a few days later. "Charles was shot through the left hand and lost his middle finger. It was taken out back to the wrist and the fore and ring finger closed together so it will make quite a shapely three fingered hand. I am very thankful that it is no worse. He is now out of danger for this summer and maybe longer. He will undoubtedly have a chance to come home until he gets well."[16]

On May 27 Sherman attempted to turn the Confederate right flank near Pickett's Mills. The attacking column consisted of Wood's division of the Fourth Corps supported by Johnson's division of the Fourteenth Corps. Major General O.O. Howard reported that the troops of the two divisions were massed to the extreme left and rear of the Twenty-third Corps in a field that was concealed from the enemy by a dense woods. Wood's Division was on the right, formed in a column of six lines deep and Johnson's was on the left with a brigade front. At eleven o'clock in the morning the troops advanced a mile forward in an easterly direction which General Howard thought "must have reached the enemy's flank, whereupon General Wood wheeled his command toward the right till he was facing nearly south."[17] Brigadier General Nathaniel C. McLean's brigade of the Twenty-third Corps was deployed to form a connection with Wood's division. After a short advance through the trees the column came to a cleared field where they could see Confederate trenches in their front. Howard then withdrew the entire attacking force including McLean another mile eastward. He and Wood recconnoitered the area and found "a line of works to our right, but they did not seem to cover General Wood's front and they were new, the enemy still working on them."[18] Howard again massed his troops for the attack but left Johnson's division a little retired on the left. At five o'clock in the afternoon the attack moved forward. Unfortunately, Wood's column still did not overlap the Confederate trenches and soon came under a deadly cross fire.[19] Johnson's leading brigade led by Col. Benjamin F. Scribner was rushed forward to Wood's support only to come into the same deadly cross fire. The union attack was centered on a reentrant angle rather then the end of the Confederate defensive line. The attack was very determined and, in spite of the technical advantages of the defensive position, the Union forces reached within a dozen feet of the Confederate trench before being driven back. Wood's division suffered heavy losses. "The total loss on the Union side was 1,732, of which Wood's share was 1,457, more than 25 percent of the force taken into action."[20]

One of Wood's brigades rallied near the Eleventh and some companies could not muster a dozen men. A captain of one of these regiments remarked that Tennyson's *Light Brigade* never rode into a more terrible gap of death than that one. John Downey saw "one poor fellow . . . coming out of that gap. His whole under jaw was shot off clear back to the throat. The front of his body was completely covered with blood, and his tongue was hanging down and dangling as he walked."[21] The Eleventh was not engaged in the attack and only suffered three wounded.[22] King's brigade must not have been brought forward to support Scribner and Wood. Lieutenant Marsh of Company A recorded the day's action in the following terms: "4:30 firing commence in our front, 5:00 move to front - heavy firing - form line - lie down - get up advance 100 yards - halt. Shell comes thick - goes to work build breast work - lots of wounded - hard fiting till after dark."[23] It was the last day that Colonel William Stoughton commanded the Eleventh. During the battle General Johnson was seriously wounded by a piece of artillery shell, and Brigadier General John H. King assumed command of the division. Stoughton as the ranking officer replaced King in command of the brigade. Captain Patrick Keegan would command the Eleventh until Lieutenant Colonel Melvin Mudge returned from convalescent camp.

After the failure on May 27, Sherman changed his battlefield tactics. With the exception of the frontal assault against the Confederate lines near Kennesaw Mountain on June 27, the massed attack by columns of brigades or demi-brigades was not used by the Union armies in the western theater again. "The usual formation was in two lines, the second only half as strong as the first and kept under cover from fire till the front line needed instant help. Coming up then with a rush, it would sometimes give the advance a new impulse which would carry it to victory."[24] After the Battle of New Hope Church the advanced line on both sides entrenched as soon as possible. Thomas had shown the advantages to be gained from even the crudest defensive works at Chickamauga. The typical method of entrenchment for the Union was described by Jacob Cox.

A division having been moved to a place it was expected to hold, the general in command, by a rapid reconnaissance of the topography, determined the most available line for defense, and directed brigade commanders to form their troops upon it . . .The skirmish line was kept in front, the rest stacked arms a few paces in rear of the intended place for the breastwork, intrenching tools were taken from wagons that accompanied the ammunition train, or were carried by the troops in the movement and each company was ordered to cover its own front. Trees were felled and trimmed, and the logs, often two feet thick, rolled into the earth thrown from the ditch in front varied in thickness according to exposure. When likely to be subjected to artillery fire it was from ten to thirteen feet thick at the base, and three feet less on the upper line of the parapet. Skids or poles, resting on top of the revetment at right angles to it, sustained the head log, a horizontal loophole for firing under it being about three inches wide . . . . As the troops became familar with the work, they were able to cover themselves with an intrenchment of this kind within an hour from the time they stacked arms. [25]

On May 28 Sherman planned a move towards the left by taking troops from the extreme right. The objective of the maneuver was to gain control of the Alatoona Pass and to repair the railroad to that point. However, the constant fighting prevented any movement until June 1. From May 26 to June 5 the Eleventh Michigan occupied the same position and was under constant fire. Dan Rose spent an uncomfortable birthday on May 28. "Lay in the rifle pits all day with skirmish line in front. Had to keep our heads under cover for fear of rebs 'minnies' that came to close for comfort." [26] He was twenty-one years old that day.

The constant firing of the Union and Confederate armies meant that the troops were in continual danger. There was no relief. The minnies were always too close for comfort. A member of Thomas's staff reported that there were "during May and June, a daily averge expenditure of 200,000 rounds of musketry and 1200 cannon-shot; althought for two weeks of that period there was scarely any firing." [27] On the average, the Army of the Cumberland used 94,500 musket rounds daily during the entire campaign. [28] After the Confederates withdrew from the Dalla lines, Marsh recorded that the ground was covered with balls. [29] Rose said that a house near the Confederate line "would equal a sieve for holes." [30]

The constant firing and danger made life miserable but, when the rains began, the Eleventh discovered the real meaning of misery. Rose reported after a heavy rain on June 2, "our works was full of mud and nearly water enough to run a small mill." [31] On the day that the Army of the Ohio charged across Alatoona Creek in "a furious thunderstorm, which made it difficult to distinguish between the discharges of the enemy's artillery at close quarters and the rattling thunder, the Eleventh was shaken when a bolt of lightening hit near their position." [32] On June 3, after more rain, Dan Rose could hardly believe his misfortune. He wrote "Oh! Misery where is thy end." [33]

On June 5 Johnston withdrew to his next fortified line just north of Marietta, Georgia. Rose recorded, "Comparative Joy, Peace and Liberty again. The rain has ceased and the enemy has retreated from our front."[34] That night he was able to wash his clothes for the second time in a month and take a bath. After nine days in the trenches, he needed it.

From June 6 to June 10 the Eleventh was near Big Shanty on the railroad line. Here they rested and drew some new camp equipment.

> "At this point we were made happy by a valuable acquisition, a camp kettle and a supply of beans. The beans were a luxury; for we had eaten nothing but hard-tack and bacon or beef since starting; but the camp kettle rejoiced us even more, and never has a piece of furniture put to more diverse uses than was that camp kettle. Our clothing had become pretty thoroughly infected with certain, from a scientific standpoint interesting, but from our standpoint annoying, zoological specimens, and nothing but boiling would have any effect on these vermin. Our company cook - each man had been doing his own cooking, but a cook was detailed when the beans and the camp kettle were received - was an accommodating man. After making the breakfast coffee for the company in the camp kettle he would let us have it until ten o'clock to cook - our clothing. At that time it had to be returned so that he could cook the beans in it for dinner. After dinner we could use it again for boiling the clothes, but it had to be back at three so that he could cook the beef for supper. We could use it again after supper, but it had to be back to the cook for making the breadfast coffee, and the same way it went through another day"[35]

On June 10 the First Division, with King still in command, moved to the left. After twelve days of marching and skirmishing they reached Kennesaw Mountain, and the brigade with Stoughton commanding relieved the Second Brigade of the First Division of the Fourth Corps in the entrenchments. They stayed in the front line from June 22 until the Confederates retreated on July 3. Most of the time the two opposing lines were not more than a hundred yards apart. It was again a time of constant firing and danger. Rose recorded a close call for the Eleventh and the Second Brigade.

> " . . .About 4 OC pm a detail of 150 men from the front of the brigade detailed to charge the front line of the enemy's works which are only about 15 rods from ours, supposing there was a very light line behind them. After we was drawn up in line behind our works, the rebs hoisted a flag of truce and

firing was stopped and one of their officers (Col. Smith) of their regular army Gen. Clabourne's division, and three of our regular officers met between the works, shook hands and wanted to make arrangements for burying some of their dead that lay in front of our works but come to no conclusion. Their men mounted their works showing as strong a line as we had which put a stop to our comtemplated charge. Luckey for us.[36]

One afternoon during the period in front of Kennesaw Mountain, the Eleventh witnessed a one officer assault on the Confederate fortifications. It happened when Colonel Stoughton was away from the front briefly on brigade business. The officer of the day was one of the regulars, a West Pointer, and he ordered a detail of one man from each company in the brigade to report to his headquarters,

> where he took personal command and proceeded to make them a speech. Said he, 'Now, men, I want you to charge those works. The rebels have all gone 'cept jest a few skirmishers and I want you to march right up and take p'session. 'For'ard - march!' The men, seeing that he was drunk and knowing that rebels had not evacuated, refused to go over the works to be shot down. The officer became very angry, flourished his sword around threateningly, and did some emphatic swearing, closing by saying: 'Jest stay here then, you miserable cowards. Damn'd if I don't charge the works myself!' So with drawn sword, over our works he went. Some rebel saw him and shot at him but, unfortunately, missed him. Dropping on his hands and knees, he crawled along in the underbrush. When he had gone about half way across, he found that more rebels were there than he had counted upon and, fearing that he might not be able to carry the works, decided not to assault.[37]

On June 27 Sherman tried to pierce Johnston's defensive line with two frontal assaults by the Army of the Cumberland. Both were repulsed with heavy losses. The Eleventh lay in readiness to support the charge made by Davis' division of the Fourteenth Corps but was not called on. Years later Captain Borden M. Hicks of Company E recalled this moment.

> Word came to us one morning that a division of the Fourteenth Corps would make a charge on the works of the enemy and try and break through their line of works. Our skirmishers were detailed and reported to Brigade Headquarters and assigned their place in front, and, then we stood and waited nearly all day long for the command to charge, the works in our front were not over four rods apart, and we knew that it meant death to the charging column. It was the most trying day that we experienced in our whole term of

service. Fortunately for us another division made the charge and were badly cut up and defeated as is most always the case in charging fortified positions. [38]

Following the failure of the frontal assaults, Sherman resumed his flanking movement. On the night of July 2 the Eleventh moved to the left and relieved the Thirty-first Iowa Infantry of the Second Brigade, First Division of the Fifteenth Corps. In the morning Dan Rose wrote, "A glorious sight this morning before sunrise our flag floated on top of Kennesaw Mt. the enemy retreated last night."[39]

At 8 o'clock on the morning of July 3 the Eleventh joined in the pursuit of the retreating Confederates, passing through Marietta along the railroad. The brigade with Stoughton in command and the Eleventh in front was leading the division. About four miles south of Marietta the brigade saw Brigadier General King, the division commander and his staff about a hundred yards ahead of them. At this moment a small Confederate cavalry force appeared in the distance and fired an ineffective volley at King before they rode away.

As Stoughton came up General King said, 'I thought other troops were in advance of us.' About this time General Thomas and his staff appeared on the scene. The division commander quickly explained the situation to his chief. 'You are in the advance,' said Thomas, and in his deliberate way added, 'Throw out two or three companies of the 11th Michigan as skirmishers, and continue to push right along as you have been doing. Hooker is on the left and Schofield is on the right. Keep things steadily moving and, if the rebels cause you too much trouble, order up some of the artillery and scrawl the canister to them."[40]

The pursuit continued for another two miles with the troops marching so rapidly that they were keeping up with the skirmish line. When a sudden volley of musketry hit them, the division quickly executed the left front into line. The Confederates had made it to another of Johnston's prepared defensive works. The Union troops immediately dug in and a sharp fire fight began and lasted until dark. That night the brigade moved through the woods in which they had first stopped and constructed another breastworks. As John Downey recalled, "We could easily see that we were preparing for serious business."[41]

The battle of Ruff's Station on July 4, 1864 was to cost the regiment dearly. Even before the order to charge the enemy lines to support the advanced placement of artillery, the regiment lost Colonel Stoughton. The day had opened with heavy shelling from both sides. The Colonel and some other officers rode out to the right and beyond the breastworks to a small rise to reconnoiter. Soon the colonel's orderly came riding back to the line calling for a stretcher. "...Colonel Stoughton is terribly wounded."[42] Young John Downey never forgot "the effect as word passed along the line that our colonel had been wounded. He had led the regiment in many a battle and, by his bravery and his many excellent qualities, he had endeared himself to his men and this was a great shock to them. There were many sad hearts and not a few moist eyes as, a little later, his leg shattered by an exploding shell, he was carried on a stretcher along the regiment, his pale face turned toward his men."[43]

The Eighteenth and Nineteenth United States Infantry and the Eleventh Michigan were ordered over the works to support the artillery. Needless to say, the Confederates opened in a lively manner. When the regiment reached their goal, they found a shallow washed-out ditch and dived into it. John Downey recalled the events that followed.

> ... the command of the regiment [had] devolved upon the major. Now the major was a man who thought a good deal of his personal safety, and wishing, besides, to set a good example to his men to protect themselves, he threw himself at full length into the ditch. He was a tall man and when his great altitude was placed in a horizontal position in the bottom of that ditch, he took up so much room that two other men of our company and myself could not get in. Now I wanted dreadfully to get into that ditch - indeed, I had never before been seized with so all absorbing a desire to get into a ditch as on that occasion; but the major gave no indication of yielding any of the space which he had appropriated. The other two men, after risking themselves a while on the exposed bank, waived the courtesy ordinarily shown to an officer and crowded in on the major's legs. As for myself, ostrich like, I hid behind a little decayed stump which you could easily have kicked over with your foot.[44]

After watching the effect of solid shot on some neighboring stumps, Downey decided that his duty to the company required him to withdraw to the breastworks. He was after all carrying the company axe and shovel.

The Eleventh Michigan suffered severe losses. Colonel Stoughton's right leg was amputated, and Lieutenant Myron Benedict, Company F, lost an arm. The regiment had three killed: William Schochenbarger, Company C; Edwin White, Company F; and Bryon J. Liddle, Company D. There were eleven enlisted men wounded. Dan Rose called it, "the hottest place we have been on the campaign."[45] Stephen Marsh of Company A was so weakened by dysentery that he had followed the regiment in a brigade ambulance. On the fourth of July he wrote, " '11 Infty opens brisk 12 rebs open arty-Strike all around me-have to move-Wm Scocensparcer [sic] killed in Co. C-I am not able to goe up . . ." Later he added, "our regt suffers today . . ."[46] The brigade had fifty casualties in all. [47]

The following day a detail from the Eleventh carried Colonel Stoughton back to Marietta on a litter. Stoughton requested that Quartermaster Sergeant James King stay with him until he was well enough to travel. The rest of the regiment joined in the pursuit of the Confederates. Rose reported that they marched ten miles but were only four miles from where they started. During the day the Eleventh finally saw the objective of the campaign; they were in sight of Atlanta.[48]

On the evening of July 6 the brigade took its place in the lines surrounding the last Confederate fortifications north of the Chattahoochee River. The tension of two months of constant combat began to tell on the Eleventh. Once again the absence of the regimental chaplin, Holmes Pattison, was a serious matter. Many of the men were very religious, but all could have used the steady hand and counsel of their chaplin. Other regimental chaplins comforted the wounded and wrote the final letters for the dying of the Eleventh. For some members of the regiment Pattison's absence forced them to provide for their own spiritual comfort and strength. The result was the formation of at least one prayer circle.

These sixteen men thought that it was important enough to incorporate themselves in some formal manner.

CAMP OF THE 11TH MICH. INFT.
IN THE FIELD GA. JULY 7TH, 1864

To all whom it may concern.

We the undersigned members of the 11th regiment Michigan Volunteer Infantry professing to be followers of our Lord and Saviour Jesus Christ, feeling that it is the duty of all Christians to assemble themselves together often to offer up prayer and thanksgiving to the heavenly father and to encourage and strengthen each other and feeling that it would be for our benefit. We do hereby organize ourselves into a little band, and adopt the following resolutions.

1st Resolved That whereas our chaplin is not with us, we do appoint Brother Chas. Patterson of Co. B as the leader of our band of breathren.

2nd Resolved That we meet for prayer as often as the circumstances will permit as the duties of a campaign make regular meetings uncertain. We will endeavor to meet as often as twice a week and oftener if possible and that we do cordially invite all who love the name of Jesus to join with us in our meetings.

3rd Resolved That we offer our sincere thanks to Almighty God for our preservation through so many firey trails and that we will not cease to praise him for his mercy endureth forever.

Charles Patterson	Co. B.		M. H. Waren [Warren]	Co.	C
B. M. Earl	"	A	G. W. Dickerson	"	A
John Clark	"	A	W. R. Matthew	"	C
C. A. Reed	"	B	F. A. Maltman	"	B
R. C. West	"	B	John F. Downey	"	E
H. S. Danks	"	B	Daniel Moyer	"	E
Jacob Palmer	"	G			
George Dresher	"	E			
John J. Bloom	"	E			

Many of these men were Methodists and this would be in keeping with their form of organization when operating without a minister.[49]

On the July 10 Johnston withdrew across the river, burning the railroad bridge. For the next week the Army of the Cumberland stopped, rested and refitted.[50] After two months of campaigning, the uniforms were in rags. John Downey reported that "an order came for a sergeant and two men to go to the rear and bring up some clothing that was being distributed to the regiments. Visions of new suits floated through our minds and we began to despise the dirty rags we were wearing...We waited very anxiously for return of the men who had gone after the clothing. When they came, they brought with them, for our company, two pairs of socks and one pair of pantaloons."[51]

The Eleventh crossed the Chattahoochee River by a pontoon bridge at 2:00 P.M. on July 17. Many of the original enlistees, who had joined the regiment on August 24, 1861, were counting the final days of their service. For Stephen Marsh it was already the end of active service. Sick and unable to keep up with the regiment, he was finally sent back to the hospital in Chattanooga. The Army of the Cumberland had been forced to wait at the Chattahoochee River while part of the Union army crossed the river farther north and came down to drive the Confederates away from the crossing points. The Second Brigade marched about three miles after crossing the river. Once across the Chattahoochee River, Sherman's army advanced with the Army of the Cumberland on the right. The Army of the Ohio was in the center, and the Army of the Tennessee was on the left. Thomas was to be the anchor on which Sherman's forces would swing left down along the east side of Atlanta. The Army of the Cumberland had the Fourteenth Corp on the right, the Twentieth Corps in the center and the Fourth Corps on the left. On July 18, 1864, the Fourteenth Corps concentrated at the fork of Nancy and Peachtree Creeks and the following day began to cross Peachtree Creek in the face of strong Confederate resistance.[52]

General John B. Hood replaced Johnston as the Confederate commander on July 17. The change resulted in an almost immediate shift in Confederate tactics as Hood moved to the offensive. On July 20 the Confederates assaulted the Union lines along Peachtree Creek with the bulk of the Confederate attack being against the Union left. For the Eleventh Michigan, the Battle of

Peachtree Creek started with a great deal of marching and very little fighting. They were ordered to strike their tents and move to the front at nine P.M. on July 19. After moving two miles to the front, the regiment counter-marched until "we were quite tired and out of patience."[53] The regiment stopped for the night close to where they had started. On the morning of the twentieth the regiment moved to front lines on a different road, crossed Peachtree Creek, and put out skirmishers to drive the Confederate skirmishers back. About noon the Confederate artillery forced them to entrench. Very heavy fighting was heard to the left, and the brigade immediately moved to the rear and then to the left at quick time passing the area of heaviest fighting in front of Hooker's corps. The brigade moved to the front again filling a gap between two divisions of the Fourth Corps. This put the brigade near the extreme left of the Army of the Cumberland. Although the heaviest fighting ceased at dark, skirmishing kept up all night.

The regiment served as the brigade pickets all day and night of July 21. There was little or no fighting during this time although artillery firing was constant. On the morning of July 22 the brigade rejoined their division. The line had been pushed forward and, when the Eleventh went to the front, they were within two miles of Atlanta. The division was under assault throughout July 23. During the early morning hours the Confederates charged the Third Brigade and at 9:00 A.M. charged the Second Brigade. The picket line of the Second Brigade was driven in, but as Dan Rose wrote, "the line was soon established in its former position."[54] The Eleventh had two men wounded in the fighting. Addison McCombs of Company G was seriously wounded and died. James Long of Company F was slightly wounded and would later serve in the reorganized Eleventh Michigan.

July 23 was a memorable day for the regiment. Henry Damon, who had been captured at Chickamauga, returned to Company A after escaping from Andersonville Prison. Damon had been taken prisoner at Chickamauga on September 20, 1863, when he had carried his wounded tentmate back to a log house where the wounded were being cared for during the fighting on Snodgrass Hill. It was dusk and Lieutenant Marsh told Damon to stay and help the wounded. When the regiment withdrew after dark, he and the wounded were forgotten. After an unsuccessful escape attempt from the prison at Danville, Virginia, he was transferred to Andersonville. Damon escaped by getting a rebel uniform and, when the guard detail came to take roll in his hut, he simply stood up, took out a notebook and joined the detail. This was on the evening of June 28. Once outside the walls he joined another escaping prisoner, William Smith, of the Fourteenth Pennsylvania Cavalry. The two of them entered Marietta, Georgia, on July 20.[55]

From July 24 to July 27 the fighting died down to siege warfare. Everyone took his turn as picket, skirmisher, and reserve. Rose recorded an incident of these days, "Last night at 10 oc the bugles sounded the assembly then the forward call and we rose up in our works and got up a yell like a charge. At the same time the skirmishers fired a volley and kept up their fire for some time. The rebs opened with some of their batteries and we answered. It was done to develope the positions of their batteries. About 11 oc quiet was restored and we lay down to sleep."[56] Yet men were wounded and killed; it was not a play. Lyman Evans of Company D was wounded on July 26.

In the latter days of July 1864 one of the most bizarre incidents in the history of the Eleventh Michigan occurred. When the regiment was being raised in August of 1861, two boyhood friends joined. James King entered the service as a private in Company A, and Charles Rice joined the regimental band. In July of 1862 Rice was discharged for a disability, and soon after this all regimental bands were mustered out of the service. He reentered the service a year later as a member of the band for the First Brigade, Third Division, Fourteenth Army Corps. In the fall of 1863 that band was transferred to the Second Brigade, and the old friends were reunited.

On July 26 the band made camp about a half mile behind the front line. They had just finished eating supper when a stray rifle bullet from the Confederate line struck Charles Rice in the back below the shoulder blade. The bullet passed through his lung and finally stopped between his body and undershirt. The next morning, King heard of his friend's wound and went to the band's camp. When Rice tried to speak, his mouth filled with blood. The surgeon told King that it was hopeless and that the wound was mortal. He returned to his front lines believing that his friend would soon die. When Rice did not die, he was sent back to the hospital at Vining's Station and then to the general hospital in Kingston.

James King returned to the regiment only to have his shoulder broken by a large shell fragment on July 30. He was sent back to Vining's Station and then to Chattanooga. After a short time in the hospital, he was released to the care of Addison Drake, the Quartermaster of the Eleventh Michigan, who was still in the city on detached duty. King recounted the remainder of the story in a piece he titled "Stranger than Romance."

> One day a desire seized [King] to visit the Chattanooga and Atlanta depot. Upon reaching the building, while walking along the platform, a freight train rolled in and came to a stop. A skelton of a soldier came tottering from that car and said, 'Jim, I knew if I could find you, I would be taken care of." The reply was: 'Why, Charley, where did you come from.' The answer was: 'I ran away from that hell of a general hospital at Kingston.' His story in brief was this: The night before, about nine o'clock, he overheard a conversation between two assistant surgeons, and one of them alluding to him by name said, 'He will not live until morning, and I am going to cut him open and find out just the course of that ball was and the effect it had on the lungs.' The hospital tent was close to the railroad platform, and the wounded and almost dying comrade, summing all of the strength and will power at his command rolled himself from under the flap of the tent, onto the railroad platform, and from there into a box car, and soon it was coupled onto a train and fortunately brought to Chattanooga. He was so feeble that he could stand but a moment without support. His friend [King] borrowed a couple of blankets from soldiers nearby and procured an ambulance and carried him to the quarters of his officer friend, Quartermaster A. T. Drake.

After a few days with Drake, Rice was taken to one of the Chattanooga hospitals. A friendly surgeon arranged for his transfer and Rice was no longer listed as deserter. He served for the rest of the war in the invalid corps at Jeffersonville, Indiana. Both King and Rice died in 1903.[57]

Sherman began to move his army around to the right of Atlanta on July 27. The Army of the Tennessee moved from the extreme left that day. As each unit passed to the rear of the Army of the Cumberland, the skirmishers would advance their lines as close to the Confederates trenches as possible and then fall back. It took two days for the Army of the Tennessee to accomplish this maneuver. On July 26, George Dickinson of Company A was wounded in the demonstration to protect the movement to the right. Hood attacked the Federal army at Ezra Church on July 28 when the leading corps of the Army of Tennessee came around the Fourteenth Corps. No units of the Fourteenth were engaged at the Battle of Ezra Church.[58]

On August 2 the Army of the Ohio passed around the Army of the Cumberland. The following day Johnton's division of the Fourteenth moved to the extreme right of the Union army and went into the front in the area of Utoy Creek. On August 7 Sherman advanced the Twenty-third and the Fourteenth Corps against the Confederate entrenchments. Cox said of this action that the troops met "opposition which General Sherman described in his despatches to Washington as a noisy but not a bloody battle."[59] For the Eleventh Michigan, however, it was the bloodiest day of the entire Atlanta campaign.

The position of the brigade on August 7 was along a low ridge that curved away from the Confederates. In front of the Union breastworks open ground descended to a small creek and then rose to a woods. The first line of enemy entrenchments was along the edge of the woods. The men could see in places a second line of trenches farther back in the woods. The object of the assault was the first line. Everything about that day and the next three were etched forever on the memory of young John Downey. He recalled that "the 7th of August was a warm and sultry day, the sun pouring down his heat to an almost insufferable degree. All nature seemed to droop beneath his power. The leaves upon the trees were almost motionless, so little air was there astir."[60] About three o'clock in the afternoon, a messenger rode up to Lt. Colonel Melvin Mudge, commanding the brigade. Soon orderlies were rushing to the various regimental commanders with orders for the assault.

The Eighteenth Regular Infantry advanced as skirmishers followed by the Fifteenth Regulars on the left. The post assigned to the Eleventh Michigan was on the right, but they were not coming out of the trenches. When the order to fall in was given, "then we well knew what was to come. Our boys dreaded it worse than any duty that had ever been assigned them. The reason was plain: this was on the 7th of August, and the regiment's time would expire on the 24th of the same month . . . and now, when they had only seventeen days more to serve to complete their three years, to be thrown against the enemy's fortified lines seemed too cruel. Many of them said they would not go and a mutiny seemed imminent."[61]

It was then that Lt. Colonel Melvin Mudge did his noblest work of the war. It was remembered by many, but most graphically recalled by John Downey. Mudge drew his sword and mounted the breastworks in plain sight of the enemy marksmen to address the regiment.

He said: 'Men, you have always done well. For almost three years you have stood nobly at your posts and have performed every duty that has been required of you. Yonder are the rebels. You are again called on to meet them in battle. The regulars on your left have already gone and there they are, nobly struglling with the foe. Do you see that gap to their right? Do as well as they are doing; go as far as they have gone - Aye, and go farther. Let not a man shirk from duty.' General King, riding along the line, commands, "Move right forward, every man!' Then our Lieutenant Colonel commands, "Eleventh Michigan - forward - double time - guide center - march!' And the Eleventh Michigan did forward. It was like an electric thrill. With one impulse every man leaped the works. See them now pressing through that open field, undauntedly following their loved flag. Immediately clouds of smoke rise from the edge of the woods in front. The break forth the thundering roar of artillery and the deafening rattle of musketry. They are greeted with round after round of shell, which come screeching and crashing through the lines, and volley after volley of musketry, thinning their ranks . . . They charged with heoric determination up to the works - beyond the works - and killed, captured or drove back to the second line the rebels who occupied them.[62]

However, the line of fortifiations faced the wrong way and only a shallow ditch protected the brigade from the fire of the Confederates, but having gone that far the Eleventh was not going to surrender their ditch. At one point it looked as if the rebels were going to attempt to win back the line with a bayonet charge. "They climb their breast-works and form a long, grim line in front. Our men have loaded their pieces and are saving their fire until they shall come close. The command, 'Charge! Charge!' sounds along the enemy's lines and reverberates through the woods. But, ah! they do not charge. Too well the men knew what would be the result . . . . Again and again the officers try to urge them forward."[63] That night the brigade dug in and changed the direction of the breastworks.

The brigade losses in this fight were four officers wounded, twenty-two enlisted men killed and another 146 wounded and seven missing.[64] For the Eleventh it was fifteen killed and fifteen wounded.[65] Lieutenant Edward Catlin, commanding Company H, soon died of his wounds. He was a veteran of the First Michigan during the three months service and had been in the First Battle of Bull Run. The Eleventh had three more men wounded on August 8 when the Confederates tried to retake their former position.[66] At least two of the missing, Daniel Baldwin and George Quay, were from the Eleventh as their bodies were found a few days later.[67]

When the brigade took the first line of Confederate defenses, they actually overran it and several men were wounded in the attack on the second line. One of these was a Company I man, probably George W. Lockwood. When the regiment fell back to the captured breastwork, the Company I man was left behind. During night everyone was so busy turning the breastwork towards the Confederates that no one went out to get him and during the day the position was much too exposed. So the Company I man lay where he fell in the hot August sun from Sunday until Wednesday. Just before daybreak on August 10 the regiment was relieved to go back to the original line from which they had charged to cook a hot breakfast and sleep out of the direct line of fire. John Downey wrote,

"When daylight came, we built fires and began preparing our breakfasts. Then we were not only astounded but terrified to see this Company I man, who had been shot on Sunday and had lain on the field until now, coming toward us. His eyes were sunken far back in his head, his cheeks were hallow, the ghastly palor of death was upon his face, and he was so weak that he reeled and staggered as he walked. A dead man from the grave could not have startled us more. We found that he had first received a flesh wound in the neck, that a bullet had then gone in at his mouth and come out at the back of his head, causing him to fall instantly and rendering him motionless and unconcious, and after he had fallen one of those large, wicked minnie balls had plowed lengthwise down his back, laying open a gash more than a foot long. All this time, in the hot August weather, he had lain there on the field, his wounds undressed and exposed. The condition of those wounds was simply appalling. One from the abode of the damned could not have suffered tortures more horrible or more revolting. If fell to my lot to help strip off his clothes and hold him while the regimental surgeon applied disinfectants to those sickening wounds. The sight not only nauseated, but so shocked me that I was in a highly wrought nervous state for several days."[68]

The brigade remained in the position of August 7 until the army began the movement towards Jonesborough. The time of the Eleventh was running out, yet each day in the trenches men were killed and wounded. On August 19 the regiment came off the front lines and moved to the concentration area for the move to Jonesborough. Dan Rose recorded on August 23, "This completes my term of three years service for the U.S. in the army as I was mustered in August 24th, 1861 and still there is no order to be sent back. We consider that we have done our duty to our country."[69] On August 25 there was a mutiny in the regiment. That day the regiment was ordered to go on the front line, " . . . some few bolted and wouldn't go. The rest went on the line."[70] Captain Borden M. Hicks recalled in later years, "I at once made up my mind that I would refuse to go on that detail, as the term of our service was up, and it meant sure capture of the skirmish line . . . "[71] On August 26 Rose was complaining, "on the line doing extra duty for 'Uncle Sam' after our time is out just on account of some miserable officers. With the hot sun pouring down on us and shells whizzing over our heads."[72]

On August 27 orders finally came that relieved the Eleventh from duty. The regiment had lain all day under orders to fight or to move to the right. According to Dan Rose their release was due to the efforts of Captain Ephraim Hall of the Eleventh who was serving as the Acting Assistant Adjutant General, Second Brigade. "At night brought us the glad tidings that we was releived from duty in the department then there was some lighter hearts."[73]

On August 29 the Eleventh Michigan slept in a railroad depot at Chattanooga. Along the way they had picked up their sick, wounded and detailed men. Rose reported that Company A had increased from twenty-three men on the line at Atlanta to forty-five men in Chattanooga. On the last day at the front Company A had had only thirteen privates for duty.[74]

Notes

1. Jacob D. Cox, *Atlanta*, (New York: Charles Scibner's Sons, 1882), p.25; William T. Sherman, *Memoirs of General William T. Sherman*, with forward by B. H. Liddell-Hart, 2 Vols. (Bloomington: Indiana University Press, 1951), 2:23.

2. O. R.., Vol. 38, pt. 1, p. 560.

3. Atlanta Campaign, Downey Papers, p. 7.

4. Atlanta Campaign, Downey Papers, p 10.

5. Rose Diary, 13 May 1864.

6. Marsh Diary, 14 May 1864.

7. Rose Diary, 14 May 1864.

8. Ibid., 16 May 1864.

9. Atlanta Campaign, Downey Papers, p. 16.

10. O.R., 38, pt. 1, p. 142.

11. O. R., 38, pt. 1, p. 560.

12. Ibid, 17 May 1864.

13. Ibid, 18 May 1864.

14. Marsh Diary, 21 May 1864.

15. Rose Diary, 26 May 1864.

16. Rose Letters, 30 May 1864.

17. O. R., Vol. 38, pt. 1, p. 194.

18. Ibid.

19. O. R., Vol. 38, pt. 1, pp. 194-195, 595, 886.

20. Henry Stone, "Part IV: Strategy of the Campaign," in Sydney C. Kerksis comp., *The Atlanta Papers* (Dayton, Ohio: Morningside Bookshop, 1980), p. 412.

21. Atlanta Campaign, Downey Papers, p. 21.

22. Marsh Diary, 27 May 1864. Details of this action can be found in O. R., 38, pt. 1, pp. 193-194, 864-866, 594-595.

23. March Diary, 27 May 1864.

24. Cox, *Atlanta*, p. 81.

25. Ibid., P. 82.

26. Rose Diary, 8 May 1864.

27. Stone, *Strategy*, p. 83.

28. Ibid.

29. Marsh Diary, 5 June 1864.

30. Rose Diary, 5 June 1864.

31. Ibid., 2 June 1864.

32. Cox, *Atlanta*, p. 89.

33. Rose Diary, 3 June 1864.

34. Ibid., 24 June 1864.

35. Atlanta Campaign, Downey Papers, pp. 31-32.

36. Rose Diary, 24 June 1864.

37. Atlanta Campaign, Downey Papers, pp. 30.

38. Hicks, Personal Recollections, p. 539-540.

39. Rose Diary, 3 July 1864.

40. Michigan In The War, p. 321. James W. King reported this story to Robertson, King was present at the time with Stoughton.

41. Atlanta Campaign, Downey Papers, p. 42.

42. Ibid.

43. Ibid.

44. Ibid., pp. 43-44.

45. Ibid., 4 July 1864.

46. Marsh Diary, 4 July 1864.

47. O. R., 38, pt. 1, p. 561.

48. Rose Diary, 5 July 1864; Marsh Diary, 6 July 1864.

49. Downey Papers, 7 July 1864. This is a hand written, two page document. In the table of contents to his much longer paper on the Atlanta Campaign, Downey included the title, "Sweet Hour of Prayer," The chronology of the paper would indicate that it should be just before the Battle of Ruff's Station on July 4, 1864. However, John Downey did not deal with the prayer group in that paper. There were other items listed in the table of contents that also were not in the paper.

50. Rose Diary, 10-17 July 1864; O. R., Vol. 38, pt. 5, p. 507.

51. Atlanta Campaign, Downey Papers, pp. 32-33.

52. O. R., Vol. 38, pt. 5, p. 507.

53. Rose Diary, 19 July 1864.

54. Ibid., 23 July 1864.

55. James W. King, "Reminiscence of Army Life," James W. King Papers, Regional History Collections, Western Michigan University, Kalamazoo, n.d.

56. Rose Diary, 25 July 1864.

57. "Stranger than Romance", King Papers, This is an undated, hand written document that was written around the time of Charles Rice's death on March 13, 1903. Addison Drake must have returned to Chattanogo.

58. O. R., 38, pt. 1, p. 508.

59. Cox, *Atlanta*, p. 194.

60. Atlanta Campaign, Downey Papers, p. 57.

61. Ibid., p. 58.

62. Ibid., pp. 59-60.

63. Ibid., p. 60.

64. O. R., 38, pt. 1, p. 563.

65. *Regimental Service Records*, Eleventh Michigan Infantry, Michigan State Record Center, Lansing, Michigan.

66. Rose Diary, 8 August 1864.

67. Ibid., 11 August 1864.

68. "Atlanta Campaign and The Spectre Guide," Downey Papers. Lockwood died of his wounds on 23 August 1864.

69. Rose Diary, 23 August 1864.

70. Ibid., 25 August 1864.

71. Hicks, Personal Recollections, p. 542.

72. Rose Diary, 26 August 1864.

73. Ibid., 27 August 1864.

74. Rose Diary, 30 August 1864.

Chapter Twenty

"No money consideration could buy my experience during that term of service, and no amount of money would induce me to again undergo it."

And so they came out of Georgia, out of the war. The regiment left Marietta, Georgia, on August 29, riding in and on boxcars that were returning to Chattanooga for more supplies. Lt. Colonel Melvin Mudge had tried to get the regiment mustered out as early as August 3. This request was forwarded through the chain-of-command of the army but was disapproved. In his request, Mudge pointed out that seven of the ten companies of the regiment were mustered on August 24, 1861, and the last company joined on September 11, 1861. Written on the bottom of the request in an unidentified hand was "Sept. 10." According to army regulations, a regiment's term of service was not complete until the last company's time was served. The refusal of the men to go forward when their time had expired probably hastened their departure from the Atlanta front.[1]

The Eleventh's relief from active duty was rather short. They arrived in Chattanooga at 4:00 A.M. on August 30 and left at 7:30 A.M. Setpember 1, as part of a force that was organized to catch General Joseph Wheeler and his cavalry. Wheeler had been sent by Hood early in August to strike at Sherman's long railroad supply line. The Confederate cavalry had created a great alarm in eastern Tennessee, but very little real disruption in the supply system. Both Rose and Bloom in their diaries say the regiment volunteered to go to eastern Tennessee.[2] Hicks pointed out that Wheeler was threatening "the only line of road that we could take to get home, our boys went willingly, as this was fighting for our homes or at least for a way to get there."[3]

The Eleventh spent their last two weeks of service as they had spent so many months at the beginning, in the hopeless pursuit of cavalry by rail and foot. The force was organized into three brigades. The Eleventh was part of the First Brigade along with the Fifty-first Indiana, the Fourteenth U.S. Colored, and the Second Ohio with Colonel Abel D. Streight commanding. Their old friends, the Eighteenth Ohio Infantry, were part of the Second Brigade.[4] On the first day the troops went from Chattanooga to Murfreesboro with stops at Bridgeport, Stevenson, and Deckert.[5] The Eleventh must have felt as if they were home. They camped that night in Fort Rosecrans.

On the following day the chase began. The troops marched to Lavergne before noon and seven miles back toward Murfreesboro. On the third they got sight of the Confederates, and on the fourth the Confederates fired at the Federal skirmishers. On September 6, the troops boarded the trains and roamed around eastern Tennessee for two days, finally arriving at Athens in the afternoon of the seventh. The infantry marched for the next three days. On September 9, they caught Wheeler's rear guard and there was a skirmish.[6] On the tenth the troops went into camp and did some heavy foraging "from the rebel citizens of the country."[7] Rose recorded, "Lay in camp all day. Being nearly out of rations we had to forage our living. Sweet potatoes, chickens, hogs and other things in proportion had to suffer accordingly."[8] However, John Bloom's company must not have done so well as he said on the eleventh that they had "nothing to eat, only apels and peaches. - pordy near starve to death."[9] On September 13 the regiment arrived back in Chattanooga.[10]

Rose had noted on September 10 that the "last company's time expired today."[11] The war was over for the Michigan Eleventh; all that remained was getting home. On the thirteenth, Lt. Colonel Mudge had to return to Atlanta, as Dan Rose said, "to do business that should have been done two weeks before but I won't blame him. It is the best he knows."[12] The regiment left Chattanooga on September 18 for Nashville. After a two-day wait they were transported to Louisville.

On September 22, the men visited their old Colonel, William May, and then crossed the Ohio River by ferry. They were headed north towards Indianapolis by sundown. From Indianapolis they went east to Sidney, Ohio, for their last fight. The regiment arrived in Sidney in the morning and had to wait for a train headed north.

When the Eleventh arrived in Sidney, it was obvious that some big event was planned. The local Republican newspaper editor came to the station to organize a meal for the troops and talk to the men. He informed the members of the regiment that Clement L. Vallandingham was to arrive on the next train from Cincinnati to speak to a Democratic Party rally for George B. McClellan. The editor encouraged the boys to give "three cheers for Lincoln."[13] He then left the depot to organize lunch for the regiment.

Daniel Rose recorded the event. "We arrived in Sidney about noon, dismounted and saw Old Traitor Vallandingham ride past. We gave him three hearty groans and secart [sic] his team. Then captured a small cannon that was fired for a salute for him. Received dinner from the Loyal young ladies of S. Changed cars and resumed our journey to the north taking our gun with us."[14] The cannon was used to fire salutes to members of the Eleventh at their weddings and reunions "until it was bursted by an overcharge of gravel."[15]

In Toledo, Ohio, the regiment moved from boxcars to coaches for the final leg home. They arrived in Sturgis at sunrise on September 25, 1864. Their first act was to march directly to Colonel Stoughton's home to pay their respect to the man who had led them through the great battles. By afternoon people were coming from all over the county. On the following day, many of the regiment attended a "Grand Republican Rally" at White Pigeon, where Stoughton and many others spoke.[16] After the Republican meeting, some of the Eleventh "cleaned out a Vallandinghamites shows."[17] Many of "the boys" had been waiting for such an opportunity for two years.

On September 27, 1864, the regiment was given a reception in Sturgis with dinner and speeches by the local dignitaries. They in turn drilled and performed the manual of arms. The troops later turned in their weapons and received a ten day furlough until they could be mustered out. Then it was off to home to be welcomed by family and friends and begin the process of relearning civilian life.

When the regiment reassembled on October 7, the discharges and pay were still not ready, and the men were sent home again. On October 13 the regiment was finally paid and discharged. Rose noted that the discharges were dated September 13, 1864.[18] "Of the 1004 men who left the redezvoud [sic] at White Pigeon in 1861 there were 340 mustered at the end of three years."[19]

Forty-six years after enlisting, Borden M. Hicks probably summed up the feeling of most men of the Eleventh Michigan Volunteer Infantry. "No money consideration could buy my experience during that term of service, and no amount of money would induce me to again undergo it."[20]

Notes

1. Regimental Papers, Arranged by Year, Month, and Date, Michigan Eleventh Infantry, Record Group 94, Box 1999, National Archives, Washington, D.C.

2. Rose Diary, 1 September 1864; Bloom Diary, 1 September 1864.

3. Hicks, Personal Recollections, p. 542.

4. O. R., Vol. 38, pt. 1, p. 856.

5. Ibid., p. 855. Also Rose Diary, 1 September 1864.

6. O. R., Vol. 38, pt. 1, p. 855; Rose Diary, 1-9 September 1864; Bloom Diary, 1-9 September 1864.

7. Ibid., p. 856.

8. Rose Diary, 10 September 1864.

9. Bloom Diary, 11 September 1864.

10. Ibid., 13 September 1864.

11. Rose Diary, 10 September 1864.

12. Ibid.,. 13 September 1864.

13. "Democratic Meeting," Sidney Journal, (Sidney, Ohio), 30 September 1864.

14. Rose Diary, 24 September 1864.

15. Hicks, Personal Recollections, p. 542.

16. Three Rivers Reporter, 1 October 1864.

17. Rose Diary, 26 September 1864.

18. Ibid., 13 October 1864.

19. James W. King, "The Eleventh Michigan Infantry," King Papers, Item #203. Regional History Collection, Western Michigan University, Kalamazoo, Michigan, n.d.

20. Hicks, Personal Recollections, p. 544.

Bibliography

I. Published Primary Sources

Beatty, John. *Memoirs of a Volunteer, 1861-1863.* Edited by S. Ford. New York: W. W. Norton, 1946.

Bierce, Ambrose. *Ambrose Bierce's Civil War.* Edited by WilliamMcCann. Chicago: Gateway, 1956.

Byrd, Cecil K., ed. "Journal of Israel Cogshall, 1861-1863." *Indiana Magazine of History,* vol. 42, no. 1, March, 1946.

Fullerton, Joseph S. "The Army of the Cumberland." *Battles and Leaders of the Civil War.* 4 vols. New York: The Century Co., 1884; reprint ed., New York: Castle Books, 1956.

Hicks, Borden M. "Personal Recollections of the War of the Rebellion." *Glimpses of the Nation's Struggle.* Sixth Series, Papers Read Before the Minnesota Commandery of the Military Order of the Loyal Legion of the United States. Minneapolis, Minn.: Aug. Davis, 1909.

Long, E. B., ed. *Personal Memoirs of U. S. Grant.* New York: Grossett Dunlap, 1962.

Richardson, James D., ed. *Compilation of the Messages and Papers of the Presidents: 1789-1897.* 10 vols. New York: Johnson Reprint Corp., 1969.

Robertson, John, ed. *Michigan in the War.* Lansing: W. S. George and Co., 1882.

Sherman, William T. *Memoirs of General William T. Sherman.* Foreward by B. H. Liddell-Hart. Bloomington: Indiana University Press, 1951.

U. S. Congress. Joint Committee on the Conduct of the War. *Report of Major General George H. Thomas.* Washington, D. C.: 1866; reprint ed., Millwood, N.Y.: Kraus Reprint, 1977.

U. S. *War Department. War of the Rebellion: Official Records of the Union and Confederate Armies.* Series One, 69 vols. and index. Washington, D. C.: Government Printing Office, 1880-1902.

Weber, Daniel B., ed. *Diary of Ira Gillaspie of the Eleventh Michigan Infantry.* Mt. Pleasant, Michigan: Central Michigan University Press, 1965.

_____. *Record of Service of Michigan Volunteers in the Civil War, 1861-1865: Eleventh Infantry.* Kalamazoo, Michigan: Ihling Bros. and Everard, n.d.

_____. *Record of Service of Michigan Volunteers in the Civil War, 1861-1865: First Light Artillery.* Kalamazoo, Michigan: Ihling Bros. and Everard.

_____. *Report of the Adjutant General of the State of Indiana.* Vol. 3. Indianapolis: Samuel H. Douglas, 1866.

_____. *Annual Report of the President and Directors of the Southern Michigan and Northern Indiana Railroad Co., March 1, 1861.* New York: W. H. Arthur and Co., 1861.

Manuscript Collections

Ann Arbor, Michigan. University of Michigan. Bently Historical Library. Michigan Historical Collection.

Centreville, Michigan. L. W. Thornton. Daniel Devine Rose Papers.

Detroit, Michigan. Detroit Public Library. Burton Historical Collection. Charles Lanman Papers.

Kalamazoo, Michigan. Western Michigan University. Regional History Collections.

Kalamazoo, Michigan. Kalamazoo Museum. Regimental Reunion Records, 11th Michigan Infantry.

Lansing, Michigan. State Archives of Michigan. Records of the Michigan Military Establishment.

Minneapolis, Minnesota. University of Minnesota Archives. John Florian Downey Papers.

Springfield, Illinois. Illinois State Historical Library.

Three Rivers, Michigan. Mrs. Elizabeth Ulrich, Diary of Issac F. Ulrich.

Three Rivers, Michigan. Mr. and Mrs. David Collins. Diary of John J. Bloom.

Vicksburg, Michigan. Stewart Talbot. Diary of Duncan Stewart, Company E, Eleventh Michigan Infantry.

Washington, D. C. National Archives. Record Group 94, Box 1999. Regimental Papers. Michigan Eleventh Infantry.

Washington, D. C. Library of Congress. Papers of Bishop Matthew Simpson, Box 7.

III. Secondary Sources

Adams, George Worthington. *Doctors in Blue*. New York: Henry Schuman, 1952.

Belknap, Charles E. *The History of the Michigan Organizations at Chickamauga, Chattanooga, and Missionary Ridge*. Lansing, Michigan: R. Smith Printing Co., 1987.

Catton, Bruce. *Never Call Retreat*. New York: Doubleday, 1965.

Cleaves, Freeman. *Rock of Chickamauga: The Life of General George H. Thomas*. Norman, Oklahoma: University of Oklahoma Press, 1948.

Cox, Jacob D. *Atlanta*. New York: Charles Scribner's Sons, 1882.

Duke, Basil W. *A History of Morgan's Cavalry*. Bloomington: Indiana University Press, 1960.

Genco, James G. *To the Sound of Musketry and the Tap of Drum: A History of Michigan's Battery D Through the Letters of Artificier Harold J. Bartlett, 1861-1864*. Rochester, Michigan: Ray Russell Books, 1983.

Hayne, J. Henry, ed. *The Nineteenth Illinois*. Chicago: M. A. Donohoe & Co., 1912.

Hesseltine, William B. *Lincoln and the War Governors*. New York Alfred A. Knopf, 1948.

Horn, Stanley F. *The Army of Tennessee*. Norman, Oklahoma: University of Oklahoma Press, 1952.

Knapp, John I. and Bonner, R. I. *Illustrated History and Biographical Record of Lenawee County, Michigan*. Adrian, Michigan: The Times Printing Co., 1903.

Lamers, William M. *The Edge of Glory: A Biography of General William S. Rosecrans, U.S.A.* New York: Harcourt, Brace and World, 1961.

Lanman, Charles. *Red Book of Michigan.* Detroit: E. B. Smith and Co., 1871.

Mann, Wayne C. "The Road to Murfreesboro: The Eleventh Michigan Volunteer Infantry from Organization Through its First Battle." Masters Thesis, Western Michigan University, 1963.

McDonough, James Lee. *Stones River: Bloodly Winter in Tennessee.* Knoxville: University of Tennessee Press, 1980.

McElroy, Joseph C. *Record of the Ohio Chickamauga and Chattanooga National Park Commission.* Cincinnati: Earhart & Richardson, 1896.

McKinney, Francis F. *Education in Violence: The Life of George H. Thomas and The History of the Army of the Cumberland.* Detroit: Wayne State University Press, 1961.

Meneely, A. Howard. *The War Department, 1861: A Study in Mobilization and Administration.* New York: Privately printed, 1928.

Millbrook, Minnie Dubbs. *A Study in Valor: Michigan Medal of Honor Winners in the Civil War.* Lansing: Michigan Civil War Centennial Commission, 1966.

Rappaport, Armin. "The Replacement System during the Civil War." *Military Analysis of the Civil War.* ed. by the Editors of Military Affairs. Millwood, N.Y.: KTO Press, 1977.

Shannon, Fred Albert. *The Organization and Administration of the Union Army, 1862-1865.* 2 vols. Reprint. Gloucester, Mass.: Peter Smith, 1965.

Stone, Henry. "Part IV: Strategy of the Campaign." *The Atlanta Papers.* Edited by Sydney C. Kerksis. Dayton, Ohio: Morning-side Bookshop, 1980.

Tucker, Glenn. Chickamauga: *Bloody Battle in the West.* Dayton, Ohio: Morningside Bookshop, 1976.

Tucker, Glenn. *The Battles for Chattanooga.* Philadelphia: Eastern Acorn Press, 1981.

Vance, Wilson J. *Stone's River: The Turning Point of the Civil War.* West Orange, New Jersey: Albert Saiffer Publisher, 1914.

Warner, Ezra J. *Generals in Blue: Lives of the Union Commanders.* Baton Rough: Louisiana State University Press, 1964.

Weigley, Russel F. *History of the United States Army.* Bloomington: Indiana University Press, 1984.

Wells, Clayton. *My Father, Benjamin F. Wells.* Ann Arbor, Michigan: The Alumni Press, 1929.

_____. *History of Branch County, Michigan.* Philadelphia: Everts and Abbott, 1879.

_____. *History of St. Joseph County, Michigan.* Philadelphia: L. H. Everts and Co., 1877.

Newspapers

Adrian (Michigan) *Daily Expositor.*

Coldwater, (Michigan) *Republican.*

Constantine, (Michigan) *The Weekly Mercury and St. Joseph County Advertiser.*

Detroit, (Michigan) *Daily Advertizer.*

Detroit, (Michigan) *Daily Tribune.*

Detroit, (Michigan) *Free Press.*

Hudson (Michigan) *Gazette.*

Lansing (Michigan) *State Republican.*

Monroe (Michigan) *Commercial.*

New York *Tribune.*

Sidney (Ohio) *Journal.*

Sturgis (Michigan) *Journal.*

Three Rivers (Michigan) *Reporter.*

Three Rivers, (Michigan) *Western Chronicle.*

Index

When Gallantry Was Commonplace

Ohio Volunteer Infantry, Twenty-
    first 183

Palmer, John M. 113, 130, 138,
    168, 174, 198, 208, 217, 221
Paris (Kentucky) 98-101
Parkhurst, John G. 208
Parkville (Michigan) 13, 35
Patten, Henry 81
Pattison, Holmes 24-25, 204-205,
    229
Pemberton, John 119
Perryville, Battle of 111, 117
Philippine Islands 206
Phillips, William W. 40, 71, 84
Pickett's Mills 221-223
Pioneer Brigade (Battle of Stones
    River) 120, 122, 133-134
Platt, Henry 36, 49, 61, 100, 107
Polk, Leonidas 119, 162
Prayer circle 229-230
Pup tents 145

Quincy (Michigan) 17, 34
Raffen, Alexander W. 179, 210
Reed, T. Buchanan 148
Reissdorff, Benjamin 72
Resaca, Battle of 219-220
Rice, Charles 71, 233-234
Richards, Mark 147
Robert, George 122, 128
Robertson, John 7-12, 23, 34, 41,
    51-52, 84-85
Rome (Indiana) 47
Rose, Daniel D.V. 48, 51, 53, 63,
    67-70, 94, 117, 119-120,
    141, 145-148, 152, 155-156,
    159-160, 163-164, 185, 189,
    191-192, 194-196, 199, 206-
    212, 220-221, 224-227, 229,
    232-233, 238-239, 245-248
Rosecrans, William S. 117-120,
    127-128, 133, 137-138, 145,
    151-153, 155-156, 161, 167-
    169, 171-172, 176-177, 190-
    191

Rossetter, John O. 208
Rossville (Georgia) 228
Rosseau, Lovell H. 110, 120-122,
    129-132, 141
Ruff's Station (Georgia) 228

Schochenbarger, William 228
Schoolcraft (Michigan) 39
Scribner, Benjamin F. 222
Scott, Joseph 138-139
Scott, Winfield 49
Sheridan, Philip 122, 128, 130,
    154, 184, 195
Sherman, William T. 153, 190,
    193-196, 217-221, 223-224,
    226-227, 235
Shippy, Daniel 96
Shirey, Solomon 211
Sidney (Ohio) 247
Simpson, Matthew 25, 205
Slocum, Henry 190
Slyter, Sam 47
Smallpox 66-72, 82
Smetts, Benneth 134
Smith, Green Clay 98-101, 108
Smith, Kirby 96
Smith, Sylvester B. 38-39, 130,
    141
Snyder, Irvin 192
Spencer, Henry N. 38, 83, 86
Springfield rifles 85
St. Joseph County Guard 14
Stanley, Timothy R. 111, 113,
    120, 128-129, 131-132, 138-
    141, 149, 161-163, 170, 172-
    175, 177-178, 182, 184
Stanton, Edwin 28, 96, 151, 191
Starr, Levi 11-12
Stevenson, Carter 118
Stewart, Duncan 68, 72, 80, 86,
    94
Stockton, Thomas B.W. 19-20,22-
    25, 29, 38